Love and Marriage Across Social Classes
in American Cinema

Stephen Sharot

Love and Marriage Across Social Classes in American Cinema

palgrave
macmillan

Stephen Sharot
Department of Sociology and Anthropology
Ben-Gurion University of the Negev
Tel Aviv, Israel

ISBN 978-3-319-82432-1   ISBN 978-3-319-41799-8   (eBook)
DOI 10.1007/978-3-319-41799-8

Cover design by Jenny Vong

Printed on acid-free paper

This Palgrave Macmillan imprint is published by Springer Nature
The registered company is Springer International Publishing AG
The registered company affiliation is: Gewerbestrasse 11, 6330 Cham, Switzerland

For Guy, Livia, Noam, and Leo

CONTENTS

ACKNOWLEDGMENTS

I have drawn upon the following of my articles for portions of this book and I would like to thank the journals' editors.

"Class Rise as a Reward for Disinterested Love: Cross-Class Romance Films, 1915–1928," *Journal of Popular Culture* 43.3 (June 2010): 583–99.

"The 'New Woman', Star Personas, and Cross-Class Romance Films in the 1920s," *Journal for Gender Studies* 19.1 (March 2010): 73–86.

"Wealth and/or Love: Class and Gender in Cross-Class Romance Films of the Great Depression," *Journal of American Studies* 47.1 (2013): 89–108.

"Social Class in Female Star Personas and the Cross-Class Romance Formula in Depression America," *Screen* 56.2 (Summer, 2015): 172–194.

PREFACE

The cross-class romance film has, at its center, a story of the development of an intimate relationship between at least two central protagonists, generally one female and one male, who come from different classes distinguished by their economic positions and status in society. This is a formula that has been the basis of hundreds of American films, albeit with variations on the theme. In contrast to the tendency in film studies to provide a detailed analysis of a small number of films, the analysis here is based on a large sample of cross-class romance films without regard to their acknowledged quality or status in film history. Cross-class romance films were made prodigiously from the beginnings of the feature film around 1915 until the USA entered World War II at the end of 1941. At the height of the studio system, all of the "Big Five" (Paramount, MGM, Warner Bros., Fox, RKO) produced cross-class romance films, as did one of the "Little Three" studios (Columbia), along with small independent production companies such as Chesterfield.

Film scholars have analyzed a small number of cross-class romance films in accord with their various interests in genres, directors and censorship. Prominent examples discussed with regard to particular genres (romantic comedy, musical, drama or melodrama) or directors include *It Happened One Night* (Columbia, 1934), *Gold Diggers of 1933* (Warner Bros., 1933) and *Stella Dallas* (Goldwyn/United Artists, 1937). Prominent examples in discussions of censorship are *Red Headed Woman* (MGM, 1932) and *Baby Face* (Warner, 1933). In addition to such well-known films, the analysis here includes films long forgotten, the commercial failures as well as the commercial successes, those directed by 'journeymen' as well as those directed by 'auteurs,' those that posed no problem for moral gatekeepers as well as those that encountered problems of censorship. Scholars sometimes justify their focus on a small number of commercially successful or critically acclaimed films by citing their popularity with audiences or their significance in film history, but at a time when a large proportion of the population went to a cinema at least once a week, the chances were that frequent cinema-goers would see many cross-class romances, including commercial failures and those that have been long forgotten.

The analytical foci of this work reflect the academic background of its author: a sociologist with a strong historical interest. My aim is not to propose a new sociological theory of popular cinema but rather to give far more attention to the socio-historical contexts of popular cinema than is usually the case in film studies. I am in agreement with Andrew Tudor that sociologists have contributed little to the understanding of film and that the uninformed view among film scholars, especially the more theoretically inclined, of sociology as an unreflective empiricist and scientistic discipline has minimized its potential contribution.[1] The publication in the 1960s and early 1970s of a few books by sociologists on film, including Tudor's own work, was not followed through in the decades that followed.[2] From the 1970s into the 1990s, the marked theoretical preferences within academic film studies for semiotics, formal structuralism, deterministic conceptions of ideology, and psychology, particularly psychoanalysis, limited attention to the historical socio-cultural contexts of films. Some systematic attention to wider contexts was provided by neo-formalists on the relationship between film style and the structure of the film industry and by reception and audience studies. However, among theorists in film studies, the common assertion that films simply do not reflect society appeared to justify the absence of any serious consideration of the socio-historical contexts of film 'texts', even though generalizations were often made about the relationship of films to very broadly conceived notions of capitalism, patriarchalism or patriarchal capitalism.

The importance of attention to socio-historical contexts is now being recognized by even the major exponents of the psychoanalytical approach,[3] The development of cultural and media studies have provided frameworks for sociologically informed research on film, but in spite of the blurring of disciplinary boundaries with sociology, it is still rare to find detailed attention being given to the larger social context of film representations by cultural studies and media scholars.[4] My detailed consideration of the socio-historical context does not assume that films simply reflect society, and an emphasis is placed on the film industry's mediation of the wider society. At one level, mediation occurs through genres or formulas, which are not necessarily limited to films. Popular cinema has been characterized as mostly comprised of genre movies that are defined by Barry Keith Grant as "those commercial feature films which, through repetition and variation, tell familiar stories with familiar characters in familiar situations."[5] The audience is familiar with the stories, characters and situations, not because they occur in their own lives, but because they have seen them so many times in the cinema. The mimicry of other films rather than 'real life' is presented as one of the defining characteristics of genre films. As Robert Warshow wrote, the genre creates its own field of reference; the relationship of the conventions of the genre to the experience of the audience or any real situation is of secondary importance to the previous experience of the type itself.[6] In tracing the evolution of a genre, Thomas Schatz notes that, although the subject matter of any film story is derived from certain real-world characters, conflicts and settings, the repetition of the story into a formula means that "its basis in experience gradually gives way to its own internal narrative logic."[7] However, Schatz recognizes that genre never evolves to a point where it becomes divorced entirely from the "real-world."[8] Similarly, John G. Cawelti writes that even the most formulaic works "have at least the surface texture of the real world,"[9] and that the most successful formulaic fiction provides escapism "within a framework that the audience can still accept as having some connection with reality."[10] My analysis is informed by the aforementioned perspectives on genre; the cross-class romance was a successful formula and was 'escapist' in the sense of providing a utopian solution that was outside the experiences and expectations of most of its audience; despite this, the audiences could also connect the films' motifs to their own social experiences and goals. Of course, that 'real world' or 'reality' changes, and although the basic elements of the formula or genre will remain in place, its content, including the characteristics of protagonists and the milieu of the narrative, will also change.

At another level, the socio-historical context is mediated by the structure and operations of the American film industry, including its self-regulation or censorship bodies, which attempted to reconcile the industry's economic goals with pressures from moral reform groups outside the industry. Among those working within this structure, the most important persons with respect to the narrative patterns and thematic concerns were the producers, directors and script writers who, from their

unequal positions within the structure, engaged with each other in complex negotiations. Ideally, in order to provide a comprehensive contextual
analysis, one would need to discover the social background, including the
class background, of these filmmakers, their social and political views, as
well as their relative influences within the studios. Such an investigation
might be possible if one was to focus on very few films, but it is beyond
the scope of this work given its wide historical perspective and the large
number of films under consideration. The studios expected that cross-class
romance films would appeal principally to women and one relevant fact
with respect to the filmmakers is that, although almost all producers and
directors were male, a relatively large number of script writers were female.

While most works on romance in American films have tended to
explore the subject in relationship to gender, this study places an emphasis
on class, albeit often in relationship to gender. Disputes over definitions
and conceptualizations of class are endless but, for the purposes of this
study, it is sufficient to note that investigations of people's notions of class
have found three widely employed considerations: socio-economic, cultural and moral.[11] These considerations are to be found, often implicitly,
in cross-class romance films.

With respect to socioeconomic boundaries, up until about 1919, class
in many American films was a matter of position in the mode of production, but in the 1920s and thereafter, Hollywood understood class almost
exclusively in terms of levels of consumerism. Although there had been
no fundamental changes to ownership and inequality in the USA after
World War I, many believed that the meanings of class and its boundaries
had changed as a consequence of consumerism, and these views became
even more entrenched during the Depression. Cultural boundaries of class
were related, in part, to consumerism; it was not just the quantity of the
items consumed but their nature that had relevance. Some working-class
heroines of cross-class romance had to overcome accusations of vulgarity
while others demonstrated that they could acquire the appropriate manners and tastes of the upper-class with ease. Classes were distinguished not
only by lifestyles but also by moralities. The upper-class relatives of the
wealthy male in cross-class romances were often portrayed as snooty, shal-
low, egoistic, cold, insincere and hypocritical. The working-class families,
particularly the men folk, of poor heroines were sometimes at fault, but
the heroine was frequently an exemplar of working-class morality, even if

she engaged in morally dubious occupations. Working-class heroines and heroes were straightforward, authentic and sincere, with a strong work ethic, personal integrity and good interpersonal relationships. By dissociating moral worth from money and wealth, the material rewards that working-class heroines and heroes received or were expected to receive as part of the happy ending of the cross-class romances were justified.

An essential precondition for the cross-class romance was the emergence of romantic love as a basis for marriage and Chap. 1 traces the diffusion of this value across the class spectrum in the nineteenth century and early twentieth century. Chapter 2 traces motifs of the cross-class romance in literature, from *Pamela* (1740), considered by many to be the first modern novel, through to the popular American literature of the nineteenth century and early twentieth century, prior to its surge of popularity in American cinema from about 1915. Chapter 3 follows the development of the cross-class romance in American cinema from its most elementary expressions in earliest cinema, 'the cinema of attractions', through the 'transitional period' from 1909–1914 when most films were no more than one reel or 15 minutes in length, to the appearance from 1914–1915 of films of four or more reels, lasting one hour or more. Subsequent chapters follow a rough chronology as significant historical events (i.e., World War 1, Hollywood's conversion to sound, the Wall Street Crash, World War II) as well as characterizations of decades or periods (i.e., the roaring twenties, the Great Depression of the 1930s, post-World War II affluence) serve to divide the chapters. However, chronology is partially compromised by themes in cross-class romances that are not confined to particular years: sexual exploitation and class conflict (Chap. 4), consumerism and ethnicity (Chap. 5), the dilemmas of working-class heroines during the Depression (Chap. 6), male seducers and female gold diggers (Chap. 7). The decline of the number of cross-class romances that began about the time that USA entered World War II and the changes the formula underwent after the war are the subject of Chap. 8. In general, this work attempts to demonstrate the range of narrative patterns and thematic concerns in cross-class romance films, their continuities and changes, and the intertextual and contextual (e.g., industrial, societal) factors that account for both continuity and change in the formula's themes and narratives.

NOTES

1. Andrew Tudor, "Sociology and Film," in John Hill and Pamela Church Gibson, eds., *The Oxford Guide to Film Studies* (Oxford: Oxford University Press), 190–194.
2. George A. Huaco, *The Sociology of Film Art* (New York: Basic Books, 1965); I. C. Jarvie, *Towards a Sociology of the Cinema: A Comparative Essay on the Structure and Functioning of a Major Entertainment Industry* (London: Routledge & Kegan Paul, 1970); Andrew Tudor, *Images and Influence: Studies in the Sociology of Film* (London: George Allen & Unwin, 1974). Prominent earlier social scientific studies of film were the Payne Fund studies, conducted from 1929 to 1932, which focused on the influence of films on American youth, Leo C. Rosten, *Hollywood, The Movie Colony, The Movie Makers* (New York: Harcourt, Brace and Company, 1941), and Hortense Powdermaker, *Hollywood, the Dream Factory; An Anthropologist Looks at the Movie-Makers* (Boston: Little, Brown and Company, 1950). A later prominent sociologist who wrote on films was Norman K. Denzin, *Images of Postmodern Society; Social Theory and Contemporary Cinema* (London: Sage, 1991), *The Cinematic Society: The Voyeur's Gaze* (London: Sage, 1995). Will Wright has applied sociology to the study of Westerns: *Sixguns and Society: A Structural Study of the Western* (Berkeley: University of California Press, 1975), *The Wild West: The Mythical Cowboy and Social Theory* (London: Sage Publications, 2001). A recent relevant text relating films to sociology is *Cinematic Sociology: Social Life in Film*, eds., Jean-Anne Sutherland and Kathryn Feltey (Los Angeles: Pine Forge Press, 2010). The editors of this text note that they are concerned primarily in teaching sociology *through* film rather than providing a sociology *of* film.
3. Laura Mulvey, "Unmasking the Gaze: Feminist Film Theory, History, and Film Studies," in Vicki Callahan, ed., *Reclaiming the Archive: Feminism and Film History* (Detroit: Wayne State University Press, 2010), 17–31.
4. Tudor noted sociological influences in the works of film scholars Richard Dyer and John Hill and among more recently published works on film by non-sociologists one can find sociological acumen in the works of Steven Ross, a historian, Rob King and Dennis Broe in cinema and film studies, and Derek Nystrom, a professor of English. Richard Dyer, *Stars* (London: British Film Institute, 1979), *Heavenly Bodies: Film Stars and Society* (London: British Film Institute and Macmillan, 1986); John Hill, *Sex, Class and Realism: British Cinema 1956–1963* (London: British Film Institute, 1986); Steven J. Ross, *Working-Class Hollywood; Silent Film and the Shaping of Class in America* (Princeton: Princeton University Press, 1998); Rob King, *The Fun Factory; the Keystone Film Company and the*

Emergence of Mass Culture (Berkeley: University of California Press, 2009); Dennis Broe, *Film Noir, American Workers, and Postwar Hollywood* (Gainesville: University Press of Florida, 2009); Derek Nystrom, *Hard Hats, Rednecks, and Macho Men: Class in 1970s American Cinema* (Oxford: Oxford University Press, 2009). Ross's work, in particular, has been a major influence on mine; his analysis of class conflict in early cinema and his argument that an emphasis on class conflict gave way, especially in post-World War One Hollywood, to cross-class romance are important to my own analysis. Although Ross includes consideration of some cross-class romance films of the 1920s, his major focus is on representations of class conflict in the silent era. My work extends the analysis of cross-class romance to a much larger sample of films, both in the silent era and the 1930s.

5. Barry Keith Grant, *Film Genre: From Iconography to Ideology* (London: Wallflower Press, 2007), 1.

6. Richard Warshow, *The Immediate Experience: Movies, Comics, Theatre and Other Aspects of Popular Culture* (Cambridge, MA: Harvard University Press, 2001 [1962]), 97–124.

7. Thomas Schatz, *Hollywood Genres: Formulas, Filmmaking, and the Studio System* (New York: McGraw-Hill, 1981), 36.

8. Schatz, *Hollywood Genres*, 30.

9. John G. Cawelti, *Adventure, Mystery, and Romance: Formula Stories as Art and Popular Culture* (Chicago: University of Chicago Press, 1976), 13.

10. Cawelti, *Adventure, Mystery, and Romance*, 34. Cawelti uses the term formula in preference to genre. He defines it as "a combination or synthesis of a number of specific cultural conventions with a more universal story form or archetype." (6) Although there are problems in applying the term 'genre', the cross-class romance can be distinguished as a subgenre within the wider category of romance, and just as romances in general can be distinguished as dramas or comedies, so can cross-class romances. As we will see, for most periods in the history of cross-class romance films there have been more dramas or melodramas than comedies, although in a number of cases it is difficult to categorize the films unequivocally as one or the other.

11. On these distinctions see Michèle Lamont, *Money, Morals and Manners: the Culture of the French and American Upper-Middle Class* (Chicago: University of Chicago Press, 1992), and *The Dignity of Working Men: Mobility and the Boundaries of Race, Class and Immigration* (New York: Russell Sage Foundation, 2000).

BIBLIOGRAPHY

Broe, Dennis. *Film Noir, American Workers, and Postwar Hollywood.* Gainesville: University Press of Florida, 2009.

Cawelti, John G. *Adventure, Mystery, and Romance: Formula Stories as Art and Popular Culture.* Chicago: University of Chicago Press, 1976.

Denzin, Norman K. *Images of Postmodern Society; Social Theory and Contemporary Cinema.* London: Sage, 1991.

———. *The Cinematic Society: The Voyeur's Gaze.* London: Sage, 1995.

Dyer, Richard. *Stars.* London: British Film Institute, 1979.

———. *Heavenly Bodies: Film Stars and Society.* London: British Film Institute and Macmillan, 1986.

Grant, Barry Keith. *Film Genre: From Iconography to Ideology.* London: Wallflower Press, 2007.

Hill, John. *Sex Class and Realism: British Cinema 1956–1963.* London: British Film Institute, 1986.

Huaco, George A. *The Sociology of Film Art.* New York: Basic Books, 1965.

Jarvie, I. C. *Towards a Sociology of the Cinema: A Comparative Essay on the Structure and Functioning of a Major Entertainment Industry.* London: Routledge & Kegan Paul, 1970.

King, Rob. *The Fun Factory: The Keystone Film Company and the Emergence of Mass Culture.* Berkeley: University of California Press, 2009.

Lamont, Michèle. *Money, Morals and Manners: The Culture of the French and American Upper-Middle Class.* Chicago: University of Chicago Press, 1992.

———. *The Dignity of Working Men: Mobility and the Boundaries of Race, Class and Immigration.* New York: Russell Sage Foundation, 2000.

Mulvey, Laura. "Unmasking the Gaze: Feminist Film Theory, History, and Film Studies," in Vicki Callahan, ed. *Reclaiming the Archive: Feminism and Film History.* Detroit: Wayne State University Press, 2010, 17–31.

Nystrom, Derek. *Hard Hats, Rednecks, and Macho Men: Class in 1970s American Cinema.* Oxford: Oxford University Press, 2009.

Powdermaker, Hortense. *Hollywood, the Dream Factory: An Anthropologist Looks at the Movie-Makers.* Boston: Little, Brown and Company, 1950.

Ross, Steven J. *Working-Class Hollywood; Silent Film and the Shaping of Class in America.* Princeton: Princeton University Press, 1998.

Rosten, Leo C. *Hollywood, The Movie Colony, The Movie Makers.* New York: Harcourt, Brace and Company, 1941.

Thomas Schatz. *Hollywood Genres: Formulas, Filmmaking, and the Studio System.* New York: McGraw-Hill, 1981.

Sutherland, Jean-Ann. and Kathryn Feltey, eds. *Cinematic Sociology: Social Life in Film.* Los Angeles: Pine Forge Press, 2010.

Tudor, Andrew. *Images and Influence: Studies in the Sociology of Film*. London: George Allen & Unwin, 1974.

———. "Sociology and Film," in John Hill and Pamela Church Gibson, eds. *The Oxford Guide to Film Studies*. Oxford: Oxford University Press, 190–194.

Warshow, Richard. *The Immediate Experience: Movies, Comics, Theatre and Other Aspects of Popular Culture*. Cambridge, MA: Harvard University Press, 2001 [1962].

Wright, Will. *Sixguns and Society: A Structural Study of the Western*. Berkeley: University of California Press, 1975.

———. *The Wild West: The Mythical Cowboy and Social Theory*. London: Sage Publications, 2001.

CHAPTER 1

Love, Marriage and Class

Most people in the USA in the past and in the present marry within their class, or what some prefer to call socio-economic stratum. The terminology of class has shifted over time and, as this work covers a wide time period, I have not confined myself to a single terminology. Historians of eighteenth-century England commonly distinguish aristocracy, bourgeoisie and laboring classes, whereas sociologists of twentieth-century America have commonly used a terminology based on differences in wealth, income and occupation and have distinguished upper, upper-middle, lower-middle, and working classes (or socio-economic strata). However named, most cross-class marriages have occurred between people located in adjacent or contiguous classes, say between aristocracy and bourgeoisie or between the lower-middle and working class, and it is rare for them to occur between widely divergent classes, say between aristocracy and laboring class or between the upper or upper-middle class and the working class. There has been an increase in recent decades in the number of marriages of couples whose level of education attainment and occupational prestige match but whose class origins are different. Marriages that cross widely divergent classes not only in terms of the class origins of the couple but also in terms of their present class locations have always been infrequent and remain rare. One reason for this is that people are more likely to meet others from their own class in settings that provide opportunities for more intimate association; their neighbors, close work associates and social circles are likely to be from the same class. When people meet others from a number of classes, tastes and sensibilities that have been shaped by

© The Author(s) 2017
S. Sharot, *Love and Marriage Across Social Classes in American Cinema*,
DOI 10.1007/978-3-319-41799-8_1

upbringing in a particular class are likely to guide them to select a spouse from their own class who shares those tastes and sensibilities.

In contrast to its infrequency in society, romance between couples from widely divergent classes that ends in marriage or the promise of marriage has been a staple narrative in popular culture for more than two centuries. Cross-class romances, most of which are between wealthy men and working women, can be found in what are regarded as the first modern novels in the eighteenth century, and films with this theme have been made throughout almost the entire history of cinema in the USA. The number of such films in recent years cannot compare with the period from the beginnings of the feature films around 1915 until 1942, when, in some years, most months would see the release of at least one and often more cross-class romances.[1]

An understanding of this heyday of cross-class romance films requires an examination of prior historical developments: the development of notions of romantic love across the class spectrum, the subject of this chapter; and cross-class romance in fictional media prior to the cinema, the subject of the following chapter.

ROMANTIC LOVE AND SOCIAL CLASSES

The basic formula of the cross-class romance is that romance between two individuals from unequal social classes leads to marriage, or the promise of marriage, despite the obstacles that relate to their differences in class. One essential condition of this formula is the notion of romantic love as the basis of marriage. Although most historians of marriage would agree that romantic love became a more important factor in marriage as western societies modernized, they differ over its importance in premodern or pre-industrial periods and how and when it diffused across the class structure. Romantic love certainly existed in premodern society, but it was seen as unrelated or even harmful to marriage. A form of love in the middle ages dissociated from marriage was courtly love or love songs addressed to the wives of lords. This may have been primarily a literary phenomenon, but even if it was rarely, if ever, practiced, it shows recognition of the possibility of romantic feelings between men and women. As marriages among aristocrats were commonly arranged and based on considerations of property, such feelings were not expected to precede marriages, and although some men chose women whom they found desirable, love was viewed unfavorably as a basis for marriage.[2]

Notions of romantic love are believed to have spread after the feudal period and to have become common among the privileged classes in Europe, and more specifically in England, by the end of the seventeenth and eighteenth century. Within the British aristocracy in the eighteenth century, aristocratic rank and wealth provided the basic parameters for suitable marriage partners, but letters written by aristocratic women indicate that, for some at least, love was one of the fundamental elements in marriage. It was unusual, however, for parents to take the romantic feelings of their children into consideration when they negotiated a union, and it was rare for children to oppose their parents' choice. Daughters, in particular, were expected to subjugate their personal desires; they had been taught female submissiveness, they were dependent on their families for dowries and they had little means to support themselves. It was hoped that marriage partners would gradually develop a general affection for each other, and while there was little investigation of the personalities of potential spouses to guarantee that this would, in fact, occur, a number of aristocratic women expressed a wish to love the appropriate man they were to marry. Once married, some aristocratic women wrote of themselves as exceptional in their matrimonial love, which they saw as necessarily coupled with their submission and obedience to their husbands.[3]

By the end of the eighteenth century, many aristocratic women considered the absence of love a sufficient cause to refuse a match. In the nineteenth century, aristocratic circles came to expect that, in addition to the family approval, the couple would be in love. This greater emphasis on love did not, however, reduce aristocratic endogamy. The vast majority of men from titled families in the eighteenth and nineteenth centuries married women who were from titled families themselves, or from non-titled families who were close to the aristocracy with respect to the basis of their wealth, particularly large landowners. Up to the last two decades of the nineteenth century, few aristocrats married women from business families; of the 2,933 marriages of British peers from 1700–1889, only 19 or 0.6 % married women from the lower or laboring class.[4] Marriages of an aristocratic woman to a laboring man were probably even rarer and necessitated the woman breaking entirely with her family. Rumors of ladies eloping with their footman occasionally surfaced in newspapers, but the intense taboo on a sexual relationship between an aristocratic woman and a servant kept them from public knowledge.[5]

Aristocratic families could tolerate marriages between their sons and non-aristocratic women because the children of those unions retained the family's status. However, because the children of a daughter who married out of the aristocracy would not retain that status, aristocratic families in the eighteenth century preferred their daughter to remain single rather than to marry inappropriately. Aristocratic men married non-aristocratic women for a number of reasons, not the least of which was money, and it was the aristocratic women who, through their in-marriages, took on the function of maintaining the rank identity of the aristocracy. When the land basis of aristocratic wealth began to weaken in the last two decades of the nineteenth century, it was the aristocratic sons who married in increasing numbers daughters from wealthy business families, and it was the aristocratic daughters who continued to marry within their social rank, at least until about 1920 when circumstances and attitudes began to change quite radically.[6]

Some historians have pointed to the bourgeoisie rather than the aristocracy as the major class carrier of romantic love during the early modern period and have noted that Puritan writers emphasized the importance of intimacy and emotional intensity within marriage. Middle-class moralists criticized the aristocratic arrangement of marriage based purely on family interests and advocated instead marriage based on 'companionate love' or, at a somewhat more passionate and spontaneous level, 'sentimental love.'[7] Such forms of love were understood to be constrained by considerations of family and rank, and most historians would acknowledge that, even for the bourgeoisie, economic interests remained the major factor in marriages until about the end of the eighteenth century. Children required their parents' permission if they wanted to marry, and parents could use their economic power over their children to influence the choice of a marriage partner. Love marriages remained confined largely to novels and only started to influence conjugal practices with the decline of land and other forms of real property as the basis of wealth. As corporations replaced families as the major focus of wealth, marriage was increasingly freed from the pressures of economic alliances.[8]

As for the majority of the population, although few of their marriages were arranged and there was greater freedom of choice than among the higher classes, mate selection was supervised by parents, peers and communal gatherings, and the choice of a spouse was likely to be influenced by practical considerations. Men chose partners who they believed would contribute to the economy of the household and provide them with children who would also contribute to that economy. Romantic love in the choice of partners became more important among the working class as production was separated from the household and the ties of the nuclear family to its wider kin and broader community were weakened, as occurred in eighteenth and nineteenth century Britain. As a larger number of the young found work outside the home and became economically independent from their families, more emphasis was placed on affection and personal compatibility as criteria in the choice of a marriage partner. The street literature of chapbooks and ballads in eighteenth-century Britain indicate that ideas of love that gave preference to individual feeling over the constraints of community were already familiar within the laboring class.[9]

In England as well as in North America, there is evidence of the increasing importance of romantic love as a basis for marriage in the eighteenth century and of its strengthening and diffusion among different classes in the nineteenth century. Magazines written for the middle and upper classes in New England between 1741 and 1749 included a large number of discussions regarding romantic love, some arguing for, and other against it, as a basis for marriage. There were more discussions of happiness of the couple as a motive for entering marriage than there were of accruing wealth or social status as motives.[10] By the last quarter of the eighteenth century, romantic love was regarded by many middle-class Americans as an essential condition for marriage and parents were giving their children considerable freedom in their choice of mates. Although parents might promote a match, they rarely opposed the wishes of their children, and parents who sought to impose a marriage partner were likely to encounter their children's resistance. By the 1830s, many young men and women only sought their parents' blessing after they had decided that they would marry, and even though many couples continued to seek the consent of the young woman's parents, it was increasingly viewed as a formality. The custom that continued into the twentieth century was for the male suitor to call on or to write to his prospective father-in-law to request the daughter's hand in marriage.[11]

With respect to the American upper class, a study of this class in Boston, the 'Boston Brahmins,' shows that the substantial parental involvement in marriages evident in the late eighteenth century gave way in the nineteenth century to greater individual choice of marriage partners. The correspondence and diaries of upper-class Boston women provide evidence of a greater emphasis on romantic love as a basis for marriage over the nineteenth century, but the marriages of this elite continued to be remarkably endogamous. Residential concentration and, from the middle of the nineteenth century, the formation of a complex of cultural institutions and exclusive social clubs and events, such as debutante balls, strengthened the boundaries of the upper class and its marriage market. The insularity of the upper-class social circles made it unnecessary for parents to intervene directly in order to ensure that their children would marry appropriate partners.[12]

Boston Brahmins were more endogamous than their counterparts in New York, but, as in Boston, the last decades of the nineteenth century in New York saw the establishment of elite organizations, exclusive social clubs and events that practically guaranteed that the romantic choices of upper-class sons and daughters would be from within their own class. The number of new millionaires multiplied, the children of 'new' money were often mated with the children of 'old' money, and as it became more difficult to ascertain a family's status, Social Registers were compiled as an index of membership within the upper class.[13] The continued endogamy of the American upper class in the twentieth century was demonstrated by two studies of marriage announcements in the *New York Times*, covering the periods 1932–1942 and 1962–1972. These studies showed that whereas in the nineteenth century there were a number of upper-class marriage markets, each localized in one of the major cities, the upper-class marriage market in the twentieth century had became national. The more recent study reported that, although less than 110,000 names were listed in all twelve volumes of the Social Register (about 0.5 % of the population), in one quarter of the marriages, both bride and groom were listed. Social Register endogamy appeared to be on the decline, however, from 30 % of all *New York Times* announcement marriages in the early 1960s to 19 % in the early 1970s.[14]

The upper class was probably the most endogamous class in nineteenth-century America, but the combination of a greater emphasis on romantic love, together with a continued high level of endogamy was also evident among the middle class. Two studies, one by Karen Lystra and the other by Ellen Rothman, provide detailed evidence of romantic love among middle-class Americans in the nineteenth century.[15] Both authors use the correspondence of courting couples and other data, such as advice literature, to show that love was becoming a necessary condition of marriage among the American middle class. Rothman traces this development to the late eighteenth century and both authors show its importance in the middle decades of the nineteenth century. At the beginning of the nineteenth century love had been differentiated from friendship between men and women, but it was also differentiated from passion, which was seen as a grave threat to love, and from romance, which was unreliable and connoted a lack of seriousness and maturity. By the middle of the century, romance had been redefined as a foundation of domestic harmony, and it was no longer associated with youthful passion and impermanence. The ability to recognize and express 'true love' became all important, and 'falling in love' became a normative part of middle-class courtship.[16]

Susan Weisser finds that periodicals addressed to the middle class in the nineteenth century expressed a persistent worry over whether romance is necessary or inimical to marriage. When romance was identified with passion it was seen as selfish and fickle, inimical to the spiritual affection and domesticity of an enduring and stable marriage. Only gradually was this view replaced by the belief that passion naturally passes through stages into a type of love that enables a marriage of companionship. These discussions on the nature of love often made references to gender differences. Love was increasingly defined as an ideal feeling associated with women's God-given nature. As women's love was purer than that of a man, her love had the capacity to reform or refine the man. The unselfishness of a women's love was supported by reports and stories of women who refused the marriage proposals of wealthy men and preferred to wait until the men they loved were in a position to marry them. However, within the moral lesson of these narratives, there was an implicit recognition that many women did marry for money.[17]

Lystra notes that a prospective marriage across a class or other sensitive social boundary may have been an exception to the expectation that parents would accept their children's choices. She writes that courting couples insisted on the priority of their feelings over all social barriers and familial restraints, but almost all of her examples and those of Rothman appear to be of couples from the same class. Manipulation of their children's associational networks may have been "all that remained of parental control in the mate-selection process,"[18] but this could be an effective strategy in reducing the chances of an inappropriate match from the standpoint of economic and social status. Couples expected to be left alone without a chaperone when courting, and parental supervision could afford to be lax and allow love to take its course once an appropriate prospective partner had been selected. Of importance here is the institution of 'calling', a practice that originated among the English upper class and was adopted by the American middle class. As it took place in the home of the girl's parents, it provided the parents, particularly the mother, with some control over the prospective suitors of their daughter. A day or days 'at home' were designated to receive callers, and it was a 'girl's privilege' to ask a young man to call. It was considered improper for a man to take the initiative, and mothers were able to patrol the appropriateness of suitors through the convention of being 'not at home'.[19] Thus, romantic involvements were bound up with a person's commitment to others and a woman's sentiments toward a man were especially likely to be influenced by the opinions that others expressed about him.[20]

Middle-class Americans in the nineteenth century believed that similarity in background was essential for the 'marriage of companionship',[21] and their conceptions of gender differences within their class made cross-class romance and marriage unlikely. A new definition of womanhood as sexually passionless began to emerge in the last years of the eighteenth century and became prevalent among the middle class in the 1820s and 1830s. Whereas men were assumed to be carnal creatures, the 'true woman' was above sexual passion. There was some distance between the doctrine and the behavior of young middle-class woman who engaged in flirtation and sexual playfulness, but many people from both sexes were persuaded that a man's relationship with a pure woman would constrain and contain his 'animal instincts'. Lower-class women might provide an outlet for the male instincts, but the pure woman could only be found in the male's own class. By the end of the nineteenth century, there was a growing recognition of female sexuality, but this meant that women had to exercise self-control as well as control the more powerful male impulses.[22]

The works of Lystra and Rothman demonstrate that the romantic choice of middle-class Americans in the nineteenth century was individualistic, but the form and meaning of that individualism was changing toward the end of the nineteenth century and was to change more radically in the twentieth century. In the growing industrial, urban environments the number of opportunities for men and women to meet at work and at leisure was increasing and it was no longer possible for parents to know all the potential partners from which their sons and daughters could choose. Romantic choices came to be disembodied from moral and social group frameworks and were increasingly taken within a relatively free market of encounters. Concerns about marriage crossing class lines, together with objections to relationships based on deceptive love, were expressed in marriage guidance guides of the last two decades of the nineteenth century. Readers were discouraged from matches based on carnal passion that was quickly satiated and from marriage across class lines in which the poorer partner might have been motivated by social climbing. Warnings against marriages that were incompatible in class and culture appeared at the time of the mass immigration from southern and eastern Europe, when there was anxiety for the ethnic survival of the older Protestant, American population.[23]

Unlike nineteenth-century middle-class Americans, the working or lower class left little written evidence of their affective lives. If some wrote love letters, the absence of family archives meant that they were unlikely to survive. It has been suggested, however, that the conditions of social flux on the frontier were conducive to romantic relationships, and an examination of popular ballads points to a preoccupation with romantic love among working people from the perspectives of courting couples and their parents. The ballads express the joy and pain of romantic love and contain parents' warnings about its dangers. Romantic love was no doubt advanced by the spread of literacy; the romantic fiction that appeared in cheap printed media from the last decades of the nineteenth century found many readers among the working poor, especially young women.[24] For young people from the urban working class whose families lived in small, crowded apartments, calling was not practical and their courting was conducted in public places and, from the end of the nineteenth century, in the rapidly developing venues of commercial amusements. Dating developed first among the working class young in response to the limitations of their homes and the opportunities provided by the new cheap, urban amusements. Among the more privileged youth, dating replaced calling as the young recognized the advantages of courting outside the home and parental authority weakened. Although the first recorded uses of the word 'date' in its modern meaning are from lower-class slang, by the mid-1910s the word had entered the vocabulary of the middle class, and between 1890 and 1925 dating became a common practice throughout the class system.[25] Dating limited further parental regulation of their children's potential spouses, and it increased the chances of cross-class romance—a romance that was likely to be initiated by the male as he was expected to invite the girl and provide the money for their entertainment.

In the vast majority of cross-class romances in fiction and film, the upper-class or wealthy protagonist is male and the working-class or poor protagonist is female. While it should be remembered that the partners in the vast majority of interclass marriages in society are from contiguous classes, the differences between men and women in these marriages is likely to be of relevance in understanding the cross-class romances in fiction and film. Although data on actual interclass marriages is weak for the heyday of the cross-class romances in cinema (1915–1942), two statements can be made with a reasonable degree of certainty: firstly, most upward female mobility was through marriage; secondly, upward mobility through marriage was higher for women than it was for men.

A number of early studies of the relationship between marriage and class were limited by their focus on single towns[26] and there appear to be only two national surveys conducted after World War II that include some, rather inconclusive, data on marital selections during the decades prior to the War. From a sample that included marriages entered into from 1885–1945, Richard Centers compared husbands' occupations to the occupations of the wives' fathers. He found that although this comparison produced a large proportion of marriages that crossed classes, most of these marriages were between individuals of contiguous classes. His finding that more women than men married up was attributed to the large increase in white-collar occupations, with a heavy concentration of males in the higher ranks.[27] Zick Rubin's analysis of a national sample from 1962 provided a more appropriate measure of marriages across classes because he compared husbands' fathers' occupations and wives' fathers' occupations. He found a low stable level of interclass marriage from 1920–1962, and that the pattern of American women marrying up was true only for marriages within the middle and upper classes.[28]

As studies conducted in the 1960s and early 1970s reported that most female mobility at that time was through marriage,[29] we can surmise that this was even more so prior to World War II. The mobility of women through marriage has been analyzed by some sociologists through a model of exchange, and one type of exchange that is believed to operate is the exchange of females' physical attractiveness for males' status-conferring ability. Females of working-class origin may have little access to high-status males and may lack the money and knowledge to cultivate their appearance and personality, but it may well be easier to overcome these handicaps than for a male of working-class origin to acquire the skills necessary for a high-status occupation.[30]

Glen Elder wrote that American men valued physical attractiveness at or near the top of the qualities they desire in women, and this seemed to be especially true of upwardly mobile or strongly ambitious men. A woman's beauty, her primary status-conferring quality, is exchanged for a man's social rank, and Elder reasoned that physical attractiveness would be even more important to women of low social origins because they had fewer other valued characteristics to offer. Elder drew on data from an Oakland study whose female subjects, born in the early 1920s, were evaluated for their relative attractiveness in the 1930s and examined in 1958 with respect to their social status through marriage. As a group, girls of middle-class origin had been judged more attractive than girls of working-class origin, but whereas college education was relatively more influential in the marital careers of women from the middle class, physical attractiveness was the most predictive factor of marriage to a high-status man among women from the working class. Elder wrote that the adoption of middle-class standards of grooming by working-class girls in the premarital years probably reflected their social ambition and anticipatory socialization toward higher status. The cultivation of a well-groomed appearance appeared to have paid off in the social ascent of women from the working class.[31] Attributions of physical attractiveness are influenced by class-based codes, but beauty and sexiness are more detached from class than other attributes, such as linguistic codes and patterns of etiquette.[32]

Taylor and Glenn cast doubt on Elder's findings by noting that physical attractiveness of males may be a factor of importance in females' choice of husbands, but more importantly they doubted that there is much consensus with regard to the factors that determine the desirability of spouses. Whereas some females may give priority to maximizing their social and economic standing, others may forego marriage to a high-status male in favor of a lower-status male who gives them greater sexual satisfaction. And whereas some men may give priority to physical attractiveness, others may place greater emphasis on finding an intellectually stimulating companion.[33] Despite this casting of doubt on generalizations with respect to gender differences in the choice of marriage partners, studies continued to assert that, whereas males are more likely to emphasize physical attractiveness in the choice of spouses, women are more likely to consider class, status and ambition. More women than men said that they are willing to marry regardless of love.[34]

Greater gender equality is likely to have an effect on marriage choices. Studies of marriage selection from the 1960s onwards have noted the increasing importance of education in the choice of marriage partners and have found that more young people were marrying those with a similar education rather than those with similar social origins.[35] The greater opportunities for obtaining high-level jobs and occupational mobility among women have resulted in a change in the meanings of a woman's higher education in the marriage market. A woman's higher education is now perceived as a direct contribution to the family's economic standing and not only as a matter of cultural compatibility with a similarly educated male.[36] In the search for mates, men are attaching increasing importance to a woman's education and income prospects and they may now be competing for highly educated, potentially high-earning women just as women have in the past competed for high-earning men. Although the greater educational and occupational achievements of women should give them more freedom to choose men for love rather than money, studies have yet to show that the importance of men's earnings for women's choices has declined. If men have come to care more about women's income potential and women do come to care less about men's, the resulting greater similarity of women's and men's preferences may reduce the number of cross-class marriages. Thus, reduced gender inequality should make classes even more endogamous.[37]

Of course, what people tell an interviewer about their preferences in a spouse and the characteristics of the spouses they actually marry may differ, and given the value placed on romantic love many people may not admit or even be conscious of the influence of instrumental factors or rational considerations in their choice of spouse. Emotions and class or status aspirations often merge in the choice of a mate, and while love can be seen as ideally disinterested, it can be activated and maintained by economic and social interests.

Although people may not recognize the intermixture of motives in their choice of marriage partners, from the eighteenth century until the present day many observers and advisors on marriage have distinguished the motives of love and material interests. In an essay published in 1727, entitled *Conjugal Lewdness, Matrimonial Whoredom: A Treatise Concerning the Use and Abuse of the Marriage Bed*, Daniel Defoe condemned those parents who forced their children to marry without love and charged those who married without affection as "little more than legal Prostitutes."[38] More than a century and a half later, an article in a 1903 issue of the American periodical *Women's Life* entitled "Do Women Marry More for Love than Money?" stated that while women like to think that they place love above money, "this is a practical age in which we live, and the present-day girl, while recognizing the value of love, is apt to look first at a man's worldly possessions."[39] Another century later, the early years of the new millennium have seen a spate of books addressed principally to women with such titles as *How to Marry Money, How to Marry a Millionaire, How to Marry a Multi-Millionaire*, and *How to Get a Rich Man*. Lisa Johnson Mandell notes that her book *How to Snare a Millionaire NOW*, published in 2012, is a sequel to her first guide, *Marrying for Love and Money*, published in the late 1990s when there were no legitimate online dating sites and most love letters were sent via the Postal Service. Mandell claims that not only have there been considerable changes since the 1990s in the way we look for love and connection, but the years have also seen a huge difference in the way we perceive wealth; whereas her first book taught how to snare a millionaire, it is now necessary to snare a multi-millionaire or even a billionaire.[40]

These books differ, however, in how they combine their advice on how to attract wealthy men with the notion of marrying for love. Elizabeth Ford and Daniela Drake, the two authors of *Smart Girls Marry Money* make a case for what they term the "GDI" or "Gold-Digging Imperative." They argue that many women have paid dearly for being duped by the "Romantic Dream," and they counsel against a woman wasting her youth and beauty by pursuing romantic love. They admire successful career women but emphasize that they are few and that the vast majority of "real power players," such as the top CEOs, are men. They warn against a woman depending on her career and marrying just for love without considering her spouse's ability to earn. Such a woman is likely to end up abandoned and broke.[41] In comparison, Mandell feels obliged to write that a woman should not marry for money alone but to insist on love as well. She begins her book with a quote that it is "just as easy to fall in love with a rich man as a poor man," and the title of one of her chapters is "Why Choose Between Love and Money When You Can Have Both." Mandell explains that finding a partner from the wealthiest 1 % of the population can be altruistic as the woman can commit the man to increasing his wealth and sharing it. If a woman is herself successful in making money it becomes even more imperative to snare a wealthy man in order to avoid the hassle that occurs when a wife earns more than her husband.[42]

The authors of books that advise on how to marry wealthy spouses recognize that, in the absence of formal social boundaries regulating access to partners, competition in meeting and attracting appropriate others is intense. Although utilitarian factors and emotions may converge in romantic choices, individuals may face dilemmas, such as the choice between a socially appropriate person and a physically beautiful person. The ambiguities and dilemmas that arise in the encounter of love and socio-economic interests have provided material for a considerable number of cross-class romance narratives in literature and films. As the cinema inherited many of the motifs of the cross-class romance from literary forms, an historical overview of those forms is provided in the following chapter.

NOTES

1. Larry May has provided a graph that shows that, of a sample of the films reviewed in the trade journal *Motion Picture Herald* between 1914 and 1958, films featuring marriage or romance across class lines varied from ten percent to almost one quarter. After the rapid drop in such films from the late 1930s May found only one cross-class romance film in his sample for 1946, and although his graph shows some increase in the early 1950s, this is followed by another drop with no cross-class romance film in 1958 when the survey ends. Lary May, *The Big Tomorrow: Hollywood and the Politics of the American Way* (Chicago, University of Chicago Press, 2000), 282.

2. John F. Benton, "Clio and Venus: An Historical View of Medieval Love," in F. X. Newton, ed., *The Meaning of Courtly Love* (Albany, NY: State University of New York Press, 1968), 19–42.

3. Ingrid H. Tague, *Women of Quality: Accepting and Contesting Ideals of Femininity in England, 1690–1760* (Woodbridge, Suffolk: Boydell Press), 72–82; Kimberly Schutte, *Women, Rank and Marriage in the British Aristocracy, 1485–2000:An Open Elite?* (Basingstoke, Hampshire: Palgrave Macmillan, 2014), 26–27.

4. David Thomas, "The Social Origins of Marriage Partners of the British Peerage in the Eighteenth and Nineteenth Centuries," *Population Studies* 26.1 (1972), 99–111; John Cannon, *Aristocratic Century: The Peerage of Eighteenth-Century England* (Cambridge: Cambridge University Press, 1984), 76–78.

5. Of the over 500 crim con trials and divorce petitions between 1692 and 1857 only 11 involved accusations of a relationship between an aristocratic woman and a servant. Lawrence Stone, *Road to Divorce, England 1530–1987* (Oxford: Oxford University Press, 1990), 272; Schutte, *Women, Rank and Marriage in the British Aristocracy,* 149.

6. Schutte, *Women, Rank and Marriage in the British Aristocracy,* 40–41, 45–48, 82–83, 161–163.

7. Wendy Love, "The Dialectic of Love in *Sir Charles Grandison*," in David Blewett, ed., *Passion and Virtue: Essays on the Novels of Samuel Richardson* (Toronto: University of Toronto Press, 2001), 295–316.

8. David R. Shumway, *Modern Love: Romance, Intimacy, and the Marriage Crisis* (New York: New York University Press, 2003), 7, 16–19, 22; Eva Illouz, *Consuming the Romantic Utopia: Love and the Cultural Contradictions of Capitalism* (Berkeley: University of California Press, 1997), 213; Jean Louis Flandrin, *Sex in the Western World: The Development of Attitudes and Behavior* (Newark, NJ: Harwood Academic Publishers, 1991).

9. Edward Shorter, *The Making of the Modern Family* (New York, 1975); Richard Bulcroft, Kris Bulcroft, Karen Bradley and Carl Simpson, "The

Management and Production of Risk in Romantic Relationships: A Postmodern Paradox," *Journal of Family History* 25.1 (2000): 63–92; Katherine Binhammer, *The Seduction Narrative in Britain, 1747–1800* (Cambridge: Cambridge University Press, 2009), 110–111.

10. Herman R. Lantz, Raymond Schmitt, Margaret Britton and Eloise C. Snyder, "Pre-Industrial Patterns in the Colonial Family in America: A Content Analysis of Colonial Magazines," *American Sociological Review* 33.3 (1968): 419–421.

11. Karen Lystra, *Searching the Heart: Women, Men, and Romantic Love in Nineteenth-Century America* (New York: Oxford University Press, 1989), 28, 158–161; Ellen K. Rothman, *Hands and Hearts: A History of Courtship in America* (New York: Basic Books, 1984), 25–29.

12. Betty Farrel, *Elite Families: Class and Power in Nineteenth Century Boston* (Albany: State University of New York, 1993), 58, 83–84, 93, 107, 111.

13. Sven Beckert, *The Monied Metropolis: New York City and the Consolidation of the American Bourgeoisie, 1850–1896* (Cambridge: Cambridge University Press, 1993), 33–35, 211; Frederic Cople Jaher, *The Urban Establishment: Upper Strata in Boston, New York, Charleston, Chicago, and Los Angeles* (Urbana: University of Illinois Press, 1982), 96, 206, 255, 259; E. Digby Baltzell, *Philadelphia Gentlemen: The Making of a National Upper Class* (New Brunswick: Transaction Publishers, 2011 [1958]), 385.

14. David L. Hatch and Mary A. Hatch, "Criteria of Status as Derived from Marriage Announcements in the New York Times," *American Sociological Review* 12.4 (1947): 396–403; Paul M. Blumberg and P. W. Paul, "Continuities and Discontinuities in Upper-Class Marriages," *Journal of Marriage and Family* 37.1 (1975): 63–77.

15. Lystra, *Searching the Heart*; Rothman, *Hands and Hearts*.

16. Rothman, *Hands and Hearts*, 31–40, 101–107.

17. Susan Ostrov Weisser, *The Glass Slipper: Women and Love Stories* (New Brunswick: Rutgers University Press, 2013), 50–69.

18. Lystra, *Searching the Heart*, 164.

19. Beth L. Bailey, *From Front Porch to Back Seat: Courtship in Twentieth Century America* (Baltimore: John Hopkins University Press, 1988).

20. Eva Illouz, *Why Love Hurts* (Cambridge: Polity Press, 2012), 29.

21. Rothman, *Hands and Hearts*, 108.

22. Rothman, *Hands and Hearts*, 49–51, 186–188, 232–234.

23. Sondra R. Herman, "Loving Courtship or the Marriage Market? The Ideal and its Critics, 1871–1911," *American Quarterly* 25.2 (1973): 235–252.

24. Herman R. Lantz, "Romantic Love in the Pre-Modern Period: A Sociological Commentary," *Journal of Social History* 15.3 (1982): 349–370.

25. Bailey, *From Front Porch to Back Seat*, 16–22.

26. Thomas C. Hunt, "Occupational Status and Marriage Selection," *American Sociological Review* 5.4 (1940): 495–504; Simon Dinitz, Franklin Banks and Benjamin Pasamanick, "Mate Selection and Social Class: Changes during the Past Quarter Century," *Marriage and Family Living* 22.4 (1960): 348–351.
27. Richard Centers, "Marital Selection and Occupational Strata," *American Journal of Sociology* 54.6 (1949): 530–535.
28. Zick Rubin, "Do American Women Marry Up?" *American Sociological Review* 33.5 (1968): 750–760.
29. Glen H. Elder, Jr., "Appearance and Education in Marriage Mobility," *American Sociological Review* 34.4 (1969): 519–533; Norval D. Glenn, Adreain A. Ross, Judy Corder Tully, "Patterns of Intergenerational Mobility of Females Through Marriage," *American Sociological Review* 39.5 (1974): 683–699.
30. Glenn, Ross, Tully, "Patterns of Intergenerational Mobility of Females Through Marriage."
31. Elder, "Appearance and Education in Marriage Mobility."
32. Illouz, *Why Love Hurts*, 53–55.
33. Patricia Ann Taylor and Norval D. Glenn, "The Utility of Education and Attractiveness for Females' Status Attainment Through Marriage," *American Sociological Review* 41.3 (1976): 484–498.
34. Letitia Anne Peplau and Steven L. Gordon, "Women and Men in Love: Gender Differences in Close Heterosexual Relationships," in Virginia E. O'Leary, Rhoda Kesler Unger, Barbara Strudler Wallston, eds., *Women, Gender, and Social Psychology* (Hillsdale, NJ: Erlbaum, 1985), 257–292; Ayala Malakh-Pines, *Falling in Love: Why We Choose the Lovers We Choose* (New York: Routledge, 1999); Frank D. Cox, *Human Intimacy: Marriage, the Family, and its Meaning* (Belmont, CA: Wadsworth, 2009).
35. Peter Blau and Otis Dudley Duncan, *The American Occupational Structure* (New York: Wiley, 1967); Matthijs Kalmijn, "Intermarriage and Homogamy: Causes, Patterns, Trends," *Annual Review of Sociology* 24 (1998): 395–421.
36. Christine R. Schwartz and Robert D. Mare, "Trends in Educational Assortative Marriage from 1940 to 2003," *Demography* 42.4 (2005): 621–646.
37. Christine Schwartz, "Trends and Variations in Assortative Mating: Causes and Consequences," *Annual Review of Sociology* 39 (2013): 451–470.
38. Ruth Perry, *Novel Relations: The Transformation of Kinship in English Literature and Culture 1748–1818* (Cambridge: Cambridge University Press, 2004), 255–259, 281. Michael McKeon states that the eighteenth century was "truly innovative … [in] its extraordinary concentration upon the question of marriage choice, and upon the paradigm of a basic opposi-

tion between love and money." Michael McKeon, *The Secret History of Domesticity: Public, Private and the Division of Knowledge* (Baltimore: The Johns Hopkins University Press, 2005), 131–132.
39. Weisser, *The Glass Slipper*, 55.
40. Lisa Johnson Mandell, *How to Snare a Millionaire NOW: A Sequel to the Ultimate Guide on Marrying for Love and Money* (Bloomington, IN: Booktango, 2012)
41. Elizabeth Ford and Daniela Drake, *Smart Girls Marry Money: How Women Have Been Duped into the Romantic Dream and How They're Paying for It* (Philadelphia, PA: Running Press Book Publishers, 2009).
42. Mandell, *How to Snare a Millionaire Now.*

BIBLIOGRAPHY

Bailey, Beth L. *From Front Porch to Back Seat: Courtship in Twentieth Century America.* Baltimore: John Hopkins University Press, 1988.

Baltzell, E. Digby. *Philadelphia Gentlemen: The Making of a National Upper Class.* New Brunswick, NJ: Transaction Publishers, 2011[1958].

Beckert, Sven. *The Monied Metropolis: New York City and the Consolidation of the American Bourgeoisie, 1850–1896.* Cambridge: Cambridge University Press, 1993.

Benton, John F. "Clio and Venus: An Historical View of Medieval Love," in F. X. Newton, ed. *The Meaning of Courtly Love.* Albany NY: State University of New York Press, 1968, 19–42.

Binhammer, Katherine. *The Seduction Narrative in Britain, 1747–1800.* Cambridge: Cambridge University Press, 2009.

Blau, Peter and Otis Dudley Duncan. *The American Occupational Structure.* New York: Wiley, 1967.

Blumberg, Paul M. and P. W. Paul. "Continuities and Discontinuities in Upper-Class Marriages," *Journal of Marriage and Family* 37.1 (1975): 63–77.

Bulcroft, Richard, Kris Bulcroft, Karen Bradley and Carl Simpson. "The Management and Production of Risk in Romantic Relationships: A Postmodern Paradox," *Journal of Family History* 25.1 (2000): 63–92.

Cannon, John. *Aristocratic Century: The Peerage of Eighteenth-Century England.* Cambridge: Cambridge University Press, 1984.

Centers, Richard. "Marital Selection and Occupational Strata," *American Journal of Sociology* 54.6 (1949): 530–535.

Cox, Frank D. *Human Intimacy: Marriage, the Family, and Its Meaning.* Belmont, CA: Wadsworth, 2009.

Dinitz, Simon, Franklin Banks and Benjamin Pasamanick. "Mate Selection and Social Class: Changes During the Past Quarter Century," *Marriage and Family Living* 22.4 (1960): 348–351.

Elder, Jr., Glen H.. "Appearance and Education in Marriage Mobility," *American Sociological Review* 34.4 (1969): 519–533.

Farrel, Betty. *Elite Families: Class and Power in Nineteenth Century Boston*. Albany: State University of New York, 1993.

Flandrin, Jean Louis. *Sex in the Western World: The Development of Attitudes and Behavior*. Newark, NJ: Harwood Academic Publishers, 1991.

Ford, Elizabeth and Daniela Drake. *Smart Girls Marry Money: How Women Have Been Duped into the Romantic Dream and How They're Paying for It*. Philadelphia, PA: Running Press Book Publishers, 2009.

Glenn, Norval D., Adreain A. Ross and Judy Corder Tully. "Patterns of Intergenerational Mobility of Females Through Marriage," *American Sociological Review* 39.5 (1974): 683–699.

Hatch, David L. and Mary A. Hatch. "Criteria of Status as Derived from Marriage Announcements in the New York Times," *American Sociological Review* 12.4 (1947): 396–403.

Herman, Sondra R. "Loving Courtship or the Marriage Market? The Ideal and Its Critics, 1871–1911," *American Quarterly* 25.2 (1973): 235–252.

Hunt, Thomas C. "Occupational Status and Marriage Selection," *American Sociological Review* 5.4 (1940): 495–504.

Illouz, Eva. *Why Love Hurts*. Cambridge: Polity Press, 2012.

Jaher, Frederic Cople. *The Urban Establishment: Upper Strata in Boston, New York, Charleston, Chicago, and Los Angeles*. Urbana: University of Illinois Press, 1982.

Kalmijn, Matthijs. "Intermarriage and Homogamy: Causes, Patterns, Trends," *Annual Review of Sociology* 24 (1998): 395–421.

Lantz, Herman R. "Romantic Love in the Pre-Modern Period: A Sociological Commentary," *Journal of Social History* 15.3 (1982): 349–370.

Lantz, Herman R., Raymond Schmitt, Margaret Britton and Eloise C. Snyder. "Pre-Industrial Patterns in the Colonial Family in America: A Content Analysis of Colonial Magazines," *American Sociological Review* 33.3 (1968): 413–426.

Love, Wendy,. "The Dialectic of Love in *Sir Charles Grandison*," in David Blewett, ed. *Passion and Virtue: Essays on the Novels of Samuel Richardson*. Toronto: University of Toronto Press, 2001, 295–316.

Lystra, Karen. *Searching the Heart: Women, Men, and Romantic Love in Nineteenth-Century America*. New York: Oxford University Press, 1989.

Malakh-Pines, Ayala. *Falling in Love: Why We Choose the Lovers We Choose*. New York: Routledge, 1999.

Mandell, Lisa Johnson. *How to Snare a Millionaire Now: A Sequel to the Ultimate Guide on Marrying for Love and Money*. Bloomington, IN: Booktango, 2012.

May, Lary. *The Big Tomorrow: Hollywood and the Politics of the American Way*. Chicago: University of Chicago Press, 2000.

McKeon, Michael. *The Secret History of Domesticity: Public, Private and the Division of Knowledge*. Baltimore: The Johns Hopkins University Press, 2005.

Peplau, Letitia Anne and Steven L. Gordon. "Women and Men in Love: Gender Differences in Close Heterosexual Relationships," in Virginia E. O'Leary, Rhoda Kesler Unger, Barbara Strudler Wallston, eds. *Women, Gender, and Social Psychology*. Hillsdale, NJ: Erlbaum, 1985, 257–292.

Perry, Ruth. *Novel Relations: The Transformation of Kinship in English Literature and Culture 1748–1818*. Cambridge: Cambridge University Press, 2004.

Rothman, Ellen K. *Hands and Hearts: A History of Courtship in America*. New York: Basic Books, 1984.

Rubin, Zick. "Do American Women Marry Up?" *American Sociological Review* 33.5 (1968): 750–760.

Schutte, Kimberly. *Women, Rank and Marriage in the British Aristocracy, 1485–2000:An Open Elite?* Basingstoke, Hampshire: Palgrave Macmillan, 2014.

Schwartz, Christine. "Trends and Variations in Assortative Mating: Causes and Consequences," *Annual Review of Sociology* 39 (2013): 451–470.

Schwartz, Christine R. and Robert D. Mare. "Trends in Educational Assortative Marriage from 1940 to 2003," *Demography* 42.4 (2005): 621–646.

Shorter, Edward. *The Making of the Modern Family*. New York, 1975.

Shumway, David R. *Modern Love: Romance, Intimacy, and the Marriage Crisis*. New York: New York University Press, 2003.

Stone, Lawrence. *Road to Divorce, England 1530–1987*. Oxford: Oxford University Press, 1990.

Tague, Ingrid H. *Women of Quality: Accepting and Contesting Ideals of Femininity in England, 1690–1760*. Woodbridge, Suffolk: Boydell Press.

Taylor, Patricia Ann and Norval D. Glenn. "The Utility of Education and Attractiveness for Females' Status Attainment Through Marriage," *American Sociological Review* 41. 3 (1976): 484–498.

Thomas, David. "The Social Origins of Marriage Partners of the British Peerage in the Eighteenth and Nineteenth Centuries," *Population Studies* 26.1 (1972), 99–111.

Weisser, Susan Ostrov. *The Glass Slipper: Women and Love Stories*. New Brunswick: Rutgers University Press, 2013.

CHAPTER 2

Before the Movies: The Cross-Class Romance in Fiction

Cross-class romance, together with the differentiated and overlapping themes of cross-class seduction and cross-class marriage, can be traced to two forms of literary fiction: the fairy tale, and, more importantly, the novel. *Cinderella* is the fairy tale most frequently associated with the cross-class romance, but this association became more evident in the twentieth century after the tale had undergone significant changes from its earliest published forms. In what is probably the earliest full literary version of the tale in Europe, *The Cat Cinderella* by Giambattista Basile, published between 1634 and 1636, Cinderella is the daughter of a prince. In the two popular and influential versions, *Cinderella, or the Little Glass Slipper* (1697) by Charles Perrault and *Ash Girl* (1812) by the Brothers Grimm, Cinderella is the daughter of a wealthy man. In these early versions, Cinderella's class origin are high, but she is degraded by her stepmother and stepsisters and, in marrying the prince, she reclaims her birthright.[1]

Beyond the common theme of class reinstatement, there are differences among the early versions, particularly with respect to Cinderella's character. Whereas Basile's heroine fights for her rights (she kills her first stepmother), Perrault's Cinderella is submissive and domestic. Basile's version was closer in spirit to oral folk versions that depicted the struggles of a spirited, independent young girl, aided by her dead mother, whose goal is not marriage but recognition of her true status. Perrault made Cinderella an incarnation of Christian values; she patiently bears the abuse of her

© The Author(s) 2017
S. Sharot, *Love and Marriage Across Social Classes in American Cinema*,
DOI 10.1007/978-3-319-41799-8_2

stepfamily and helps to dress them in their finery for the ball. Although dressed in rags Cinderella is "a hundred times handsomer than her sisters," and this inconsistency between beauty and dress is corrected by the fairy godmother who, among her transformations, changes Cinderella's clothes into cloth of silver and gold. Suitably attired, Cinderella displays at the ball all the graces expected of the refined, aristocratic lady, and her goodness is not spoilt by her marriage to the prince as she forgives her stepsisters and finds them husbands among the lords of the courts.[2]

Perrault's Cinderella provided both a model of the comportment and behavior of the aristocratic lady, and, by her passive suffering and forgiveness, a more general ideal of feminine submissiveness.[3] The Cinderella of the Brothers Grimm is far less submissive and there is more violence (the stepsisters are punished by having their eyes pecked out by the birds that help Cinderella), but even in Perrault's version there is some ambiguity with respect to Cinderella's behavior; she conveys humility and self-effacement, but she is also adroit at pretense, fails to tell the truth to her stepfamily, and grasps the opportunity to become a princess.[4] Although the versions of Perrault and the Brothers Grimm differ in a number of ways, they both incorporate the aristocratic belief in virtue by birth. Cinderella is the daughter of a rich man, apparently bourgeois rather than aristocratic, but she displays the salient characteristics of gentility. Her innate virtue, a virtue that indelibly marks the nobility, is contrasted with the coarse, ambitious parvenu stepsisters. Cinderella's magical clothes reveal the "natural" superiority of the higher ranks, and it is the sight of Cinderella in the clothes that enchants the prince. The shoe or slipper that fits Cinderella's foot is an emblem of her true identity as a noble lady; it implies a delicate physique that is usually associated with a female of the upper ranks. The prince is bewitched by Cinderella, but there is nothing in the text to suggest that the prince loves Cinderella or that Cinderella loves the prince.[5]

Later versions of Cinderella incorporate romantic love—often love at first sight—and twentieth-century film versions no longer have Cinderella born into a wealthy family. The heroine's beauty and birth are no longer associated with aristocratic or high birth, and the relationship between Cinderella and the prince becomes a true romance across classes. Perrault's self-effacing Cinderella rather than the more active Cinderella of Basile and the Brothers Grimm was adopted in American children's books in the nineteenth century and although a more savvy, independent Cinderella began to appear in twentieth-century film versions, the Disney version in 1949 presented a passive Cinderella who awaits her rescue with patience and a song.[6] Although cross-class romances are often tagged as 'Cinderella stories' in order to emphasize their far-fetched, fairy-tale elements, it is evident that the most essential elements of the cross-class romance were not derived from the fairy tale. It is more accurate to say that the Cinderella story underwent adaptation to the cross-class romance as it crystallized in other fictional forms, particularly the modern novel.

THE EARLY MODERN NOVEL: CROSS-CLASS SEDUCTION

Samuel Richardson's *Pamela or Virtue Rewarded* (1740), regarded by many as the first modern novel, contains three aspects of the cross-class male-female relationship that will continue to overlap and be differentiated in subsequent fictions: attempted seduction, romance and marriage.[7] The theme of seduction was prominent in what has become known as 'amatory fiction' written in the last decades of the seventeenth century and the early decades of the eighteenth century prior to the publication of *Pamela* in 1740. The most prominent authors of amatory fiction were women writing for a predominantly female readership. The most typical plot involves an innocent young girl who is seduced by an older man, often her guardian or a relative, who promises her true love and marriage and then abandons her once his desires have been sated. The heroines struggle, verbally and physically, against their seducers, but their resistance heightens the males' desire and the seducers or rapists invariably achieve their goal. The representations of rape and seduction are often hard to distinguish because the maidens are frequently made complicit in their undoing as they initially enjoy the rake's attentions or are unknowingly in love with their seducers.[8] The heroines are often tormented with guilt after their seduction, but in contrast with the seduction fiction of the later eighteenth century and nineteenth century they are not invariably punished with social ostracism or death and some recover their reputations.[9]

Apart from Richardson's attempt to replace the deliberate fantasy of amatory fiction with realistic settings and characters, the treatment of seduction in *Pamela* differs from that fiction in a number of ways. Firstly, the attempts of Mr. B, the squire, to seduce the 15-year old Pamela, which make up a large part of the novel, fail; his promises, attempted bribes, tricks and violence are of no avail, and the attempted seduction is replaced by love and marriage between the would-be seducer and his intended victim. Whereas the male's love or exclamations of love in amatory fiction is typically reduced to sexual desire, Mr. B's lust is transformed into love and is domesticated in marriage. Secondly, in contrast with the heroines of amatory fiction who almost always belong to the same class as their seducer, the aristocracy or at least leisured stratum,[10] Pamela is a maidservant. The inequality of the male and female in amatory fiction was confined to gender, and prior to *Pamela,* fictional sexual intimacy between the upper and lower class was for the most part a subject for pornographers.[11] *Pamela,* while highly successful, did not set a trend with respect to its integration of the narrative of seduction and the narrative of cross-class romance. It was Richardson's second novel *Clarissa* that was a more important touchstone in the development of the novel of seduction and had many imitators among both British and American writers.

There are class differences between Clarissa and her would-be seducer, Lovelace, but they are minor compared with those in *Pamela.* Lovelace is heir to an earldom and Clarissa is the youngest child of a landed family whose wealth was originally gained from trade. The aim of Clarissa's brother is to achieve a title and, in order to advance this aim and prevent any diversion of the family's wealth to Clarissa, he convinces his family to put pressure on Clarissa to marry Solmes, a physically repulsive, uneducated, newly wealthy man. Clarissa's family opposes her courtship by Lovelace, an attractive, educated aristocrat who exploits her alienation from her family to advance his licentious goal. He tricks Clarissa into fleeing from her family with him, but his belief that every woman will eventually surrender to desire is proved wrong by the virtuous Clarissa who successfully struggles against the passion that Lovelace arouses in her. After Lovelace's rape of Clarissa as she lay unconscious, the heroine eventually dies, and it is this narrative of seduction or rape followed by a detailed account of the heroine's suffering and death that became the common trajectory of the seduction novel. In many subsequent novels of seduction, the unequal positions of males and females is compounded by the inequality of class; the seduced maiden who, unlike Clarissa, finally gives her consent to the illicit intercourse, is often a simple village girl of about fifteen to eighteen and the seducer is a man in his twenties from the upper class. Richardson's Lovelace, remorseful of his actions, is killed in a dual with a cousin of Clarissa, but in many subsequent seduction novels the pathetic fate of the girl contrasts with the ability of the male to avoid negative consequences to his life or social position. Although the seduced maidens are frequently from the lower classes, they are made appealing and objects of compassion by their fine sensibilities that are purported to be exceptional for their class.[12]

THE EARLY MODERN NOVEL: CROSS-CLASS ROMANCE AND MARRIAGE

Richardson's Pamela is represented as exceptional for her class, not only because of her sensibilities, but also by her success in prevailing against the sexual advances of her social superior. This provided a touchstone for the genre of 'seduction foiled', which became as popular as that of the genre of seduced maidens.[13] In the melodramatic versions that became popular in the theatre, the maiden does not fall in love or marry her would-be seducer but thwarts him and is rescued just in time by a hero. It was the introduction of love followed by marriage between Pamela and the would-be seducer Mr. B that made *Pamela* the most prominent early example of the successful cross-class romance formula. Even as she resists Mr. B's sexual advances, Pamela betrays her attraction to him by comments on his appearance, his health and her admission that she cannot hate him. Mr. B sends Pamela back to her parents after he abandons his attempts to seduce her or make her his mistress, and it is on her journey home that she receives a letter from him in which he declares his love and requests her return. Pamela had slowly and reluctantly come to acknowledge that she was in love with Mr. B. She declared that love is not voluntary "for I know not how it came, nor when it began; but creep, creep it has … and before I knew what was the Matter, it look'd like Love."[14] After the marriage, Mr. B's sisters, Lady Davers, asks Pamela if she did not love him the whole time. Pamela answers that she had always had great reverence for her master "but I did not know that it was Love. Indeed, I had not the Presumption."[15] Mr. B expresses his love for Pamela on a number of occasions, both prior to his proposal of marriage and after.[16] One of the rules that Mr. B submits to Pamela after their marriage is that "Love before marriage is absolutely necessary."[17]

The cross-class romance and marriage in *Pamela* is conducted with little questioning of the inequalities of gender and class. Pamela felt that Mr. B lowered himself and demeaned his status when he pursued her.[18] His attempt to violate her virginity violated the ethical standards of his own class and aligned him with the worst of his servants, Mrs. Jewkes, who tries to force Pamela into sexual submission. Once Mr. B shows signs of his redemption and offers Pamela marriage, she is able to admit to her attraction to him and accepts unconditionally his superiority. She tells Mrs. Jewkes that Mr. B "shall always be my Master; and I shall think myself more and more his Servant."[19] Lady Davers' initial violent opposition to her brother marrying a maidservant occasions Pamela's reflections that the rich have no cause to despise the poor. She declares that all were originally equal and all will be judged equally. There is no reason for the rich to be high minded and proud because fortunes are lost and gained; class position is not immutable.[20] She does not, however, object to inequality if the wealthy behave in accord with their rank. She repeatedly praises the ability of the wealthy to do good and after her marriage to Mr. B she adopts the role of the Lady Bountiful. Her criticism is not of the class system but of Mr. B's failure, and the failure of others like him, to meet the ethical standards of their own class. Once the aristocrat has come to accept his moral obligations, his class position is secure.[21]

The potential subversion of the class system by cross-class marriage is reduced by Richardson in a number of ways. Pamela's beauty is like that of a lady; she has fine hands, small feet,and a slender waist. She also has the delicate constitution of a lady as shown by her tendency to faint at any sexual advance. We learn that during the period when Pamela was a maidservant to Mr. B's widowed mother, prior to Mr. B's return to England occasioned by his mother's death, the mother had taught Pamela skills such as dancing, singing, drawing, needlework, and writing in a "genteel Manner." Pamela recognizes that she now has skills above her class, and they indicate that Mr. B's mother regarded her as a surrogate daughter. After his mother's death, Mr. B gives Pamela many of his mother's fine clothes—an action that arouses the suspicion of Pamela's father that Mr. B has designs on her. Mr. B tries to soften Pamela with presents but, ultimately, he assumes that his class and authority gives him the right to Pamela's sexual favors; he believes that his offer to Pamela to secure her economic independence in return for sex is pure generosity on his part, because he could claim his pleasure without entering into a consensual exchange.[22] The prevalence of these beliefs among the males of Mr. B's class is made evident when Mr. Williams, a clergyman who befriends Pamela, attempts to persuade other gentlemen in the area to interfere on Pamela's behalf. He is unsuccessful and is told that no injury is done to a servant maid if a squire takes his pleasure with her because the maid has no family name to protect.[23]

The skills taught to Pamela by Mr. B's mother prepare her for her future role as his wife, and at the point when Mr. B marries Pamela we learn that her parent's class had not always been so low. Pamela relates that her parents had once "lived creditably" and her father had tried unsuccessfully to set up a small country school before he was forced to take up hard labor.[24] However, this information makes little difference to the vast class gulf between Pamela and the Squire. When Mr. B first declares his love for Pamela he tells her that the "World's Judgment" and "Censure" prevents him from marrying her.[25] Lady Davers writes to her brother that if he would think of marrying Pamela it would be "utterly inexcusable." She reminds him that their family, one of the best in the kingdom, had never "disgraced themselves by unequal matches," and she would renounce him forever if he would "descend so meanly."[26] When Mr. B proposes marriage to Pamela he warns her that she will be slighted by the neighboring gentry and that his sister, Lady Davers, will never reconcile herself to their marriage. Pamela, wholly respectful of the upper class, says that even the slights of the ladies will be an honor to one with such a low status as herself.[27] The wedding is a small private event and when Lady Davers arrives she refuses at first to believe that they have married and then remonstrates with her brother: "Suppose … I had marry'd by Father's Groom! What would you have said to that?" Mr. B's response not only provides a lesson to his sister on the relationship of class and gender it also explains why in the vast majority of both real and fictional cross-class marriages the wealthy protagonist is male and the poor protagonist is female: "The Difference is, a Man ennobles the Woman he takes, be she *who* she will; and adopts her into his own rank, be it *what* it will: But a Woman, tho' ever so nobly born, debases herself by a mean Marriage, and descends from her own Rank, to his she stoops to."[28]

The most important means used by Richardson to defuse the subversive potential of a cross-class marriage was to make Pamela an exemplary special case who proves repeatedly, both prior to and after the marriage, that she is worthy of her elevation. Early in the narrative, the neighboring aristocratic ladies comment on the beauty of Mr. B's servant maid and one exclaims that Pamela must be of better descent that she had been told.[29] After the marriage, the neighboring gentry do not hesitate to visit Mr. B's bride and shower her with complements, describing her as charming, graceful, with a fine figure.[30] Mr. B explains to his sister that Pamela has more beauty, virtue, prudence and generosity than any lady that he has known and that "she has all these *naturally*, they are *born* with her."[31] Mrs. Davers comes to recognize these virtues and removes her opposition to her brother's marriage.[32] The information that Pamela's parents had formerly embraced genteel aspirations functioned to account, at least in part, for Pamela's exceptionalism, and it is certainly the case that Pamela's values are representative of a moralistic middle class. Above all, it is Pamela's exceptional virtue that enables her to overcome the class barrier. Mr. B tells her that he is "not so much the victim of your Love, all charming as you are, as of your Virtue."[33] Sir Simon, a neighbor, tells Mr. B that "there is something in Virtue, that we had not well considered," and that Mr. B has got the "one Angel [who has] come down for these thousand years."[34] The message of "Virtue Rewarded" is reinforced by the cautionary tale of Sally Godfrey, a girl closer to Mr. B's class, whom he seduced and impregnated and then assisted her passage to Jamaica where she marries a man ignorant of her indiscretion. The child left in England by Sally is taken in by Pamela who succeeds in molding her moral character. The motif of an exemplary working-class girl with middle-class values redeeming a wealthy man was to become a common motif in both literature and films.

Unlike most subsequent cross-class romances that end with marriage, *Pamela* continues after the marriage, and Richardson's sequel, *Pamela, Volume 2*, provides both a very detailed account of married life and further refutation that a cross-class marriage had subversive implications. Richardson was concerned to deny the charge that *Pamela* had sanctioned social leveling, and a sequel offered the opportunity to take the denial even further. Pamela's beauty, virtues and capacity to learn the skills and deportment of a lady enable her to overcome obstacles to her social acceptance. She performs the role so well that one countess exclaims that Pamela must have been born with her dignity: "Education cannot give it: if it could, why should not *we* have it."[35] Pamela's ability to act the part of the lady is demonstrated when Mr. B's grotesque uncle, Sir Jacob Swynford, comes to protest the marriage. When Pamela is presented to him as Lady Jenny, the daughter of a countess, Sir Jacob exclaims that he wishes Mr. B had married "such a charming creature, who carried tokens of her high birth in her face, and whose every feature and look shewed her to be nobly descended."[36] Once disabused, Sir Jacob is contrite and immediately accepts Pamela. When Sir Jacob expresses his concern that, despite Pamela's excellences, the marriage could set an example to other young gentlemen to marry beneath them, Mr. B asks Pamela if she can defend him. Pamela reluctantly expresses her opinion that "degrees in general should be kept up; although I must always deem the present case a happy exception to the rule." She adds that there should be a law that would determine that "when a man, whatever his station, seduces a woman, whatever her station, he would be obliged to marry her."[37]

Mr. B raises the status of Pamela's parents by asking them to run his Kentish estate and when the parents ask for Pamela's advice on employing two of her cousins to work on the estate, Pamela makes clear her opposition, "for I would not wish any of them to be lifted out of his station, and made independent, at Mr. B's expense, if their industry will not do it."[38] Pamela's recognition of her exceptionalism as well as her support of the social order is made evident when, following her marriage, she happens to spy on Mr. H, Lady Davers' nephew, attempting to have his way with Polly, Pamela's maidservant. Polly struggles and complains but she also encourages the nephew by laughing. We are given to understand that most maidservants act like Polly and that Pamela was not like most maidservants. Pamela criticizes Polly for her language and conduct ("if you hope to emulate my good fortune, do you think *this* is the way?"), and berates Mr. H for having "leveled all distinction."[39]

As Pamela's exceptionalism enables her to become a lady and rapidly overcome the objections of members of Mr. B's family, there remains little room for drama over class differences in the sequel. Although marriage changes Pamela's class and way of life, her values remain essentially the same; she becomes a privileged aristocratic lady with her bourgeois values intact. And, indeed, little happens in the first half of the sequel; Pamela's virtues are endlessly celebrated and her class origins appear to be forgotten as her relations with her parents become indistinct, all the servants defer to her and she moves with ease among the aristocrats. A dramatic development of sorts occurs when Mr. B and a pregnant Pamela go to stay in London where characters do call attention to Pamela's class origins. The couple attends a masquerade where Mr. B, dressed in a costume of a Spanish don, separates himself from Pamela and flirts with a woman dressed in the costume of a nun whom we later learn is a countess. Mr. B continues to visit the Countess, and fearing that Mr. B will divorce her, Pamela makes Mr. B participate with her in a pretend trial in which Pamela is accused of marrying Mr. B in order to change her status. Her punishment would be divorce and Mr. B marrying the Countess who has the "nobleness of birth."[40] Mr. B breaks off his relationship with the Countess who leaves for Italy, and it is revealed that false rumors of a sexual liaison between them had been spread by the malicious Mr. Turner, who had been jilted by the Countess.[41]

The potential of a plot in *Pamela, Volume II* of a cross-class marriage ruined by infidelity of the male with a woman of his own class is reduced to misunderstandings. No further events disturb the happiness of the couple; Pamela continues to be popular among the local gentry and nobility, the couple have many children, and they travel.[42] If *Pamela, or Virtue*

Rewarded was a touchstone for fictions of cross-class romance that end in marriage, its sequel lacked a coherent narrative that might have made it a touchstone for novels of cross-class marriages that are disrupted by class differences between the couple. The sequel is more like a conduct book than a novel, with Pamela functioning as an exemplar of the virtuous wife and perfect mother who defers to her husband even at the expense of her own beliefs.[43]

The little interest aroused by *Pamela, Volume II* suggests why few subsequent cross-class romances in fiction and films continued their narratives beyond marriage. The portrayal of a happy, problem-free marriage was boring, and the most interesting part of *Pamela, Volume II* is when Pamela believes that her marriage is threatened by the relationship of her husband with the Countess. This upset is soon defused and the book returns to its uninteresting account of a happy marriage.

It may be surmised that one reason Richardson wrote a sequel was that other authors attempted to profit from the novel's success by writing their own sequels. These authors included the 'Pamelists' who continued to portray Pamela as a virtuous heroine and the 'anti-Pamelists' who portrayed a duplicitous anti-heroine. There was nothing new in making a fictional heroine regard her chastity as a supreme value, but the anti-Pamelists believed that it was preposterous to assign this value to a maidservant. A woman's sexual behavior and her social class were perceived as congruent. Laboring women in general were believed to have no inhibition in providing sexual favors, and their sexual proclivities and willingness to engage in sexual relations outside of marriage were contrasted with unmarried leisure-class women who were represented as sexually chaste and innocent. When a servant women proclaimed her sexual virtue it could be nothing more than an act, and it would be foolish for a upper-class man to believe her.[44] The assumption that a maidservant's defense of her chastity must be a pretense was shared by Mr. B in the early parts of the novel, when he responds to Pamela's resistance by accusing her of being "a little hypocrite" who has "all the arts of her sex."[45] Mr. B refuses to believe that Pamela's fainting episodes in response to his sexual advances are genuine, and when he recognizes that she has lost consciousness he believes that she can induce the fainting at will. He makes repeated attempts to read Pamela's letters to her parents and her journal in order to discover hidden designs, and he decides to make Pamela his wife only when he is convinced that she is innocent of all designs. Mr. B's phrasing of his proposal of marriage, asking Pamela if she can return his "honest compliment" of love as his only motive, reflects his lingering anxiety that her 'love' for him conceals other interests. Pamela's response that she has never entertained the "presumption" of marrying Mr. B conveys that her love is genuine.[46] After Mr. B is convinced, it is the turn of Lady Davers to accuse Pamela of duplicity and then to be persuaded that her love is genuine. Some readers could not, however, be persuaded and their reading of a duplicitous Pamela is supported by what Huang Mei has called "holes and gaps" in the narrative. Although Pamela repeatedly begs for permission to return to her parents in order to escape Mr. B's advances, once Mr. B gives his permission she tarries at his house under the pretense of her duties. Pamela makes a handsome waistcoat for her "vile" master, she often makes sure that they encounter each other, she expresses anxiety about his feelings towards her, and she tells him adamantly that she loves no other. These incidences suggest that, parallel to the prominent narrative of Pamela's defense of her virtue, there is "a 'silent' plot of self-advancement."[47]

The proposition that a maidservant's defense of her chastity was rewarded by wealth and status lent itself to satire. The best known of the Anti-Pamelist works, which purported to reveal the "true" Pamela, was Henry Fielding's *Shamela* (1741), a sixty-page satire of the narrative method and moralizing of Richardson's lengthy novel. *Shamela* begins with a letter from a gullible parson who recommends the novel *Pamela* to a fellow parson, who in turn explains that Pamela's name is actually Shamela and presents her authentic correspondence together with letters written by other characters. The letters reveal that Shamela is a calculating hussy who makes a pretense of her "vartue" in order to ensnare Square Booby for material goals. Shamela is repulsed by Booby's inadequate lovemaking and she takes as her love the Reverend Williams, who is transformed from the virtuous clergyman in Richardson's novel into a scheming rogue.[48] In comparison with Shamela, who is as interested in sexual satisfaction as much as material rewards, Syrena Tricksy, the anti-heroine of Eliza Haywood's *The Anti-Pamela; or Feign'd Innocence Detected* (1741) is focused more exclusively on financial gain in her relationships with a number of men. For Syrena, love or sincere affection is not part of her emotions. She has been taught "that a woman who had Beauty to attract the Men, and Cunning to manage them afterwards, was secure of making her Fortune."[49] Syrena's ambition is to establish herself as a gentlewoman, but reckless spending by Syrena and her mother leads them to penury.[50]

The origins of Fielding's Shamela are disreputable; she is the illegitimate daughter of an orange seller and a dissipated custom house official. The Pamelist writers, in contrast, deprive Pamela of a humble background and thereby negate the subversive motif of a maidservant marrying into the aristocracy no less than the anti-Pamelists. John Kelly's two-volume sequel, *Pamela's Conduct in High Life* (1741) reveals that Pamela's parents are descendants of genteel ancestry, as does another work, *The Life of Pamela* (1741). In a popular theatrical version of *Pamela*, the squire learns that the heroine is of noble birth before he marries her. Whereas most of the Pamelist writers raised Pamela's class origins in order to achieve what they saw as an appropriate correspondence with her moral qualities and marriage into the aristocracy, a dramatic poem *Pamela the Second* provided a different solution to the potential subversion of a cross-class marriage: Pamela resists the advances of her father's landlord until she is rescued by her true love, a young miller.[51]

The greatest number of seduction narratives in the street literature of ballads and chapbooks that circulated among the lower classes told of laboring women seduced and abandoned by men of their own class, but a good number told of relationships between laboring women and men from the higher classes. Unlike the Pamelist literature that raised Pamela's class background, the street literature affirmed their heroines' laboring class background. Unlike the anti-Pamelist literature in which the lower-class woman ensnares the higher-class man for purely mercenary motives, the street literature told of women who were wise enough to understand that a rich man who vows true love is after sex without marriage. The virtue of the laboring heroine is not her chastity, as little stigma was attached to premarital sex; a laboring woman's ruin occurred not when she loses her virginity, but when a man of whatever class impregnates her and then refuses to marry her. The laboring woman's virtue is her refusal to submit to the desire of the upper-class man and his class-based authority. In contrast to Pamela whose defense against male sexual aggression was to faint, some street literature heroines would use violence against the male aggressor. Some ballads depicted women as victims but others celebrated laboring-class women who outwit upper-class men, steal their money or trick them into marriage. In certain chapbooks, the heroine is motivated solely by feeling, and her lack of class pretensions lead her to reject her rich suitor. Chapbooks written by Christian moralists used the seduction plot as a warning to laboring women not to believe that they could rise in class through marriage.[52]

Pamela, the spurious sequels and satires, and the street literature of the period contain motifs that were to be repeated ad infinitum in subsequent fictions—in novels, short stories, plays and films of cross-class sexual encounters and romances. First, the most central motif is that of the poor, lower- or working-class female whose virtues are rewarded by marriage to a wealthy or upper-class male. The second motif is that of the dissipated, wealthy male redeemed by the virtuous poor female. In the third motif, members of the wealthy male's family oppose his engagement or marriage to the poor female. The fourth motif is the female who came to be known in the twentieth century as a 'gold digger,' an amoral social climber who feigns virtue (in the eighteenth century) or love (in the twentieth century) in order to marry the wealthy man. The use of 'female wiles' to seduce the male is frequently successful and differs from the more aggressively physical attempt at seduction of the female by the male. And the fifth motif is the virtuous girl from the working class who constitutes an exception from within her class. Within the compass of these motifs, variations appeared in accord with socio-cultural change, particularly with respect to expectations of gender, and the specific classes of protagonists would, of course, change as the class structure changed.

One change within these motifs has been in the nature of the female's virtues. The major virtue of the twentieth century heroine of the cross-class romance is not her defense of her chastity, although this remained important in the early decades of the century, but rather her disinterested love for the wealthy man. The integrity of the heroine came to focus less on her body than on her indifference to material and other considerations of class and status, which are entirely subordinated to the overwhelming value and emotion of love. This development reaches its apogee when the virtuous heroine is a prostitute, as in *Pretty Woman.* One motif not found in the early cross-class romance literature is the redemption through love of the predatory female. In much of the post-*Pamela* cross-class romance fiction, the virtuous heroines continue to redeem the male objects of their love, but female protagonists remain either virtuous or sexually manipulative; the redemption of the sexually manipulative woman by falling in love is a comparatively late variation.

Females have always constituted the majority of the poor protagonists in cross-class romances, but there have always been a minority who were male. In Henry Fielding's comic novel *Joseph Andrews,* it is the woman from the upper-class, Lady Booby, the aunt of Mr. B from *Pamela,* who, soon after the death of her husband, makes sexual overtures to Joseph, her

young, handsome footman. Joseph is the brother of Pamela and he follows his sister's example by insisting on his chastity. Lady Booby declares
to Joseph that it is not to be believed that when "a Lady demeans herself
to throw aside the Rules of Decency, in order to honour you with the
highest Favour in her Power, your Virtue should resist her Inclination."
Joseph replies that he cannot understand why, just because he is a man, his
virtue must be subservient to the lady's pleasure.[53] Joseph's polite refusal
leads to his dismissal but later Lady Booby admits to her maidservant that,
although Joseph's qualities are higher than those of many contemptible
aristocrats, in order to avoid the censure of society, women of her class
must "ally ourselves to those we despise; we must prefer Birth, Title and
Fortune to real Merit. It is a Tyranny of Custom."[54] Lady Booby understands that her desire for Joseph is a feeling that women of her status
are not permitted to acknowledge even to themselves. She asks herself if
she could marry a footman and sacrifice her reputation and rank "to the
Indulgence of a mean and a vile Appetite."[55] As Lady Booby's feelings for
Joseph are not reciprocated, she does not have to make a decision with
respect to this dilemma, but a recognition that the romantic crossing of
class boundaries was not entirely constrained by gender was to be found
in a number of street ballads that narrated stories of lower-class men marrying women from higher ranks.[56]

READERS AND SOCIAL EXPERIENCES

One of the major themes of the present book is that, although a cross-
class romance that ended in marriage between a wealthy individual and a
poor person has always been and remains extremely rare, many among the
audience, particularly the female audience, were familiar with the social
experiences and anxieties of the working-girl protagonist. This was true of
many of the female readers of *Pamela* in the eighteenth century, as well
as for many of the female spectators of the cross-class romance movies in
the twentieth century. Richardson's *Pamela* and a number of other novels
of the period were directed primarily to a predominantly female readership that spanned the social classes. An increase in leisure time for women,
especially middle-class women, in London and other large cities, occurred
in the early eighteenth century, and they often occupied their leisure time
with reading fiction. The literacy rate of lower-class women, including
servants, was relatively low, but as domestic service was by far the largest
female occupation after agriculture there were a considerable number of

literate female servants. As an epistolary novel, *Pamela* was almost totally made up of the heroine's letters, and readers found it quite credible that a servant girl could write her own story.[57]

The declaration of Lady Mary Wortley Montague, an aristocratic reader of *Pamela*, that Pamela's matrimonial triumph had made her the joy of chambermaids[58] points to her belief that, not only had many maidservants read the novel, they also identified with its heroine. We may assume that most female servants who worked in aristocratic houses were sufficiently realistic to understand that the possibility of them marrying their masters, even if it was not entirely beyond the realm of possibility, was close to zero. Nevertheless, one concern of the Anti-Pamelites was that *Pamela* would encourage maidservants to behave like ladies and thereby entice their masters into marriage. This was part of a wider feeling among the upper classes of a threat to the absoluteness of the boundary between themselves and their inferiors, a feeling that was evident with respect to clothes. On the one hand, well-dressed, well-mannered servants were encouraged as this was an indication of the wealth and prominence of their employers. On the other hand, there were numerous accounts of well-dressed maids being mistaken for ladies, and this led to expressions of concern that maids would aspire beyond their class. In a pamphlet published under a pseudonym, Daniel Defoe harshly criticized maidservants who dressed as finely as their mistresses; in order to prevent class confusion, he proposed strict dress codes that would prevent servants from wearing expensive fabrics. In contrast to Richardson's Pamela who worried that the clothes that Mr. B gave her from his late mother's wardrobe were too rich and good for her, Defoe wrote that the desire to acquire fine clothes motivated female servants to prostitute themselves. Authors who defended female servants against Defoe's diatribe included "The Lady's Maid," who titled her work *The Maid Servant's Modest Defense*, and "Catherine Comb-brush" who wrote that Moreton (Defoe's pseudonym) wrote his critique after his own servant had rejected his sexual advances and that his obsession with servant's clothes was a projection of his own sexual interest in maids.[59]

Richardson constructed Pamela as an exemplary woman whose distance from the characteristics commonly attributed to female servants enabled her to cross the class boundary, but Richardson also addressed Pamela's anxieties with respect to her class identity. Mr. B's mother taught Pamela skills and qualifications that distinguished Pamela from her parents. Whilst she loves her parents, she also worries that she might be forced to return to them. Pamela learns to act and speak in accord with the class into which she marries, but her feelings of discomfort and anxiety remain, particularly as she is aware that she could still lose her newly attained status.[60] Many maidservants could identify with Pamela's anxieties over her class dislocation as they had also experienced mobility, moving from agrarian labor to serving in houses of the higher classes and participating in a consumerism that in the eighteenth century was moving down into the lower ranks of society. Maidservants may have taken vicarious delight in Pamela's social ascent, but with respect to their own experiences, it was Mr. B's sexual advances that they were likely to find familiar.

It was assumed by many upper-class males that their position gave them sexual privileges over their female servants, and the sexual relations that many female servants had with their masters ranged from the coercive to the seemingly voluntary. Conduct manuals for servants advised the female servant that she had a right to resist a master's sexual advance. Eliza Haywood made it clear in her conduct book, *A Present for a Servant Maid* (1743), that unwanted sex with a master was a common occupational hazard. Haywood advised the self-abnegation of female servants and wrote that they should resist the master's sexual advances by appealing to his patriarchal duty to protect them. She conceded that "a vigorous resistance is less to be expected in your station," and advised that if the maid felt the need to leave her employment she should be careful not to let her mistress know the motive of her departure. A servant should not confide in the master's wife because "in such Cases the Innocent suffer for the crimes of the Guilty." If the sexual advances come from the master's son, Haywood cautioned not to succumb to the bait of a promise of marriage and not to "flatter yourselves that because such matches have sometimes happened, it will be your fortune." She warned that even if such a marriage occurred, "a disparity of birth, of circumstances and education can produce no lasting harmony."[61]

AMERICAN FICTION

An American edition of *Pamela* was printed between 1742 and 1743, but it was only in the last decade of the eighteenth century that American editions of Richardson's novels were published in unprecedented numbers, albeit in abridged versions. Novels were becoming the preferred reading of Americans during this period and novels with seduction plots were among the most popular.[62] The early seduction novels by American authors such as the enormously successful *Charlotte Temple* (1794) and *The Coquette* (1797) were closer to the formula of *Clarissa* than to *Pamela*; the class of the seduced maidens is similar to that of their seducers who abandon them, and they die after giving birth to their illegitimate, often stillborn, babies. The seducer may not have been born an aristocrat but he embodied aristocratic vices and, as such, was a threat to stable family life and, by extension, to the new nation. In contrast to the seducer, a purveyor of corrupt European aristocratic mores, the exemplary figure of a middle-class republican patriarch strove to teach women the appropriate behavior for an American, middle-class female. The women who ignored his advice and succumbed to the advances of the rake were inevitably punished by suffering and death.[63]

From about 1820, the seduction novel gave way in America almost entirely to what has been called domestic or women's fiction that focused on female protagonists in domestic settings.[64] This type of novel, which flourished during the middle decades of the nineteenth century, was written principally by middle-class women for middle-class female readers. The heroine begins in some versions as a poor orphan and in others as a pampered wealthy girl who has become poor, but in place of the passive, naïve and essentially victimized women of seduction novels, the heroines' piety, intelligence and initiative enable them to overcome cruel and immoral adversaries and they become exemplars of 'true womanhood'.[65] There was no questioning that men and women occupy separate spheres and that the heroine's main responsibility was to become an ideal wife and mother. The ideal family, although it might become wealthy, is represented as middle class in its values; it is situated between a lower class, often of immigrant origins, that is domestically disordered, and an upper class seen as idle, wasteful and without the virtues of self-control.[66]

Although middle class values prevail in domestic fiction, many of the novels included a cross-class romance. The novel that has been recognized as the first of the genre, *A New-England Tale* (1822), tells the tale of an orphaned heroine who supports herself as a schoolteacher and ends with her marriage to a wealthy widower who purchases the childhood home that the heroine had lost through the bankruptcy and death of her parents. The orphan heroine of *St. Elmo* (1866) reforms her wealthy benefactress' rakish son who becomes a minister and marries her, but most upper-class suitors are unsuitable; they are portrayed as idle, morally weak and subject to alcoholism and violence. There were instances in which heroines meet appropriate wealthy men through their fathers or brothers, but most heroines are not tempted to marry for money and the female protagonists who do are likely to die in poverty or of a broken heart when they are no longer able to marry the man they truly love. Although in some novels the heroine marries a poor man and is rewarded for her lack of acquisitiveness by the husband becoming wealthy,[67] in most it was made clear that middle-class, well-educated young women should avoid working-class men who are not likely to share their cultural interests and social pursuits. Even though heroines of the domestic genre in the middle decades of the nineteenth century were often rewarded by marriage to a wealthy man, the cross-class romance generally remained within a broadly conceived middle class and did not cross successfully to upper or lower classes.

The heroines of the domestic fiction might work for a short period before they are rescued by marriage, but they are unlikely to engage in work, such as that of a seamstress or a factory worker, that was associated with working-class women.[68] The professionalization of occupations, such as medicine and law, had eliminated women from the most prestigious areas of work and the only professional fields in which women were accepted were nursing and teaching. The advances in prosperity of the early nineteenth century made it possible for middle-class women to become the 'genteel lady', a status that had formerly been reserved for upper-class women. The 'cult of true womanhood' with its emphasis on the home as the place of the female served to reinforce class distinctions as industrialization resulted in an increasing number of women working outside the home in mills and factories. There were areas, such as the frontier, where the economic contribution of women was highly valued, but in the Northeast the lifestyles of middle-class and working-class women were entirely different.[69] Domesticity was a defining characteristic of true womanhood and if a woman was to rise in class through marriage she had to prove her worthiness by acquiring the necessary domestic skills. Gertrude, the mistreated orphan heroine of Maria Susanna Cummins' *The Lamplighter* (1854), eventually finds that she has a wealthy father and marries a wealthy man (both of whom are self-made men), after she overcomes her unruly emotions, learns domesticity and becomes a graceful lady.[70]

The Lamplighter was one of the best sellers in domestic fiction by female authors and was part of a publishing boom that began in the 1850s. An increase in literacy, the expansion of libraries, and technological changes in printing made possible a much larger audience that included working-class women. Some of the authors who wrote fiction directed at working-class readers were themselves workers in the mills of Lowell, Massachusetts. The stories published in local workers' magazines told of poor and struggling but virtuous heroines who were well rewarded in the end, often by marriage with wealthy men. An early short story of this type, *The Temptation* (1848), follows the formula of *Pamela*. The heroine, a factory worker, refuses to yield sexually in exchange for a spurious promise of marriage and financial benefits for her poor farming parents from the son of a wealthy merchant. The son, impressed by her virtue, seeks her forgiveness and makes a genuine proposal of marriage; the following decades saw many repetitions of this formula. The heroine of a short story, *The Factory Girl* (1861), works in a woolen mill and is the sole support for her young brother and parents following her father's business failure. The owner of the mill is attracted to her quiet virtue and, although the heroine at first believes him to be haughty, he finally confesses his love and they marry. The number of working-class female readers for this type of fiction in novel form increased substantially with the publication of dime novels from 1860, and this number continued to increase during the last decades of the nineteenth century. Social mobility was a theme in about one-third of a random sample of 130 novels published in the USA between 1876 and 1910, and although the investigator does not calculate the number of cross-class romances, he states that *Eirene* (1870) was typical. The heroine in this novel starts out as the daughter of a poor but loving farm family, goes through hardships as a worker in a New England textile mill, and ends up in a New York mansion married to the scion of one of the city's prominent Dutch families.[71]

The plot device of the domestic fiction of a young heroine who finds herself without family or other support remained in the dime novel romances, but the working-class heroines of the dime novels faced greater threats to their bodies and, in particular, to their virginity. The seduction plot of the *Clarissa* type was occasionally applied to the working girl. Vinnie of *Only a Mill Girl* (1879) is seduced by a wealthy man who had promised to marry her, and after she is drugged and raped by a lawyer's son she takes a downward path and commits suicide. In most cases, however, the working girl successfully repulses the would-be seducer. The mill worker heroine of the dime story, *Kathie, the Overseer's Daughter: or Love and Life at the Loom* (1887), published in the series "Factory Life Library: Stories for the Working People," rebuffs the sexual advances of a brutal overseer and is rescued by the son of one of the town's magnates. When the son declares his love, the heroine is concerned because of their class differences, but her discovery that she is in fact the daughter of a wealthy man removes this barrier.

The plot device of the working girl's discovery that she is a heiress or daughter of a wealthy parent was common. The heroine of *Rose Michel: or, The Trials of a Factory Girl* (1881) marries a mechanic after he saves her from the clutches of the mill owner's nephew. This is one of the few dime novels in which the factory girl marries a male factory worker, but they are able to move to a stately residence in Boston after Rose discovers that she is the daughter of a French nobleman and that the mill owner is her uncle. Even without the motif of the lost heiress, the middle-class authors were prone to portray their working-class heroines as exceptional within their class and not always popular with their fellow workers. Delia, the beautiful weaver of the short story *Only a Factory Girl* (1881), is sneered at by other workers before she becomes the wife of the junior partner of the business.[72] Female novelists catering to a more middle-class readership occasionally made their heroines nonimmigrant working girls whose refinement in character and behavior separated them from other working girls and made them appropriate to marry wealthy men. The heroine of one of Mary Wilkin Freeman's novels, *The Portion of Labor* (1901), organizes her fellow shoemaking workers for a walkout, but she is too refined to socialize with her crude female coworkers and she becomes the wife of her patrician employer. Another heroine who is refined despite her working-class background is the central protagonist in *Amanda of the Mill* (1905), a novel by Marie van Vorst, a reformer from a wealthy background who worked incognito as a working girl in a factory and mill. The novel's heroine is taken away from work in the mill by the owner's wife when she is a child, and although she later helps the female mill workers in their strike, her qualities made her a suitable mate for the man who inherits the mill.[73]

The theme of the working-class girl as a true lady was common in the stories of Laura Jean Libbey, the most successful author of the working-girl genre. During the 1880s and 1890s, she wrote over sixty novels, many of which were first serialized in popular story weeklies and then printed as dime novels. Some of Libbey's heroines were from the upper- or middle-class and she also made use of the lost heiress device, but her heroines from the working-class were no less ladylike in both appearance and behavior; they are small and girlish, and they are demure and modest. Their daintiness makes them dependent on the hero who is required to rescue her as she is constantly placed in danger by fires, floods and the villain's clutches. In contrast to the villain, whose designs and actions show his lack of respect for the working girl, the hero is identified by his recognition of, and respect for, her true character as a lady.

The message that wealth without love is worthless is a constant theme in Libbey's novels. Marriage for money leads to unhappiness, and a test of the hero's virtue is his willingness to be disinherited and pursue marriage with the working girl despite the opposition of his wealthy parents. The working girl is shown to be capable of honest toil and living in poverty, but her reward is always marriage to a man who combines heroic masculinity and wealth. Virtuous working-class males who love the heroine and may help to rescue her are never suitable mates. As Joyce Shaw Peterson notes in her account of Libbey's novels, the combination of respect for a working girl's work together with the rewards of love and riches provide a success myth that complements the male myth typified by Horatio Alger's male heroes who attain success through hard work, thrift and loyalty to their employers. The difference is, of course, that the working girls are socially mobile through marriage rather than work and, unlike Alger's male heroes who learn to improve their appearance and manners, Libbey's working girls are perfect or natural ladies from the beginning. The naïve innocence of Libbey's heroines may have made the working-girl readers reflect that they knew better, but the message that romantic love is the only basis for marriage clearly had an appeal to young working women who, although they knew that their futures were going to be very different from the heroines, had hopes to improve their situation through marriage.[74]

In Libbey's stories of the 1880s, there was an emphasis on the harsh conditions of the mill or the factory and it was clear at the beginning who was the heroine's worthy suitor and who was the villain or would-be seducer. Libbey modified the formula somewhat in the 1890s; there was less emphasis on the conditions of the work place or on goodness rewarded and evil punished, and greater emphasis on the process of finding the appropriate partner for life. At the beginning, it was not always clear who the heroine would marry. In addition, the heroine often had to overcome trials, such as inappropriate betrothals and meddling relatives, before she and her 'true Mate' discover their true feelings and marry. These modifications of the formula were insufficient to ensure the continued popularity of Libbey and authors like her after World War I. The characters and behavior of working-class heroines in cross-class romance fiction and films came to differ considerably from the ladylike heroines of Libbey and other novelists, especially as we enter the 1920s and even more so the 1930s. One difference is the inclusion of sexual content, which was not even suggested in Libbey's fiction. Passion and sensuality were confined to the villain, who attempts to seduce the pure heroine, and the villainess, who is motivated by jealousy to seek revenge on her rival. With the appearance of the 'New Woman' in both society and popular culture after World War I, passion and sensuality were no longer qualities that had to be subdued.

Cross-class romance changed with the times, but certain themes and assumptions changed little. One assumption that remained was that female socio-economic mobility was attained principally by marriage. Female readers and spectators of cross-class romance fiction and films may have had little hope that their lives would be like those of the heroines of cross-class romances, or that marriage would propel them into wealth or the upper class, but at least during the first four decades of the twentieth century they had good reason to believe that whatever chances they had of mobility were to be attained through marriage.

NOTES

1. Alan Dundes, *Cinderella: A Folklore Casebook* (New York: Garland Publishing, 1982), 3–29.
2. Dundes, *Cinderella*, 16–18, 21.
3. Jack Zipes, *Fairy Tales and the Act of Subversion: The Classical Genre for Children and the Process of Civilization* (New York: Routledge, 1991 [1983]), 27–33.
4. Huang Mei, *Transforming the Cinderella Dream: From Frances Burney to Charlotte Brontë* (New Brunswick: Rutgers University Press, 1990), 8.
5. Elisabeth Panttaya, "Going Up in the World: Class in 'Cinderella'," *Western Folklore* 52 (1993): 85–105; Mei, *Transforming the Cinderella Dream*, 3.
6. Jane Yolen, "America's Cinderella," in Dundes, *Cinderella*, 296–303; Jack Zipes, *The Enchanted Screen: The Unknown History of Fairy-Tale Films* (New York: Routledge, 2011).
7. Samuel Richardson, *Pamela; or, Virtue Rewarded* (Oxford: Oxford University Press, 2001 [1740]).
8. Toni O'Shaughnessy Bowers, "Sex, Lies, and Invisibility: Amatory Fiction from the Restoration to Mid-Century," in John Richetti ed., *The Columbia History of the British Novel* (New York: Columbia University Press, 1994), 50–51, 60–69.
9. Aleksondra Hultquist, *Equal Ardour: Female Desire, Amatory Fiction, and the Recasting of the Novel, 1680–1760* (Ph.D dissertation, University of Illinois at Urbana-Champaign, 2008), 4.
10. John J. Richetti, *The English Novel in History, 1700–1780* (London: Routledge, 1999), 20.

11. Rita Goldberg, *Sex and Enlightenment: Women in Richardson and Diderot* (Cambridge: Cambridge University Press, 1984), 24.
12. Susan Staves, "British Seduced Maidens," *Eighteenth-Century Studies* 14.2 (1980–1981), 113–118.
13. Staves, "British Seduced Maidens," 114.
14. Richardson, *Pamela*, 248; cf. Geoffrey Still, *The Cure of the Passions and the Origins of the English Novel* (Cambridge: Cambridge University Press, 2006), 176; Ruth Bernard Yeazell, *Fictions of Modesty: Women and Courtship in the English Novel* (Chicago: University of Chicago Press, 1991), 94; Catherine Ingrassia, *Anti-Pamela Eliza Haywood and Shamela Henry Fielding* (Ontario, Canada: Broadview Press, 2004), 28.
15. Richardson, *Pamela*, 452.
16. Richardson, *Pamela*, 206, 251, 341.
17. Richardson, *Pamela*, 449.
18. Richardson, *Pamela*, 35, 54.
19. Richardson, *Pamela*, 303; Laura Fasick, *Vessels of Meaning: Women's Bodies, Gender Norms, and Class Bias from Richardson to Lawrence* (DeKalb, IL: Northern Illinois University Press, 1997), 149.
20. Richardson, *Pamela*, 258.
21. Christopher Flint, "The Anxiety of Affluence: Family and Class (Dis)order in Pamela: or Vice Rewarded," *Studies in English Literature, 1500–1900* 29.3 (1989): 497.
22. Richardson, *Pamela*, 76, 188–192; Nancy Armstrong, *Desire and Domestic Fiction: A Political History of the Novel* (New York: Oxford University Press, 1987), 114.
23. Richardson, *Pamela*, 134.
24. Richardson, *Pamela*, 313, 455.
25. Richardson, *Pamela*, 213, 218.
26. Richardson, *Pamela*, 257.
27. Richardson, *Pamela*, 261–262.
28. Richardson, *Pamela*, 422.
29. Richardson, *Pamela*, 53.
30. Richardson, *Pamela*, 283–288.
31. Richardson, *Pamela*, 423.
32. Richardson, *Pamela*, 433.
33. Richardson, *Pamela*, 341.
34. Richardson, *Pamela*, 410.
35. Samuel Richardson, *Pamela, Volume II* (Guttenberg Ebook, 2004 [1741]), 111.
36. Richardson, *Pamela, Volume II*, 135–136.
37. Richardson, *Pamela, Volume II*, 139.
38. Richardson, *Pamela, Volume II*, 11–12.

39. Richardson, *Pamela, Volume II*, 154, 166.
40. Richardson, *Pamela, Volume II*, 264; Terry Castle, *Masquerade and Civilization: The Carnivalesque in Eighteenth-Century England* (Stanford: Stanford University Press, 1986), 167.
41. Castle, *Masquerade and Civilization*, 171–172.
42. Castle, *Masquerade and Civilization*, 170.
43. Toni Bowers, "A Point of Conscience: Breastfeeding and Maternal Authority in *Pamela* Part 2," in Susan C. Greenfield and Carole Barash, eds., *Inventing Maternity: Politics, Science, and Literature, 1650–1865* (Lexington, Kentucky: University Press of Kentucky, 1999), 140, 150.
44. Scarlett Bowen, "A Sawce-box and Boldface Indeed: Refiguring the Female Servant in the Pamela-Antipamela Debate," *Studies in Eighteenth-Century Culture* 28 (1999): 259, 268.
45. Richardson, *Pamela*, 36.
46. Yeazell, *Fictions of Modesty*, 91–94.
47. Mei, *Transforming the Cinderella Dream*, 13–15.
48. Henry Fielding, *Joseph Andrews and Shamela* (Oxford: Oxford University Press, 2008), 305–344; Thomas Keymer and Peter Sabor, *'Pamela' in the Marketplace: Literary Controversy and Print Culture in Eighteenth-Century Britain and Ireland* (Cambridge: Cambridge University Press, 2005), 86.
49. Ingrassia, *Anti-Pamela*, 37.
50. Ingrassia, *Anti-Pamela*, 38–41.
51. Richard Gooding, "Pamela, Shamela, and the Politics of the Pamela Vogue," *Eighteenth-Century Fiction* 7.2 (1995): 117–121, 126.
52. Katherine Binhammer, *The Seduction Narrative in Britain* (Cambridge: Cambridge University Press, 2009), 108–136.
53. Fielding, *Joseph Andrews and Shamala*, 35.
54. Fielding, *Joseph Andrews*, 258.
55. Fielding, *Joseph Andrews*, 287–288.
56. Binhammer, *The Seduction Narrative in Britain*, 116.
57. Ian Watt, *The Rise of the Novel: Studies in Defoe, Richardson, and Fielding* (Harmondworth: Penguin, 1963 [1957]), 48; J. Paul Hunter, "The Novel and Social/Cultural History," in John Richetti, ed., *The Cambridge Companion to The Eighteenth Century Novel* (Cambridge: Cambridge University Press, 996), 19, 22.
58. Watt, *The Rise of the Novel*, 154.
59. Chloe Wigston Smith, *Women, Work and Clothes in the Eighteenth-Century Novel* (Cambridge: Cambridge University Press, 2013), 123–132.
60. Flint, "The Anxiety of Affluence," 123–125, 131–132.
61. Bowen, "A Sawce-box and Boldface Indeed," 269; Perry, *Novel Relations*, 284; Tim Meldrum, *Domestic Service and Gender, 1660–1750: Life and Work in the London Household* (Abingdon, Oxon.: Routledge, 2014), 104–107.

62. Leonard Tennenhouse, "Reading Spaces: The Americanization of Clarissa," *Yale Journal of Criticism* 11.1 (1998): 177–196.

63. Nina Baym, *Woman's Fiction: A Guide to Novels by and about Women in America, 1820–1870* (Ithaca, NY: Cornell University Press, 1978), 51–52; Gareth Evans, "Rakes, Coquettes and Republican Patriarchs: Class, Gender and Nation in Early American Sentimental Fiction," *Canadian Review of American Studies* 25.3 (1995): 41–62.

64. Michael Denning, *Mechanic Accents: Dime Novels and Working-Class Culture in America* (New York: Verso, 1987), 95–97; Baym, *Woman's Fiction*, 26.

65. Baym, *Woman's Fiction*, 35; Frances B. Cogan, *All-American Girl: The Ideal of Real Womanhood in Mid-Nineteenth Century America* (Athens, Georgia: University of Georgia Press, 1989), 139.

66. Richard Brodhead, *Cultures of Letters: Scenes of Reading and Writing in Nineteenth-Century America* (Chicago: University of Chicago Press, 1993), 94–95.

67. Cogan, *All-American Girl*, 108–115, 142–148.

68. Amal Amirch, *The Factory Girl and the Seamstress: Imagining Gender and Class in Nineteenth Century American Fiction* (New York: Garland Publishing, 2000).

69. Gerda Lerner, "The Lady and the Mill Girl: Changes in the Status of Women in the Age of Jackson," *American Studies* 10.1 (1969): 5–15.

70. Amirch, *The Factory Girl and the Seamstress*, 115–116.

71. Wendy Griswold, "American Character and the American Novel: An Expansion of Reflection Theory in the Sociology of Literature," *American Journal of Sociology* 86.4 (1981): 740–765.

72. Judith A. Ranta, *Women and Children of the Mills: An Annotated Guide to Nineteenth-Century American Textile Literature* (Westport, CT: Greenwood Press, 1999), 79–82, 89–92, 100, 107.

73. Laura Hapke, *Labor's Text: The Worker in American Fiction* (New Brunswick: Rutgers University Press, 2001), 145–7; Fay M. Blake, *The Strike in the American Novel* (Metuchen, NJ: Scarecrow Press, 1972), 230.

74. Joyce Shaw Peterson, "Working Girls and Millionaires: The Melodramatic Romances of Laura Jean Libbey," *American Studies* 24.1 (1983): 19–35. For examples of Libbey's stories see Ranta, *Women and Children of the Mills*, 96–100. On the hope of working-class women in nineteenth-century America that they could escape the harsh conditions of the factories by marriage see, Sarah Eisenstein, *Give Us Bread but Give Us Roses: Working Women's Consciousness in the United States, 1890 to the First World War* (New York: Routledge, 2013 [1983]), 139, 144–146.

BIBLIOGRAPHY

Amirch, Amal. *The Factory Girl and the Seamstress: Imagining Gender and Class in Nineteenth Century American Fiction*. New York: Garland Publishing, 2000.

Armstrong, Nancy. *Desire and Domestic Fiction: A Political History of the Novel*. New York: Oxford University Press, 1987.

Baym, Nina. *Woman's Fiction: A Guide to Novels By and About Women in America, 1820–1870*. Ithaca, NY: Cornell University Press, 1978.

Binhammer, Katherine. *The Seduction Narrative in Britain, 1747–1800*. Cambridge: Cambridge University Press, 2009.

Blake, Fay M. *The Strike in the American Novel*. Metuchen, N.J.: Scarecrow Press, 1972.

Bowen, Scarlett. "A Sawce-box and Boldface Indeed: Refiguring the Female Servant in the Pamela-Antipamela Debate," *Studies in Eighteenth-Century Culture* 28 (1999): 257–285.

Bowers, Toni O'Shaughnessy. "Sex, Lies, and Invisibility: Amatory Fiction from the Restoration to Mid-Century," in John Richetti ed., *The Columbia History of the British Novel*. New York: Columbia University Press, 1994, 50–72.

Bowers, Toni. "A Point of Conscience: Breastfeeding and Maternal Authority in *Pamela* Part 2," in Susan C. Greenfield and Carole Barash, eds. *Inventing Maternity: Politics, Science, and Literature, 1650–1865*. Lexington, Kentucky: University Press of Kentucky, 1999, 138–158.

Brodhead, Richard. *Cultures of Letters: Scenes of Reading and Writing in Nineteenth-Century America*. Chicago: University of Chicago Press, 1993.

Castle, Terry. *Masquerade and Civilization: The Carnivalesque in Eighteenth-Century England*. Stanford: Stanford University Press, 1986.

Cogan, Frances B. *All-American Girl: The Ideal of Real Womanhood in Mid-Nineteenth Century America*. Athens, Georgia: University of Georgia Press, 1989.

Denning, Michael. *Mechanic Accents: Dime Novels and Working-Class Culture in America*. New York: Verso, 1987.

Dundes, Alan. *Cinderella: A Folklore Casebook*. New York: Garland Publishing, 1982.

Eaton, Jeannette. and Berta M. Stevens. *Commercial Work and Training for Girls*. New York: The Macmillan Company, 1915.

Eisenstein, Sarah. *Give Us Bread But Give Us Roses: Working Women's Consciousness in the United States, 1890 to the First World War*. New York: Routledge, 2013 [1983].

Evans, Gareth. "Rakes, Coquettes and Republican Patriarchs: Class, Gender and Nation in Early American Sentimental Fiction," *Canadian Review of American Studies* 25.3 (1995): 41–62.

Fasick, Laura. *Vessels of Meaning: Women's Bodies, Gender Norms, and Class Bias from Richardson to Lawrence*. DeKalb, IL: Northern Illinois University Press, 1997.

Fielding, Henry. *Joseph Andrews and Shamela*. Oxford: Oxford University Press, 2008 [1742].

Flint, Christopher. "The Anxiety of Affluence: Family and Class (Dis)order in Pamela: or Vice Rewarded," *Studies in English Literature, 1500–1900* 29.3 (1989): 489–514.

Goldberg, Rita. *Sex and Enlightenment: Women in Richardson and Diderot*. Cambridge: Cambridge University Press, 1984.

Gooding, Richard. "Pamela, Shamela, and the Politics of the Pamela Vogue," *Eighteenth-Century Fiction* 7.2 (1995): 109–130.

Griswold, Wendy. "American Character and the American Novel: An Expansion of Reflection Theory in the Sociology of Literature," *American Journal of Sociology* 86.4 (1981): 740–765.

Hapke, Laura. *Labor's Text: The Worker in American Fiction*. New Brunswick: Rutgers University Press, 2001.

Hultquist, Aleksondra. *Equal Ardour: Female Desire, Amatory Fiction, and the Recasting of the Novel, 1680–1760*. Ph.D dissertation, University of Illinois at Urbana-Champaign, 2008.

Hunter, J. Paul. "The Novel and Social/Cultural History," in John Richetti, ed. *The Cambridge Companion to The Eighteenth Century Novel*. Cambridge: Cambridge University Press, 1996, 9–40.

Ingrassia, Catherine. *Anti-Pamela Eliza Haywood and Shamela Henry Fielding*. Ontario, Canada: Broadview Press, 2004.

Keymer, Thomas. and Peter Sabor. *'Pamela' in the Marketplace: Literary Controversy and Print Culture in Eighteenth-Century Britain and Ireland*. Cambridge: Cambridge University Press, 2005.

Lerner, Gerda. "The Lady and the Mill Girl: Changes in the Status of Women in the Age of Jackson," *American Studies* 10.1 (1969): 5–15.

Mei, Huang. *Transforming the Cinderella Dream: From Frances Burney to Charlotte Brontë*. New Brunswick: Rutgers University Press, 1990.

Meldrum, Tim. *Domestic Service and Gender, 1660–1750: Life and Work in the London Household*. Abingdon, Oxon: Routledge, 2014.

Panttaya, Elisabeth. "Going Up in the World: Class in 'Cinderella'," *Western Folklore* 52 (1993): 85–105.

Peterson, Joyce Shaw. "Working Girls and Millionaires: The Melodramatic Romances of Laura Jean Libbey," *American Studies* 24.1 (1983): 19–35.

Ranta, Judith A. *Women and Children of the Mills: An Annotated Guide to Nineteenth-Century American Textile Literature*. Westport, CT: Greenwood Press, 1999.

Richardson, Samuel. *Pamela; or, Virtue Rewarded*. Oxford: Oxford University Press, 2001 [1740].

———. *Pamela, Volume II*. Guttenberg Ebook, 2004 [1741].

Richetti, John J. *The English Novel in History, 1700–1780*. London: Routledge, 1999.

Smith, Chloe Wigston. *Women, Work and Clothes in the Eighteenth-Century Novel*. Cambridge: Cambridge University Press, 2013.

Staves, Susan. "British Seduced Maidens," *Eighteenth-Century Studies* 14.2 (1980–1981), 109–134.

Still, Geoffrey. *The Cure of the Passions and the Origins of the English Novel*. Cambridge: Cambridge University Press, 2006.

Tennenhouse, Leonard. "Reading Spaces: The Americanization of Clarissa," *Yale Journal of Criticism* 11.1 (1998): 177–196.

Watt, Ian. *The Rise of the Novel: Studies in Defoe, Richardson, and Fielding*. Harmondsworth: Penguin, 1963 [1957].

Yeazell, Ruth Bernard. *Fictions of Modesty: Women and Courtship in the English Novel*. Chicago: University of Chicago Press, 1991.

Yolen, Jane. "America's Cinderella," in Alan Dundes, *Cinderella: A Folklore Casebook*. New York: Garland Publishing, 1982, 294–308.

Zipes, Jack. *Fairy Tales and the Act of Subversion: The Classical Genre for Children and the Process of Civilization*. New York: Routledge, 1991 [1983].

———. *The Enchanted Screen: The Unknown History of Fairy-Tale Films*. New York: Routledge, 2011.

CHAPTER 3

From Attraction and the One-Reeler to the Feature

Cinema of Attractions

The cross-class romance film required the development of narrative film of some complexity. It could appear only in its most elementary forms during the earliest form of cinema, which has become known as the 'cinema of attractions', a term that has replaced 'primitive cinema' to refer to the period from the first public screening of motion pictures (1896 in the United States) to no later than 1906–1907, when multi-shot narrative films became the norm.[1]

Motifs of seduction and romance familiar to readers of fiction and audiences of melodrama were among the subjects of the earliest forms of narrative cinema.[2] The well-established melodramatic theme of the seduction and ruin of a young girl was portrayed on film as early as 1900 in *The Downward Path* (American Mutoscope and Biograph Co.). The film is composed of five shots or scenes that were listed separately in the production company's catalog. The catalog proclaims that the "series of five pictures is intended to convey a moral lesson in the career of a young country girl who succumbs to temptations, and becomes involved in the wickedness of the big city." The country girl is seduced by a "book agent" with whom she elopes, pursued by her mother and a farm hand in their nightclothes. The girl becomes a street walker, the man abandons her, and in the fourth picture she has "descended to the depths ... under the influence of liquor, and takes part in a scene of riotous abandon." The last picture shows her suicide by drinking carbolic acid.[3]

© The Author(s) 2017
S. Sharot, *Love and Marriage Across Social Classes in American Cinema*,
DOI 10.1007/978-3-319-41799-8_3

The same production company returned to the theme of seduction, abandonment and descent in *The Fate of the Artist's Model* (1903), which is composed of five shots, each preceded by a caption of its number. "Part one" shows an artist painting at an easel in front of a painted backdrop of a park. A young lady enters, shows her appreciation of his work, and they exit together. The next three parts take place in the artist's studio; the artists paints the lady who has become his model, she resists and then surrenders to the artist's advances, and the last scene in the studio shows the artist rejecting the woman though she pleads with him on her knees. The last part shows the exterior of a house in a snow scene; the woman enters carrying her baby and she knocks on the door and collapses, another woman opens the door and takes the woman and her baby inside.[4]

The novelty of moving picture narratives enabled audiences to accept such elementary versions of the melodramatic seduction plot, but any meaningful portrayal of cross-class romance was limited by the elementary narrativization of early cinema. The comic film *The Gay Shoe Clerk* (Edison, 1903) portrays an interaction with sexual implications that appears to be across social classes. The film is composed of three shots. The first shows the shoe clerk against a background of shoe boxes and the entrance into the frame of a young lady with an older female chaperon, possibly her mother. The clerk brings a high-heeled shoe for the young lady to try on and the second shot, a close up, shows the lady gradually lifting up her dress to display her ankle and calf. The third shot returns to the medium-shot perspective of the first; the clerk kisses the lady and is beaten over the head with an umbrella by the elderly woman (Fig. 3.1). Tom Gunning and Charles Musser refer to this film to support their opposing positions on the relative importance of attractions and narrative in early cinema. Gunning argues that, although various techniques such as the close-up are

Fig. 3.1 Frames from *The Gay Shoe Clerk* (Edison, 1903): The young lady shows her leg, the shoe clerk kisses her, the clerk is beaten by the elderly woman

to be found in the cinema of attractions, they are not strictly subordinated to narrativization. The close-up of a female's foot and ankle as the salesman places a shoe on it does not advance a narrative but is pure exhibitionism. Musser argues that the shot advances the narrative by signaling the woman's erotic interest to the salesman and thus operates within the unfolding of a narrative that continues with their kiss and ends with the woman's elderly female companion beating the salesman.[5]

We may suppose that the young lady is from a higher class than the shoe clerk and Musser's formulation with its emphasis on the narrative in early cinema is amenable to the claim that *The Gay Shoe Clerk* is an early example of a cross-class romance, albeit one of a brief and elementary nature. Clearer examples of cross-class sexual encounters are to be found among dramatic and melodramatic narrative films, which in 1907 replaced comic films as the most numerous types of film narratives. The years 1906–1907 are viewed by a number of film historians as the beginning of the 'transitional period', a term used for the period following the 'cinema of attractions' and lasting, according to various accounts, until 1913 or 1915—certainly no later than 1917 when the 'classical style' of American cinema was in place. Charlie Keil, who dates the transitional period from 1907—1913, writes that this period saw new and improved techniques that aided the comprehension and greater complexity of narrative-based films. Keil details how filmmakers increasingly rendered time and space intelligible within the context of a narrative, and how changes were made in sets, lighting, props, the framing of shots, editing, and acting style in order to achieve greater verisimilitude, "the illusion of actual life." These changes are analyzed by Keil for the most part with respect to single-reel, approximately 1000-foot, films, which remained the standard length of most films during this period.[6]

SEDUCTION AND ROMANCE IN THE ONE-REELER

A transitional film produced in 1907 that incorporated attractions and elements of a narrative of continuity was *The Unwritten Law: A Thrilling Drama based on the Thaw-White Case* (Lubin). The film dealt with the rape of a young girl from the working-class by a wealthy man and the shooting of the rapist by another wealthy man who has married the girl. Reenactments of sensational and topical news events were frequent attractions in early cinema and *The Unwritten Law* included a reenactment of the widely reported trial of Harry Thaw, a millionaire, for the murder of

Stanford White, a wealthy architect.[7] Thaw was married to a former model and chorus girl, Evelyn Nesbit, and his defense sought to justify his action by calling upon Nesbit's testimony that White had drugged and raped her prior to her marriage with Thaw. The film, which was produced and exhibited while Thaw was on trial, followed many of the newspaper reports in shaping the scandal as a melodrama with an emphasis on the age and class differences between the middle-aged wealthy White and the lower-class Nesbit who was sixteen years of age at the time of the alleged rape.

The Unwritten Law is composed of one shot scenes, some of which are introduced by intertitles. Attractions predominate in the early scenes: Nesbit posing in an artist's studio, her preparing for the stage in a dancing class, and her swinging on a velvet swing in White's studio. In the later scenes there is a shift to a narrative of continuity. White is shown bringing Nesbit to his apartment, drugging her drink, and, after her collapse, placing a screen around her body. We are given to assume, supported by Nesbit's testimony reported in newspapers, that White proceeded to rape her. Scenes of Nesbit and Thaw leaving their marriage ceremony and their happiness at home are followed by the murder scene on a Roof Garden where Thaw shoots White. A scene of Thaw in prison shows a visit from his wife and mother and then his dream that replays his shooting of White and his embracing and kissing of his wife and mother. The dream suggests that Thaw's action was motivated by his love of his wife and mother. The last scene of the trial shows Nesbit giving her testimony, arguments between the prosecutor and defense—presumably over the relevance of her testimony of the rape—and Thaw's acquittal that we are to understand is justified by the unwritten law that proclaims that a man whose wife has been violated by another can take revenge. The actual trial concluded with a hung jury and after a second trial in 1908 Thaw was committed to an insane asylum.

The names of Thaw, White and Nesbit were changed somewhat in the film (Daw, Black, Hudspeth), but the film's subtitle made clear that it was based on the "Thaw–White Case," and although there was little continuity between the early scenes, and the intertitle information was sparse, the filmmakers were able to assume that audiences would understand the film because most had been reading about the case for many weeks in the newspapers. As in many newspaper accounts of the case, the film portrayed the rape of an innocent lower-class girl by a sexually rapacious upper-class villain and her rescue by a hero who marries her and takes revenge on her despoiler. Events that in reality were separated by years appeared to immediately follow each other in the film. Thaw was married to Nesbit for three years before he shot White, but the film's scene of the shooting immediately following the wedding contributed to a sympathetic portrayal of Thaw. Newspaper coverage came to portray Thaw to be as immoral and as perverse as White. The portrayal of Nesbit as a ruined innocent girl was countered by a portrayal of a corrupt and lying woman who brought the scandal on herself by her desire for pleasure and her unconstrained display of herself as a model and chorus girl. These complications were not included in the film, which conformed to the melodramatic mode of clear distinctions between good and bad protagonists. However, the film's sensational content of rape and murder drew condemnation from the trade press, reform groups and the police, who claimed that the film had a corrupting influence on its audiences, especially on school girls and young working women who were reported to find the film of great interest.[8]

As a reenactment of an ongoing trial and with its tableaux shots and partial continuity, *The Unwritten Law* is predominantly part of the cinema of attractions. A more integrated narrative is evident in *The Mill Girl* (Vitagraph, 1907), a fictional melodrama in which a mill girl repulses the sexual advances of a foreman and is rescued from him and from a fire in the mill by a young male mill worker. *The Mill Girl* was composed of a large number of 31 shots for its 700 foot length (*The Unwritten Law* at 950 foot had ten shots), and with only one intertitle and its use of parallel editing it is an early example of a film with a narrative of continuity.[9] In most early films of sexual harassment, the heroines are able to repulse the offender, often with the aid of a male hero, but a number of films such as *Traffic in Souls* (Universal, 1913) showed working girls, newly arrived immigrants and country girls being ensnared into prostitution by perfidious city men.[10]

Most male seducers or would-be seducers in films of the transitional period are either criminals or men, such as foremen, who are close to the heroines in class; however, wealthy seducers occasionally made an appearance. The daughter of a tailor in *The Blood of the Poor* (Champion, 1911) is employed as a maid by a wealthy family and falls victim to the son of the house for whom her father is making a dress suit. Driven out of the wealthy house, the girl's woes are compounded by the death of her father after he finishes making the dress suit. When he calls to collect his suit, the seducer offers money to the girl that he has ruined, but she refuses the money and he goes on his way leaving her in misery.[11] Wealthy seducers of poor girls do not always escape punishment. In *Heaven Avenges* (Biograph, 1912), the daughter of a fruit picker runs away from home after she is shamed by the wealthy owner of the orange grove, who trifles with her affections and then refuses to marry her. The girl's father and fiancée attempt to shoot the owner and he falls down dead, but the doctor's diagnosis is that the owner's death was a result of a heart condition and not from their bullets. The girl is reunited with her father and fiancée.[12]

The classical seduction plot in which a working class or poor girl is seduced by an upper-class male and she takes a downward path of misery and sometimes prostitution became increasingly rare as it was replaced by cross-class romances in which the girl finds happiness with a wealthy man. Three of the many one-reel films directed by D. W. Griffith for Biograph in 1909–1911 combined elements of the lachrymose seduction plot with upbeat endings of cross-class marriages. The wealthy young man in *A Change of Heart* (1909) deceives an innocent country girl into a false marriage with one of his unworthy companions posing as a minister. After the girl learns the truth and sets out for home, the young man is persuaded by his mother of the error of his ways. With feelings of remorse he finds the girl, asks her forgiveness and presents a real minister to marry them legally.[13] The wealthy young man in *A Child's Impulse* (1910), takes a trip to the country on the advice of friends who have warned him against a socially ambitious widow with whom he has become attached. He falls in love with Grace, the daughter of a farmer, and proposes marriage. The widow follows him to the country, succeeds in renewing his infatuation with her, and returns with him to the city. Grace's despair induces her little sister to travel to the city where her sweet face and one word of pleading is sufficient to make the young man decide to return to Grace. Back at the farmhouse, he throws himself at her feet.[14] In *Fate's Turning* (1911) a relationship develops between a hotel waitress and a wealthy guest and the affection between them leads to a betrothal. The man is called away by news that his father is ill and after the father's death he reconsiders and writes to the waitress to take back his "foolish promise." The wealthy milieu in which the man courts a woman of his own class is followed by a shot of the waitress and her baby in their miserable abode. At the wedding ceremony, the waitress arrives to confront the man with their baby. The man rushes after his bride who has left in disgust and his pleading is of no avail. He returns to the waitress and child and feelings of remorse induce him to ask the pastor to marry him to the waitress[15] (Fig. 3.2).

Griffith was not the only director who made films of wealthy individuals who displayed indifference toward the suffering of the poor and were

Fig. 3.2 Frames from *Fate's Turning* (Biograph, 1911): The meeting of the hotel waitress and the wealthy man; the waitress confronts the man with their baby as he is about to wed a woman from his own class

redeemed by their love of a poor person. *From the Submerged* (Essanay, 1912), directed by Theodore Wharton, juxtaposes wealth and poverty and uses melodramatic twists to bring about a cross-class marriage. A homeless man about to jump in a lake is prevented from committing suicide by a young woman who persuades him with what appears to be religious arguments (she points to heaven). The man, exhausted from hunger, obtains food from a bread line and there he sees a personal announcement in a newspaper that his father is dying and that "all is forgiven." The man inherits a fortune and becomes engaged to a wealthy girl. On a "slumming party" they visit a bread line where his fiancée shows her complete lack of sympathy for the poor and laughs when he tells her of his destitute past. The man's decision to break their engagement is shown by his tearing up a picture of her. He remembers the woman who saved his life (the scene from the past is superimposed within the shot) and, in his former shabby clothes, he returns to the park where he had intended to kill himself. The woman who saved him appears and as she is about to throw herself in the water he stops her, reminds her of their previous encounter and quickly marries her. When he takes her to his home she realizes that he is a wealthy man[16] (Fig. 3.3).

These films are morality tales with little attention to a romance between the couple who unite at the end. Another one-reeler directed by D. W. Griffith in 1910, *The Dancing Girl of Butte* (Biograph, 1910), was more of a precursor to the cross-class romances that were to become so popular in the classical period. In this film, it is the 'disreputable'

Fig. 3.3   Frames from *From the Submerged* (Essanay, 1912): On a "slumming party" the wealthy fiancée shows her lack of sympathy for the poor; the man remembers the poor girl who prevented him from committing suicide

occupation of the working girl that constitutes the obstacle in her relationship with the middle-class hero. Bella's demure manner and pretty face appeal to Howard, a newspaper artist, who assists her when she falls and hurts her ankle in the city park. Howard is unaware that she is a dancer in a music hall and when, at her home, he surprises her in her dance hall attire she pretends that it is a costume for her part with a dramatic company. They are betrothed and Howard refuses to believe his friends when they inform him of Bella's work. Bella admits the truth and takes him to her place of work, where he turns away from her in revulsion. She tells him that she has been forced to earn a living in this fashion but that she intends to leave while her soul is pure. Howard is softened by her sincerity and he takes her in his arms. Two years later, two of Howard's ex-friends see him and Bella pushing a perambulator in the park.[17]

Few cross-class romances were made in the one-reel format and what appears to have been a crucial factor in the sudden increase of cross-class romance films in 1915 was the appearance of feature-length films of four or more reels, lasting about an hour or more. Few films of this length were made before 1914 and, until 1915, feature-length films had made little impression on mainstream movie theater exhibition. From eight in 1912 and 56 in 1913, the number of American-made feature length films rose to 342 in 1914, 599 in 1915, 835 in 1916, and 936 in 1917. 'Variety programs', made up of two to four films one-reel (about 15 minutes) in length and a song-slide sing-along, continued to coexist with feature programs for a few years but, whereas in 1915 almost two-thirds of movie theaters had variety programs, in 1917 this was the case for about one theater in six; from 1918, very few theaters continued the variety format.[18] Very few cross-class romances were made in the split-reel, one-reel or two-reel formats. I was able to find only six one-reel cross-class romances in 1911 out of a total of 2,060 one-reel films made in that year. There were no doubt some that I missed, but there is no question that the proportion of cross-class romances in relation to the total number of one-reel films was minute. By contrast, I found eighteen cross-class romance films in 1915; three were one or two reels in length and the others were features of four or five reels. The number of cross-class romance films reached an early peak in 1916, and of the 33 cross-class romance films I found in that year, 29 were of five reels or more. For the following two years, 1917 and 1918, I found 25 and 23 cross-class romance films, respectively. I found sixteen cross-class romance films in 1919, and although they continued to be frequent throughout the 1920s and 1930s, the yearly number remained lower than the peak years, 1916–1918. Of course, even in the peak years, the cross-class romances were always a small proportion of the total of features but, from 1916 to 1942, cross-class romances were far more numerous in comparison with the pre-1916 period and the post-1942 period.[19]

THE CROSS-CLASS ROMANCE FILM DURING THE TRANSITIONAL PERIOD, 1908–1914

In accord with the entire history of cross-class romance in written fiction and films, most of the wealthy protagonists in the cross-class romance films of the transitional period are male and the couples are united happily at the end. Of the 28 split reel, one-reel and two-reel cross-class romance films that I found among the reviews of films in the trade press between 1908 and 1914, in only four films is the wealthy protagonist female and in three of those films the male has a middle-class occupation: a doctor in *Romance of a Taxicab* (Essanay, 1908), a clergyman in *Capital vs. Labor* (Vitagraph, 1910), and a settlement worker in *For Her Father's Sins* (Majestic, 1914). The male protagonist in *The Lackey* (Magestic, 1913) is a butler who rescues the girl he loves, the daughter of the wealthy family for whom he works, from an escaped convict but he leaves because of their class difference. When the male is the wealthy protagonist in a cross-class romance, the female protagonist is almost always from the working or lower-class. Typical relationships are between the son of a factory owner and a female factory worker, or between the owner of a department store or his son and a shop girl.

Class differences in cross-class romances are more likely to be overcome when the wealthy protagonist is male, but in five films from this period the poor or working-class heroine finally favors, or is reunited with, a male from her own class. These films in which the cross-class romance is broken off or ends unhappily convey a clear message of the moral dangers encountered by working-class females who succumb to the temptations of a higher standard of living through relationships with wealthy men. The shop girl in *The Measure of a Man* (Rex, 1911) compared favorably the wealth and refinement of a "fashionable clubman" with her rough, uneducated boyfriend who, broken hearted by her refusal, enters the army. The shop girl is disillusioned and leaves the wealthy man when she discovers that he is married, and five years later she meets and is reunited with her former boyfriend. Nora the country girl in *Fashion's Toy* (Lubin, 1913) is taken under the wing of a wealthy woman who transforms her into a fashionable urbanite, but Nora is thrown out of the house when Hendricks, the beau of the wealthy woman, shows a romantic interest in her. Nora is delighted when Hendricks comes to her country home to claim her, but she repulses him when he explains that he does not intend to marry her. Hendricks seizes her and she is rescued by her local admirer whom she had previously compared unfavorable with the elegant Hendricks.[20]

A similar moral message was conveyed in *The Kiss* (Vitagraph, 1914), which begins with Alice, a shop girl, reading a newspaper headline, "Low Wages and Vice: How Shop Girls live on 4 and 5 dollars a day." The implication is that many shop girls supplement their low wages by immoral means but Alice is unconcerned and appears to regard her piggy-bank as security. Alice becomes discontented when she observes another shop girl, "Flashily dressed Mazie," attracting George, a "society man," when he comes to the store to buy a tie. Alice looks at herself in her drab clothes and exclaims (an intertitle), "I *will* be noticed." She buys new clothes, much to the surprise of her regular boyfriend, Fred the Floorwalker, and she makes a conquest of George who invites her out and introduces her as his cousin to his fiancée who gives her a friendly kiss. When George is alone with Alice at a restaurant he attempts to kiss her. She resists him and exclaims (intertitle), "No, No! That's where she [George's fiancée] kissed me because she loves you!" Alice returns home and cries but an intertitle announces that there is a "Return to simple things." The final scene shows Alice in her regular clothes receiving innocent kisses from the landlady's little girl and Fred the Floorwalker.[21]

Whereas films such as *The Kiss* discouraged working girls from seeking romance beyond their class, an increasing number of films suggested that working girls could find happiness with wealthy males even in contexts of class conflict. A significant proportion of the admittedly small number of cross-class romances during the transitional period took place in industrial contexts such as factories, mills and sweat-shops, and a number of these portrayed conflicts between workers and employers. One of the earliest films of this type *The Power of Labor* (Selig, 1908) introduces a theme that was to become common in the more conservative films of class conflict; it is the actions of the villainous supervisor or manager of the workers rather than the absent or unknowing owner that results in conflict with the workers. In this film, Flack, the supervisor—an ex-burglar—reduces the wages of the mill workers without notifying the absent owner who has left the mill in his hands. When Bob, the owner's son, opposes him, Flack employs three thugs to throw Bob into a furnace. Bob is saved by Mabel, the daughter of a mill worker, and it is Flack, pursued by workers, who falls into the furnace. Bob becomes the new supervisor, returns the old scale of wages, proclaims that he recognizes the power of labor, and marries Mabel cheered on by the satisfied workers. The reviewer for *Moving Picture World* wrote that, "The whole story is a powerful argument for fair play between employer and employee."[22]

The unlikely intercessor in a conflict between workers and employer in *Capital vs. Labor* (Vitagraph, 1910) is a young clergyman who loves the daughter of the factory owner. The girl at first prefers a young military officer, seemingly a man of action, but it is the minister rather than the officer who succeeds in protecting her and her father when striking workers attack their home. The minister had previously appealed to the proprietor on behalf of the workers without success, but he succeeds in attaining concessions from the capitalist after he has calmed the strikers. His actions win the heart of the owner's daughter. The reviewer in the trade journal *Moving Picture World* focused on the class conflict depicted in the film: "The chief interest in this picture will center in the scenes depicting a strike and the riotous work of a mob. It is much too realistic to be comfortable. It gives a graphic representation of mob violence when unrestrained."[23] Another review in the same journal complained that the story was not that of "an American strike, but an anarchistic revolution, with no moral lesson to it. A minister of the Gospel should and would not have approved such scenes of vandalism by forcing the manufacturer to consent to the terms of the mob."[24] A report on the film's reception declared that the film had "taken big" and that some people from Philadelphia had written to the "little minister" in the picture asking him to come to their city and settle their troubles.[25]

The portrayal of strikers as an unruly mob influenced by agitators in *Capital vs. Labor* was not unusual in films of industrial unrest, but as a cross-class romance the film was unusual insofar as the wealthy protagonist was female. More frequently, the female protagonist in cross-class romances in contexts of industrial conflict was a factory or mill worker who was involved in, or even led, a strike. Lou, the heroine of *The Girl Strike Leader* (Thanhouser, 1910) induces other workers to strike when their salaries are reduced by 10 %. Faced with starvation, the workers return to work with the exception of Lou who is found weeping on the steps of her home by Hal, the son of the factory owner. Hal has been working incognito in the factory and has fallen in love with Lou, whom he protected from the sexual advances of the factory manager. Hal provides the solution: Lou accepts his marriage proposal and he returns the workers' wages to the old scale.[26] The opposition to workers' demands by Bert Readly, the son of the President of the Readly Steel Mills, in *The Long Strike* (Essanay, 1911) prevents him from winning the heart of Jane, the daughter of a mill worker. Bert has been commissioned to come to terms with the workers and his rejection of their terms puts him in danger from a mob of workers. Jane saves him from the workers and hides him in her home. Bert prevents a plot to burn the mills, but it is Jane's success in gaining concessions from Bert's father that ends the strike. Jane returns to her working-class boyfriend.[27]

Even the feature-length *What Is to Be Done?* (1914), an independently made, socialist-inspired radical film focusing on industrial conflict, includes a cross-class romance. Made by Joseph Leon Weiss, an actor and cofounder of the socialist *Jewish Daily Forward*, the film, in addition to its fictional treatment of an industrial conflict, includes a number of vignettes and reenactments of the plight and repression of workers: hunger; sexual harassment; miners dead from an explosion; a factory fire; and the recent Ludlow massacre in which striking workers, together with their wives and children, were killed by gunmen in the employ of John D. Rockefeller's Colorado Fuel and Iron Company of Ludlow. The film's heroine, Louise, a stenographer, leads workers in a peaceful protest and strike against a wage cut, and the employers are shown using special agencies to provide them with strikebreakers, beat the workers and kill a union leader. A love affair develops between Louise and the liberal son of the factory owner,

Henry, who admires her for her activities on behalf of the workers. In this film, however, it is the worker's struggle led by Louise rather than the benevolence of the owner's son that succeeds, at least temporarily, and the couple unites only after this achievement. Henry's father finally agrees to the demands of the workers because of the repercussions of the violence and his fear of public disapproval, but together with his Wall Street allies he compensates for the increase in wages by raising prices on necessities. The film appears to have been ignored by the trade press and to have had a limited distribution.[28]

Working girls in cross-class romances during the transitional period were often subject to harsh treatment, including sexual harassment, but although the number of industrial conflict films was relatively high during this period, most cross-class romances were not inserted within contexts of class conflict and most working-class heroines were saved by wealthy men. Mabel, the mill girl heroine of *The Factory Girl* (Kalem, 1909), repulses the sexual advances of the foreman who seizes her in the woods behind the mill. Her screams are heard by Ned, the mill owner's son who hurls the foreman into the bushes. The foreman, together with a female cousin of Ned who intends to marry him, plots to have Mabel falsely accused of a robbery that they in fact have committed. Accused of theft, Mabel leaps into a stream and she is saved from drowning by Ned. The plotters are foiled and arrested and the mill owner places Mabel in his son's arms and tells him how proud he is that his son has been able to win a girl as noble and pure as Mabel.[29] The sufferings of Angie, the factory girl in the wildly melodramatic five-reel *A Factory Magdalen* (Edyth Totten Features, 1914), include being made pregnant by Williams, the mill's villainous manager, who abandons her in favor of Mercy, the mill owner's daughter, and hires thugs to kill Angie by throwing her into the mill sluice. Angie is rescued by a dog belonging to Rufus, who is an ex-foreman of the mill. Rufus has been hesitant to declare his love for Mercy because of their class differences. After the villains are caught, the dying Angie gives her blessing to the union of Mercy and Rufus.[30]

Most factory girls in cross-class romance films could expect happy endings because the sons of wealthy capitalists were willing to subject themselves to various deprivations and dangers in order to marry them. The son could be disinherited by his wealthy family if he insisted on marrying the working girl. After the son of the owner of a shirtwaist factory in *The Working Girl's Success* (Lubin, 1911) is turned out by his family when he marries a working girl, he obtains work as a street car conductor.

Five years later, his family relents and there is a reunion.[31] The son of the owner of a department store in *The Curse of Humanity* (Domino, 1914) fares less well after he marries a shop girl and is turned out by his father. Untrained for labor, he is unable to hold a position and he drowns his sorrows in drink while his wife earns a few pennies by sewing. His mother searches for him in the streets of the East Side and discovers that the poor, little barefoot girl whom she befriends is her grandchild. A reconciliation takes place and the son resolves to reform.[32]

The millionaire's son in *If Love Be True* (Lubin, 1909) accepts a position as a working man in the same factory as the working girl he loves; he is accepted by her after he rescues her from a fire in the mill.[33] The son of the mill owner in *That Girl of Dixon's* (Edison, 1910) protects the mill girl from her drunken, abusive father who tries to kill the son in a cotton compressor. The girl arrives in time to stop the machine and the mill owner shows his gratitude by adopting the girl with the suggestion that her future is with his son.[34] A son from a wealthy family may even have to save the working girl from his own father, as in *The Lily of the Tenements* (Biograph, 1911). Lily, a Jewish textile pieceworker, faints when her landlord sexually attacks her. She is saved by the landlord's son who brings a doctor to her tenement home, to cure her sick mother, and asks for Lily's hand in marriage. Reviewers of this film in the trade press expressed doubts about the film's credibility with respect to finding such a heroine in the tenements and to the cross-class romance. The reviewer for the *Nickelodeon* wrote: "Does such a delicate, flower-like girl grow in a tenement? It is doubtful. You would have to search the East Side a long time before you found one. She is a sentimentalist's dream. The incongruity would not be so striking were the other conditions not so downright realistic. A lily growing in a rubbish pile would not be more incongruous."[35] The reviewer for the *Motion Picture World* wrote that in New York "the thing [sexual harassment] is so common that a considerable proportion of the population wink at it as a necessity, and let it pass. The happy ending for the poor girl, following the denunciation of his father by the young man, is dramatic, but, unfortunately, few instances of this sort actually occur."[36]

THE CROSS-CLASS ROMANCE FILM DURING 1915–1919 AND WOMEN'S OCCUPATIONS

As noted, the number of cross-class romance films increased considerably from 1915 together with the dominance of the feature film of four reels or more. The most general characteristics of the cross-class romance films of the transitional period continued into the 'classical' period. Of the 115 cross-class romance films that I found between 1915 and 1919, in 101 of them (88 %) the wealthy protagonist of the romantic couple is male. As in the transitional films, many of the wealthy males are owners or the sons of owners of factories, mills, mines or department stores. Some are owners of tenement buildings, financiers, wealthy artists, or simply millionaires or their sons. In the few films in which the wealthy protagonist is female, the poor male protagonists include manual workers (e.g., miner, longshoreman), but more typically they have middle-class occupations (e.g., author, artist, minister) or positions of authority (e.g., construction chief, foreman), or they become middle class (a traffic cop becomes a lawyer). The few wealthy female protagonists are almost always non-working daughters of wealthy families, daughters of factory or mine owners, or simply 'socialites'. The highest status position among the poor female protagonists is secretary, but almost all, whether blue, white or pink collar, are poor 'working girls'. During the transitional period, eight of the female protagonists are industrial workers (including factory or mill workers, seamstresses and pieceworkers), three are daughters of factory or mill workers, and five are shop girls. Between 1915 and 1919, 24 of the poor female protagonists are factory or mill girls, 23 are shop girls, six are stenographers and three are chorus girls. Others occupations include manicurist, model, newspaper seller, telephone operator, hatcheck girl and travelling saleswoman.

The trend over this period was for the number of factory or mill girls in cross-class romance films to decline and the number of shop girls, stenographers and other white-collar occupations to increase. Whereas there were six girls in manufacturing occupations in the cross-class romance films of 1915 and eight in 1916, the number dropped to five in 1917, four in 1918, and one in 1919. The number of shop girls in cross-class romances numbered four in 1915, four in 1916, nine in 1917, three in 1918, and three in 1919. The occupations of the poor female protagonists partially reflect the occupational distribution of women and the changes that were occurring in that distribution. One important female occupation that is almost never found in cross-class romances of this period is the domestic servant. I found only one film in which the poor female occupies the position of maid: *Miss Ambition* (Vitagraph, 1918). In this film Marta, a girl from the tenements, accepts a position of maid to a wealthy female settlement worker and is dismissed after she poses for a statue representing Ambition for her employer's fiancé who becomes infatuated with her. They marry, but her husband's friends do not accept Marta and he drinks himself to death. Marta sacrifices the fortune left by her husband to help her former boyfriend, a contractor, who is on the verge of bankruptcy. Exhibitors were advised by a trade paper to work on the angle that the heroine finds happiness with a poor man, and the advertisement tag read, "The Story of a Girl who Climbed the Social Ladder and then went back—for Love."[37]

Domestic service was still the largest single female occupation during this period; it represented a third of non-agricultural women workers in 1900, and one quarter in 1910. However, after a steady growth of female domestics for over a century, their number dropped after 1910; in 1920, they constituted just over 18 % of non-agricultural women workers.[38] The most readily available alternative to domestic service for those women who lacked education, knowledge of English or commercial skills was manufacturing. The number of women employed in the two major industries that employed women, clothing and textiles, rose from a little less than a million in 1900 to over one and a quarter million in 1910. This number declined by about one seventh during the 1910s, but whereas only 28 % of all women in the clothing industry worked in factories in 1910, by 1920 the proportion had risen to over 44 %. Although the overall number of female workers in manufacturing remained stable, the number of female factory workers continued to rise, with the greatest increase occurring between 1910 and 1920 when women factory workers increased by a third.[39] In New York, the center of film production for most of this period, many of the women who worked in the clothing trade at the end of the nineteenth century were contracted to tenement sweatshops, often conducted as family-based enterprises. However, an increasing number of women, especially single women, were entering large, mechanized factories and after 1900 three-quarters of ready-made garments were made in factories.[40]

The highest growth rates in women's employment were in white-collar sectors: the number of saleswomen and female clerks in stores rose from less than a quarter of a million in 1900 to more than half a million in 1920; and the number of stenographers and typists rose from less than 90,000 in 1900 to more than half a million in 1920.[41] In addition to the rapid expansion of the economy, the entrance of women into white-collar work was a result of the development of mass secondary schooling. Around 1900, secondary schooling began a transformation from a system that focused on (mostly male) youths who wished to enter college, to one that provided qualifications for entering work after leaving high school. Attendance levels and graduation numbers from secondary schools were higher among girls than boys, and high school education gave girls the literacy and numerical qualifications required for white-collar work. Many girls preferred white-collar jobs to manufacturing, even when they were paid the same wages. The proportion of men in white-collar work also increased but this increase was far less than for women. The proportion of women among all white-collar workers increased from 18.5 % in 1900 to 33 % in 1930, and the proportion of women among all clerical and sales personnel increased from 20 % in 1900 to 40 % in 1930.[42]

New York anticipated the phenomenal growth of the white collar sector and women's participation in it by a decade. Retail trade, including department store trade, grew substantially in the city, and from a predominantly male occupation, a position as a salesperson became a coveted one for young women by 1900. As New York became the nation's center for corporate industry, there was a considerable growth in the number of female secretaries, clerks, typists and telephone operators.[43] With respect to cross-class romances, the traditionally dominant female occupation of domestic service was virtually ignored in favor of the rapidly growing female occupations in factories, offices, and stores, especially department stores.

Socio-Economic Contexts of the Cross-Class Romance: Class and Gender Inequality

By the end of the nineteenth century, a class consisting of owners of large-scale capital—a bourgeoisie in the classical Marxist sense—had emerged in the United States. The American bourgeoisie was characterized by a high level of structuration; the possibilities of entering it were minute for the vast majority of Americans, its boundaries were strengthened by its distinctive style of life and status, it articulated a class consciousness and at times it acted collectively in accord with this consciousness. The unity of the bourgeoisie was reduced by its dispersal in a number of centers over the vast nation, but the consolidation of major industries increased the dominance of New York in the national economy with its industrialists and bankers controlling enterprises in different areas of the country. A number of managers and professionals who did not own substantial amounts of capital were part of the bourgeois socio-cultural world, but it was the owners of capital who were the dominant members of the sector and it was the prominent entrepreneurs of New York, such as Rockefeller, Morgan and Carnegie, who were seen by many of their contemporaries as the representatives of a gilded age.

The wealth of the bourgeoisie was enormous. At the turn of the century, less than 2 % of the population owned 60 % of the nation's wealth; in 1910, the seventy richest Americans, each with a fortune of at least $35 million, together owned one-sixteenth of the nation's wealth.[44] This wealth was displayed quite openly in an opulent lifestyle: large town mansions and country houses; spectacular banquets, balls and parties; and the collection of valuable works of art. Exclusive educational institutions, clubs and hotels excluded those bourgeois whose ethnic, particularly Jewish, origins were viewed as a threat to the status of a class that was, for the most part, Protestant and 'Anglo-Saxon'.[45] More than a third of the working class was living in poverty, and the dramatic differences between neighborhoods in the cities contributed to the perception that the population was split into two classes; in New York there were the ostentatious mansions of Fifth Avenue and the squalled tenement slums of the Lower East Side.[46]

The class of women, including working women, was determined for the most part by the males in their family—fathers for single women and husbands for married women. The higher the class, the fewer the opportunities for a woman to gain entrance into the class through her occupation (if any) in the labor force. Access to the professions, including the emergent business professions, was increasingly dependent on formalized requirements, such as appropriate degrees, certifying examinations and licensing regulations; men used various means, such as discouragement and quotas, to prevent women from attaining those qualifications. The promoters of new professionalism emphasized its inherent manliness and saw women in their ranks as a threat to their professional esteem. Although the proportion of women in universities increased, the universities professional schools remained from 90–100 % male. Women with professional aspirations were restricted for the most part to the 'female professions', particularly elementary teaching, librarianship and nursing. During the first three decades of the twentieth century, women made up around 80 % of teachers, from 70–90 % of librarians and around 95 % of nurses, but they constituted only around 5 % of physicians and surgeons, less than 10 % of accountants and auditors, and no more than 2 % of lawyers and architects.

At the same time as they kept their own ranks as free of women as possible, male professionals oversaw the feminization of the lower levels of office work, and many firms refused to hire men as typists, stenographers or machine operators. The proportion of female stenographers and typists increased from 72 % in 1900 to 80 % in 1910 and to 90 % in 1920; the proportion of female managers and other higher office positions rose only slightly from 2 % in 1900 to 3.5 % in 1910 to 5 % in 1920. Although a much smaller proportion of working men worked as clerks, their numbers were still about equal to the number of female clerks in 1930, and they earned more and could expect more raises and promotions than female clerks. The highest position in clerical work that women could hope for was secretary, but there were few secretarial positions and although their pay was better than other female office workers, they were paid considerably less than men in similar positions and with similar experience.[47]

Differential pay and advancement was also prevalent in retail sales, which was also undergoing feminization, and in manufacturing. Female workers were almost entirely absent from many industries and their numbers in manufacturing were concentrated in just a few industries, particularly textiles and clothing. In those industries with both male and female workers, men earned more than women, even in unskilled, menial work. Men were also more likely to attain promotions and positions of authority, such as foremen.[48]

This was the period of the young, single working woman. The number of married working women was growing but married women made up only 20 % of the female labor force in 1920. About half of the working women in the cities were under 20 years of age; in New York, four-fifths of wage-earning women were single and almost a third were aged 16–20.[49] The common assumption that once women married they would leave the work force and be dependent on their husbands was used to justify the exclusion of women from prestigious positions, as well as their lower wages, and the 'marriage bar' that resulted in the firing of many women upon marriage. Some married women disguised their marital status in order to obtain a job or to keep the one they had. Older single women in white-collar work were regarded as an aberration and, as discrimination against women over 30 was prevalent, their circumstances were likely to become increasingly miserable.[50] The forlorn presence of older single female workers could only reinforce the belief among the younger 'working girls' that marriage was their only appropriate future.

If women in the better paid and more prestigious clerical occupations could only see their future in marriage, this was even more so for saleswomen and female operatives in manufacturing whose wages and working conditions made their lives ones of toil and suffering. About 60 % of working women lived with their families and their work outside the home provided them with little independence from the controlling influence of the family, to whom they gave most of their earnings.[51] An increasing number of women lived away from their parents and their living conditions, health and morals were a subject of much social concern and a focus for female reformers from the middle- and upper-middle classes.[52] An investigation by the National Consumers' League on the income and conditions of work of female workers in factories, sweatshops and stores was published in 1911. It contains heart-rending accounts of the extremely low wages, long working hours, exhausting and dangerous work, and the atrocious living conditions in the tenements. Among the reports on factory workers is one on Natalya, an 18-year old worker in a shirtwaist factory, whose income of $6 a week was depleted by the seasonal nature of the work. The factory in which she worked employed 400 women (600 in the busy season) who worked from 8.00 a.m. until 6.30 p.m., sometimes until 9.00 p.m., with a half-hour interval for lunch. The "rows and rows of girls with heads bent and eyes intent upon the flashing needles" of the vibrating, noisy machines had to work at a rapid pace. Natalya shared a tenement room with two other girls; she was worn and frail and her health was breaking. Some months after reporting on the harsh working conditions and hand-to-mouth existence of Rita, an immigrant girl of 19, the investigator heard that Rita "had solved many of her difficulties by a happy marriage." Rita had told of a friend at work who, hard pressed by the dull season, had become the mistress of a man who supported her until the birth of their child and had then left her without resources.

The investigators collected reports of about fifty saleswomen in various grades of stores. The common features of the reports were low wages, casual employment, lack of promotion, heavy expenses in laundry and dress, and long hours of standing. In its chapters on female factory workers the National Consumers' League investigation included reports on the large-scale strikes of shirtwaist makers in 1909, which lasted 13 weeks, and of cloak makers in 1910. Most of the 20,000 shirtwaist strikers were women between the ages of 16 and 25 from Jewish and some Italian immigrant families. The owners, who were also Jewish, hired strike breakers to attack the strikers and were assisted by the police, who arrested many strikers on trumped-up charges. The strikers gained limited concessions and the strike in 1910 of about 60,000 cloak makers resulted in the employers' recognition of the International Ladies Garment Workers Union.[53] The National Consumers' League report appeared in press before the fire that occurred on March 25, 1911 in the Triangle Shirtwaist Factory, in which 146 female workers died.

The conditions of women working in the factories and living in the tenements as well as strikes and fires were portrayed, sometimes vividly and realistically, in cross-class film romances that were also highly melodramatic. *The High Road* (Rolfe Photoplays, 1915), based on a play produced in 1912, included both a strike and a fire in a shirtwaist factory. Mary Page escapes the brutality of her father to become a kept woman, and then leaves what she regards as a shameful life to become a worker in a shirtwaist factory. In response to a wage cut, Mary organizes the female workers to strike. When the owner hires thugs to create problems for the strikers, Mary appeals to Barnes, the mayor, whom she discovers is an ex-suitor of hers who has risen up in the world. The women succeed in retaining their former wage but when, one evening, the manager locks the women in the factory to force them to work overtime a fire breaks out and several of them die. The film showed women leaping from the window, and their bodies laid along the street covered with shrouds. Mary, badly burned, is cared for by Barnes and his sister, and although her past as a kept woman is revealed to Barnes, he marries her.[54]

Children of Eve (Edison, 1915) is another film with scenes of a factory fire that were inspired by the fire at the Triangle Factory. In this highly melodramatic film, replete with far-fetched coincidences, the cross-class romance is between Mamie McGuire, who is known as "Pride of the Alley," and Bert Madison, the nephew and ward of Henry Clay Madison, a wealthy capitalist who owns a canning factory in which we are shown women and young girls being worked to exhaustion. Unable to influence his uncle with his complaints of children being employed, Bert devotes himself to a settlement school and social work in the tenements. Bert meets Mamie, reforms her, and they fall in love. In fact, unbeknown to any of the protagonists, Mamie is the daughter of Henry and an ex-prostitute, Flossy, whom Henry had reformed when he was a student and clerk living next-door to her in the tenements. Flossy refused his marriage proposal because she believed that she was unworthy of him. She dies in poverty and her child, Mamie, is raised by another woman. Unaware of any of this, Henry tells Mamie to leave his house when she learns that Bert is ill and comes to visit him. Henry tells her (intertitle), "If you were to marry him, you would bring him down to your level." Bert recovers, and when he inquires if anyone came to see him when he was ill Henry shakes his head. A committee investigating conditions in the factories asks Mamie to obtain employment in Henry's factory and report to them. A fire breaks out and there are scenes of firemen rescuing some of the girls, the collapse of the building, and the dead girls lying out on the street. Mamie is rescued but she is severely affected by the fumes and when Henry comes to visit her in her tenement room he agrees to her request to see Bert just once more. At this point, Henry sees a picture of Mamie's mother and recognizes that Mamie is his daughter. It is too late. The doctor tells Henry that no amount of money he offers can save her and, after Bert and Mamie kiss, she dies[55] (Fig. 3.4).

The punishment of the bad capitalist in *Children of Eve* is the death of his daughter and his knowledge that his lack of concern for the welfare and safety of his workers was responsible for her death. As we will see in the next chapter, bad capitalists were frequently punished in cross-class romance films; but in most films, the capitalist's punishment was not accompanied by the death of the heroine. *Children of Eve* was one of the few cross-class romances to end sadly for the heroine. In general, it was becoming increasingly unusual for any American film to end unhappily. Lois Weber, a prominent scenarist and director, found that her aim to make 'artistic' films was often compromised by producers and exhibitors who put pressure on her to provide happy endings.[56] Some American film producers were happy to provide alternative tragic endings for the Russian market because of the Russian's 'love of tragedy,' but happy endings came

Fig. 3.4 Frame from *Children of Eve* (Edison, 1915). Mamie and young girl workers in the canning factory just before a fire kills many of them

to be seen as one of the demands of the domestic market. As early as 1909, *Moving Picture World* argued that, "the public should not patronize shows which offer only these depressing endings," and exhorted exhibitors to give the American public "good cheer and watch the increased stream of dimes and nickels which will flow into your coffers."[57]

TWO TYPES OF MELODRAMA: SERIALS AND CROSS-CLASS ROMANCES

A happy end to a cross-class romance film in this period was a happy end to a drama. Almost all of the cross-class romance films of the 1910s were dramas, and cross-class romances that were either comedies or that combined comedy with drama only began to appear in 1918 (e.g., *Amarilly of Clothes-Line Alley, Impossible Susan* and *Mickey*) and 1919 (e.g., *Maggie Pepper, The Delicious Little Devil*). However, cross-class romances were sometimes termed "melodramas" rather than dramas. *The High Road* was described by *Motion Picture World* as "unadulterated melodrama."[58]

Both *The High Road* and *Children of Eve* included most of the key constitutive factors listed by Ben Singer as characteristic of melodrama: pathos, implausible coincidences, and spectacles of physical peril. These are not the kinds of films, however, that Singer associates with the film melodrama of the 1910s. He shows that the term "melodrama" was applied principally to a type that he calls "sensational melodrama," as exemplified by serials in which the central protagonist was an intrepid, athletic heroine.[59] In contrast with the cross-class romances, most of which were feature length, most serials were made up of 12 or 15 episodes, with each episode lasting about 20 minutes shown on consecutive weeks. The two most important elements of melodrama in the serials were moral polarization—the entirely good heroine pitted against the vilest of villains—and spectacular action.

The first female adventure serial, the phenomenally successful *What Happened to Mary* (1912–1913), originated in collaboration between the Edison Company, which produced the film, and *The Ladies' World*, a monthly magazine with a primarily working-class female readership, which published written versions of the serial illustrated with stills from the movie. Mary is first seen doing things like other working girls such as finding a job as a clerical worker and finding a place to live, but she is soon the center of fantastic adventures in which she demonstrates dedication to her work, physical strength, valor and feats of daring. *What Happened to Mary* with Mary Fuller was followed by other successful serials with fearless heroines:

The Adventures of Kathlyn (1914) with Kathlyn Williams, *The Perils of Pauline* (1914) and *The Exploits of Elaine* (1915) with Pearl White, *The Hazards of Helen* (1914) with Helen Holmes, and many more in the years 1916 to 1919. The heroine's name in the title was often the name of the actress who played her, and their publicity emphasized that the actresses performed their own stunts and braved considerable dangers while filming.

Mary in *What Happened to Mary* is an orphan and although she discovers that she is an heiress, the absence of patriarchal control enables her to freely construct her identity.[60] The absence of a father became a common element in most of the serials; in the first episodes, the father or guardian is murdered or abducted and the heroine enters an extended struggle with a villain over the physical possession of some highly prized object in order to gain her inheritance or rescue her father. In this struggle, the heroines demonstrated qualities that were commonly associated with masculinity, such as strength, endurance, self-reliance and courage; however, these portrayals of female power were often accompanied by spectacles of their distress and victimization, since the villains and their henchmen were forever attempting to terrorize, entrap, kidnap and kill them.

Singer and other analysts of the serials have related the narrative structure—the oscillation between liberation and entrapment, empowerment and imperilment—to the experiences of single, young working women of the time. Although a large proportion of young working women were expected to hand over most of their earnings to their fathers, they experienced some freedom from their families both at work and at leisure. This was especially the case for the increasing number of women who were living apart from their families, but these were also the women who were likely to encounter the dangers of the city, especially at the hands of men who exploited them, economically and sexually. Singer writes that the serials can be interpreted both as fantasies in which the heroines are free of the constraints placed upon women and as reflections of the progress that women were making as they entered the work force and experienced greater freedom in public areas, which included the new commercial entertainments such as the cinemas.[61]

The heyday of the 'serial queens' from 1913 to the end of the decade coincided with the considerable increase in cross-class romance films from 1915. The central protagonist in both cases was a female, and although the audiences for these films were not confined to women, they were addressed primarily to women. It is possible that the audiences for these two types of melodrama differed somewhat in class. Singer writes that the serials were probably seen by spectators from all classes, but that they were shown for the most part in small neighborhood and cheap second-run downtown cinemas. Many of these cinemas continued to show a 'variety program' of short films, including a number of serials, well after the ascendance of the feature film.[62] The cross-class romance films, by contrast, came into their own with the ascendance of the feature film, and many were shown in large, first-run theaters as well as second- and third-run cinemas. However, working-class women made up a large part, possibly the principal part, of the audience for cross-class romances, and it is most likely that the audiences for serials and cross-class romances overlapped considerably. Young women saw all the different types of films, which differed with respect to the facets of the working woman's working experiences on which they focused and the kinds of fantasies they provided.[63]

Unlike the central female protagonist of the seduction plot films and at least some of the cross-class romances, the heroines of the serials were in no way pathetic. Like many of the heroines of cross-class romances, the serial heroines were often saved from peril by heroes; but unlike most cross-class romance heroines, the serial heroines would often act like men and rescue the heroes. The major difference between the serial and the cross-class romance was that, in the serials, romance was of minor importance compared with the heroines' thrilling adventures. In *What Happened to Mary*, the heroine did not allow romance to deter her from her work and adventures, and she expressed displeasure when John, a clerical co-worker, insisted on proposing marriage. When another suitor presented her with a large diamond ring, she threw it out a carriage window and laughed. Marriage was not the culminating reward of Mary's adventures, and the series did not end with her wedding. In an early scene of *The Perils of Pauline*, the heroine refuses a marriage proposal from the son of her departed guardian and tells him that she wishes to postpone marriage in order to travel the world and have adventures. The series closes with Pauline's marriage, but marriage for the serial queen was not a goal or a reward; it simply signified a closure to her exploits and adventures. The heroine of *The Hazards of Helen* refused her boyfriend's offer of marriage and was even more independent from male companions or assistance than other serial queens.[64]

Marriage with a fabulously wealthy, handsome man was no less a fantasy than the daring escapades and last-second escapes of the serial heroines, but these fantasies did not contradict each other and female spectators could enjoy both and identify with their respective heroines. Similarities can also be found between the serials and cross-class romances. As we will see in the following chapter, the heroines in many cross-class romances were also victimized by villains and placed in situations of danger, especially danger to her virtue. Although the hero almost invariably saved her, she often demonstrated considerable bravery, comparable with that of the serial queen. However, such similarities were less significant than the differences, particularly with respect to narrative structures and the place of romance. These were two different types of melodrama. In contrast to the "sensationalist melodrama" of the serials, the cross-class romances tended to be what John G. Cawelti has termed "social melodrama."[65] A social melodrama includes such elements as pathos, moral polarization, and physical danger within realistic settings such as work places, and includes realistic portrayals of major social phenomena such as sexual harassment of female workers and class conflict.

Realistic portrayals of suffering and injustice endured by the working class in social melodramas could be understood as a critique of the social structure, but this critique is tempered and ameliorated by the social melodrama's affirmation of a benevolent moral order. The morally appropriates fates are portioned out; the villain, often the would-be seducer or economic exploiter, is punished or redeemed by love, and the heroine is rewarded by marriage to a wealthy man. A critique of the social structure is deflected by placing the moral responsibility onto the villain, who is motivated by lust, greed or a general form of malevolence. Society's problems are personified in the evil villain and, once the villain is removed or redeemed, justice is achieved and society can function fairly and smoothly.

With respect to those films in which the central protagonist is female, it was the social melodrama of the cross-class romance rather than sensationalist melodrama of the serials that was to retain its popularity. The serial did not fit into film programs in which the feature film was the main attraction, and whereas serials in general came to be relegated to special film shows for children, and serials in which the central protagonist is female almost disappeared, cross-class romances continued to be popular into the 1920s and beyond. Both the serial-queen melodramas and the cross-class romances were addressed principally to women who, according to some estimations, had come to constitute the majority of filmgoers by the late 1910s. With the demise of the serials, it was the romantic female-centered film that continued its appeal to female audiences. There is no hard evidence to substantiate the claim that the film audience continued to be predominantly female into the 1920s and 1930s, but the Hollywood studios assumed this to be the case and planned their production accordingly.[66] The cross-class romance was one of the important sub-genres that was expected to appeal to the all-important female audience.

NOTES

1. The place of narrative and its development in early film has been an issue in dispute among film historians. Charles Musser, "Rethinking Early Cinema: Cinema of Attractions and Narrativity," *Yale Journal of Criticism* 7.2 (1994): 203–232; Charles Musser, "Historiographic Method and the Study of Early Cinema," *Cinema Journal* 44.1 (2004): 101–107; Tom Gunning, "Attractions: How They Came into the World," in Wanda Strauven, ed., *The Cinema of Attractions Reloaded* (Amsterdam: Amsterdam University Press, 2006), 31–40; Tom Gunning, "Cinema of Attractions," in Richard Abel, ed., *Encyclopedia of Early Cinema* (London: Routledge, 2005), 124–127.

2. Kristin Thompson writes that prior to 1903 the single-shot fictional narratives resembled a simple vaudeville skit or sketch, and that the multi-shot film, beginning about 1903, adopted the form of the vaudeville playlet. The vaudeville playlet, which lasted about twenty minutes, was a condensed version of successful dramas or a short play written especially to fit into the variety program of vaudeville. The melodrama was a popular type of playlet; it was episodic with quick transitions in space and time, its protagonists were easily recognizable characters representing good and evil, and it emphasized pictorial elements rather than dialogue. These characteristics were appropriate for the early multi-shot film melodramas that lasted about five minutes. Kristin Thompson, "The Formulation of the Classical Style, 1909–28," in David Bordwell, Janet Staiger and Kristin Thompson, *The Classical Hollywood Cinema: Film Style and Mode of Production to 1960* (London: Routledge, 1985), 159–160; John C. Tibbets, *The American Theatrical Film: Stages in Development* (Bowling Green: Bowling Green State University Popular Press, 1985), 59–61.

3. American Film Institute (henceforth AFI) online catalog.

4. This film can be viewed on YouTube.

5. Tom Gunning, "The Cinema of Attractions: Early Film, its Spectator and the Avant-Garde," in Thomas Elsaesser with Adam Barker, eds., *Early Cinema: Space, Frame, Narrative* (London: BFI Publishing, 1990), 58; Musser, "Rethinking Early Cinema," 210–211.

6. Charlie Keil, *Early American Cinema in Transition; Story, Style, and Filmmaking, 1907–1913*, (Madison, Wisconsin: The University of Wisconsin Press, 2001), 128.

7. The film can be seen on YouTube. My account of *The Unwritten Law* has been informed by Grieveson's detailed account of the film and its relationship to the newspaper coverage of the trial. Lee Grieveson, *Policing Cinema: Movies and Censorship in Early-Twentieth-Century America* (Berkeley: University of California Press, 2004), 39–57. See also Janet

Staiger, *Bad Women: Regulating Sexuality in Early American Cinema* (Minneapolis: University of Minnesota Press, 1995), 20–21, 61–62.

8. On the responses to the film see Grieveson, *Policing Cinema*, 58–65, 70–71.

9. Eileen Bowser, "Toward Narrative, 1907: The Mill Girl," in John L. Fell, ed., *Film Before Griffith* (Berkeley: University of California Press, 1983), 330–338.

10. Steven J. Ross, *Working-Class Hollywood: Silent Film and the Shaping of Class in America* (Princeton: Princeton University Press, 1998), 51; Staiger, *Bad Women*, 128–146.

11. *Motion Picture World* (hereafter MPW), December 30, 1911, 1100.

12. Kemp R. Niver, *Motion Pictures from the Library of Congress Paper Print Collection, 1894–1912* (Berkeley: University of California Press, 1967), 190.

13. MPW, October 23, 1909, 539; *Variety*, October 23, 1909, 13.

14. MPW, July 2, 1910, 37.

15. This film is included in the DVD *Nickelodia 2* (Unknown Video).

16. This film is included in the DVD *Treasures 3: Social Issues in American Film, 1900–1934* (National Film Preservation Foundation).

17. MPW, January 9 1910, 25.

18. Ben Singer, "Feature Films, Variety Programs, and the Crisis of the Small Exhibitor," in Charlie Keil and Shelley Stamp, eds., *American Cinema's Transitional Era: Audiences, Institutions, Practices* (Berkeley: University of California Press, 2004), 76–100.

19. I began constructing my list of cross-class romance films by reading plot outlines in the American Film Institute catalog under a number of subject categories, including class distinction, employer-employee relations, social climbers, factory workers, sales clerks, upper class, factory owners, factory workers, gold diggers, and department stores. Only films with narratives set in the contemporary United States were included. The digitalization of trade journals and other film journals enabled me to increase my list by finding relevant films through certain search terms such as working girl, shop girl, and millionaire. As only a small proportion of the relevant silent films have survived, for plot details, in addition to the AFI catalog, I depended on trade journals, particularly *Moving Picture World* (1907–1927), *Motography* (1911–1917, formerly *Nickelodeon*, which began in 1909), and *Motion Picture News* (1913–1930). Additional sources for plots and other information were the *New York Times*, *Variety*, *Exhibitors Herald*, *Exhibitors Trade Review*, and *Wid's Daily*, which became *Film Daily* in 1922. In contrast with the small proportion of silent films on my list that I was able to view, I have viewed the great majority of sound films on my list. Although there are no doubt a number of cross-class romance films that I have missed, particularly those of one or two reels made prior to 1915, I am confident

that my list for all periods includes a sufficient number which allow me to make differentiations among sub-types and to substantiate my arguments.

20. MPW, September 13 1913, 1200; Michelle Tolini Finamore, *Hollywood Before Glamour: Fashion in American Silent Film* (New York: Palgrave Macmillan, 2013), 12.
21. *The Kiss* can be seen on YouTube.
22. MPW, October 3 1908, 266–267.
23. MPW, April 2 1910, 509.
24. MPW, April 9 1910, 551.
25. MPW, April 30 1910, 690.
26. MPW, July 9 1910, 62, 107.
27. MPW, December 2 1911, 744; December 23 1911, 989.
28. The description here is indebted to Ross who bases his account on Weiss' script. Ross notes that the film was shown in a cinema in Manhattan and a cinema in Brooklyn. Ross *Working-Class Hollywood*, 98–101.
29. MPW, July 24 1909, 137.
30. AFI online catalog; Motography, December 12 1914, 829.
31. MPW, July 15 1911, 627.
32. MPW, July 4 1914, 118.
33. MPW, December 11 1909, 859.
34. MPW, February 26 1910, 309.
35. Nickelodeon, March 4 1911, 252.
36. MPW, March 11 1911, 542.
37. MPW, November 16 1918, 764.
38. S.J. Kleinberg, *Women in the United States, 1930–1945* (London: Macmillan Press, 1999), 112.
39. David M. Katzman, *Seven Days a Week: Women and Domestic Servants in Industrializing America* (Oxford: Oxford University Press, 1978), 51.
40. Kathy Peiss, *Cheap Amusements: Working Women and Leisure in Turn-of-the-Century New York* (Philadelphia: Temple University Press, 1986), 36, 39.
41. Katzman, *Seven Days a Week*, 284.
42. Claudia Goldin, "The Rising (and then Declining) Significance of Gender," NBER Working Paper April 2002.
43. Peiss, *Cheap Amusements*, 36–39.
44. John Whiteclay Chambers II, *The Tyranny of Change: America in the Progressive Era 1900–1917* (NY: St. Martin's Press, 1980), 81.
45. Sven Beckert, *The Monied Metropolis, New York City and the Consolidation of the American Bourgeoisie, 1850–1896* (Cambridge: Cambridge University Press, 2001).
46. Peiss, *Cheap Amusements*, 11.

47. Sharon H. Strom, *Beyond the Typewriter: Gender, Class, and the Origins of Modern American Office Work, 1900–1930* (Urbana: University of Illinois Press, 1992), 49, 65–79, 288–289, 319; Goldin, "The Rising (and then Declining) Significance of Gender."

48. Goldin, "The Rising (and then Declining) Significance of Gender."

49. John Sharpless and John Rury, "The Political Economy of Women's Work: 1900–1920," *Social Science History,* 4.3 (1980), 317–346; Peiss, *Cheap Amusements,* 34.

50. Strom, *Beyond the Typewriter,* 387–401.

51. Sharpless and Rury, "The Political Economy of Women's Work," 322–323.

52. Claudia Goldin, "The Work and Wages of Single Women, 1870–1920," *The Journal of Economic History,* 40.1 (1980), 81–88.

53. Sue Ainslie Clark and Edith Wyatt, *Making Both Ends Meet: The Income and Outlay of New York Working Girls* (New York: The Macmillan Company, 1911).

54. *Motography,* May 8 1915, 749–50; MPW, May 8 1915, 917; *Motion Picture News,* May 8 1915, 72.

55. This is one of the few silent films from this period discussed here that is extant. It is available on the DVD *The Devil's Needle and Other Tales of Vice and Redemption* (Kino Classics).

56. Shelley Stamp, *Lois Weber in Early Hollywood* (Oakland: University of California Press, 2015), 25, 36.

57. John Trumpbour, *Selling Hollywood to the World: U.S. and European Struggles for Mastery of the Global Film Industry, 1920–1950* (Cambridge: Cambridge University Press, 2002), 19.

58. MPW, May 8 1915, 917.

59. Ben Singer, *Melodrama and Modernity: Early Sensational Cinema and Its Contexts* (New York: Columbia University Press, 2001).

60. Nan Enstad, "Dressed for Adventure: Working Women and Silent Movie Serials in the 1910s," *Feminist Studies* 21.1 (1995): 67–80.

61. Singer, *Melodrama and Modernity,* 239–242, 253–255.

62. Singer, *Melodrama and Modernity,* 203.

63. Stamp writes that although movie theater owners of this period sought respectability principally by attracting the patronage of middle-class ladies, their cultivation of a refined movie going experience extended to unmarried female wage-earners and women from the working class who were "eager to fantasize their own upward mobility." Shelly Stamp, *Movie-Struck Girls: Women and Motion Picture Culture After the Nickelodeon* (Princeton: Princeton University Press, 2000), 15(quote)-25.

64. Enstad, "Dressed for Adventure," 78–82; Shelley Stamp, "An Awful Struggle between Love and Ambition: Serial Heroines, Serial Stars and

their Female Fans," in Lee Grieveson and Peter Krämer, eds., *The Silent Cinema Reader* (London: Routledge, 2004), 217.

65. John G. Cawelti, *Adventure, Mystery, and Romance: Formula Stories as Art and Popular Culture* (Chicago: University of Chicago Press, 1976), 261–267.

66. Melvyn Stokes, "Female Audiences of the 1920s and early 1930s," in Melvyn Stokes and Richard Maltby, eds., *Identifying Hollywood's Audiences: Cultural Identity and the Movies* (London: British Film Institute, 1999), 43–44.

BIBLIOGRAPHY

Beckert, Sven. *The Monied Metropolis: New York City and the Consolidation of the American Bourgeoisie, 1850–1896.* Cambridge: Cambridge University Press, 1993.

Bowser, Eileen. "Toward Narrative, 1907: The Mill Girl," in John L. Fell, ed. *Film Before Griffith.* Berkeley: University of California Press, 1983, 330–338.

Cawelti, John G. *Adventure, Mystery, and Romance: Formula Stories as Art and Popular Culture.* Chicago: University of Chicago Press, 1976.

Chambers II, John Whiteclay. *The Tyranny of Change: America in the Progressive Era 1900–1917.* NY: St. Martin's Press, 1980.

Clark, Sue Ainslie. and Edith Wyatt. *Making Both Ends Meet: The Income and Outlay of New York Working Girls.* New York: The Macmillan Company, 1911.

Enstad, Nan. "Dressed for Adventure: Working Women and Silent Movie Serials in the 1910s," *Feminist Studies* 21.1 (1995): 67–80.

Finamore, Michelle Tolini. *Hollywood Before Glamour: Fashion in American Silent Film.* New York: Palgrave Macmillan, 2013.

Goldin, Claudia. "The Work and Wages of Single Women, 1870–1920," *The Journal of Economic History* 40.1 (1980): 81–88.

———. "The Rising (and then Declining) Significance of Gender," NBER Working Paper April 2002.

Grieveson, Lee. *Policing Cinema: Movies and Censorship in Early-Twentieth-Century America.* Berkeley: University of California Press, 2004.

Gunning, Tom. "The Cinema of Attractions: Early Film, Its Spectator and the Avant-Garde," in Thomas Elsaesser with Adam Barker, eds. *Early Cinema: Space, Frame, Narrative.* London: BFI Publishing, 1990, 56–62.

———. "Cinema of Attractions," in Richard Abel, ed. *Encyclopedia of Early Cinema.* London: Routledge, 2005, 124–127.

———. "Attractions: How They Came Into the World," in Wanda Strauven, ed. *The Cinema of Attractions Reloaded.* Amsterdam: Amsterdam University Press, 2006, 31–40.

Katzman, David M. *Seven Days a Week: Women and Domestic Servants in Industrializing America.* Oxford: Oxford University Press, 1978.

Keil, Charlie. *Early American Cinema in Transition; Story, Style, and Filmmaking, 1907–1913.* Madison, Wisconsin: The University of Wisconsin Press, 2001.

Kleinberg, S.J. *Women in the United States, 1930–1945.* London: Macmillan Press, 1999.

Musser, Charles. "Rethinking Early Cinema: Cinema of Attractions and Narrativity," *Yale Journal of Criticism* 7.2 (1994): 203–232

———. "Historiographic Method and the Study of Early Cinema," *Cinema Journal* 44.1 (2004): 101–107.

Niver, Kemp R. *Motion Pictures from the Library of Congress Paper Print Collection, 1894–1912.* Berkeley: University of California Press, 1967.

Peiss, Kathy. *Cheap Amusements: Working Women and Leisure in Turn-of-the-Century New York.* Philadelphia: Temple University Press, 1986.

Ross, Steven J. *Working-Class Hollywood; Silent Film and the Shaping of Class in America.* Princeton: Princeton University Press, 1998.

Sharpless, John. and John Rury. "The Political Economy of Women's Work: 1900–1920," *Social Science History*, 4.3 (1980), 317–346.

Singer, Ben. *Melodrama and Modernity: Early Sensational Cinema and Its Contexts.* New York: Columbia University Press, 2001.

———. "Feature Films, Variety Programs, and the Crisis of the Small Exhibitor," in Charlie Keil and Shelley Stamp, eds., *American Cinema's Transitional Era: Audiences, Institutions, Practices.* Berkeley: University of California Press, 2004, 76–100.

Staiger, Janet. *Bad Women: Regulating Sexuality in Early American Cinema.* Minneapolis: University of Minnesota Press, 1995.

Stamp, Shelly. *Movie-Struck Girls: Women and Motion Picture Culture After the Nickelodeon.* Princeton: Princeton University Press, 2000.

———. "An Awful Struggle between Love and Ambition: Serial Heroines, Serial Stars and their Female Fans," in Lee Grieveson and Peter Krämer, eds. *The Silent Cinema Reader.* London: Routledge, 2004, 210–225.

———. *Lois Weber in Early Hollywood.* Oakland: University of California Press, 2015.

Stokes, Melvyn. "Female Audiences of the 1920s and early 1930s," in Melvyn Stokes and Richard Maltby, eds. *Identifying Hollywood's Audiences: Cultural Identity and the Movies.* London: British Film Institute, 1999, 42–60.

Strom, Sharon H. *Beyond the Typewriter: Gender, Class, and the Origins of Modern American Office Work, 1900–1930.* Urbana: University of Illinois Press, 1992.

Thompson, Kristin. "The Formulation of the Classical Style, 1909–28," in David Bordwell, Janet Staiger and Kristin Thompson, eds. *The Classical Hollywood Cinema: Film Style and Mode of Production to 1960.* London: Routledge, 1985, 155–240.

Tibbets, John C. *The American Theatrical Film: Stages in Development.* Bowling Green: Bowling Green State University Popular Press, 1985.

Trumpbour, John. *Selling Hollywood to the World: U.S. and European Struggles for Mastery of the Global Film Industry, 1920–1950.* Cambridge: Cambridge University Press, 2002.

CHAPTER 4

Sexual Exploitation and Class Conflict

Portrayals of sexual harassment of working girls and of conflict between labor and capital appeared in many of the cross-class romance films that were made between 1914 and 1918. One type of sexual exploitation of women that was prevalent, but rarely discussed or portrayed in popular culture, was that conducted by the women's own families. As the family was considered a basis of social order, incest was unacknowledged, and it was assumed that young women and girls who accused their fathers and other male relatives of sexual abuse were lying.[1]

By comparison, the sexual exploitation of the increasing number of young, unmarried women who were working outside of the home was a subject of extensive investigation and discourse and was incorporated into the narratives of cross-class romance films.

WORKING GIRLS AS VICTIMS IN CROSS-CLASS ROMANCE FILMS

The cross-class romance films of this period ranged from those that depicted the female protagonist from a poor or working-class family as a victim of sexual exploitation to those that depicted her as a voluntary agent in her relationship with the wealthy male protagonist. This was a period in which an unusually large number of films included rapes or attempted rapes; the American Film Institute Catalog lists no less than 182 films released between 1914 and 1920 that included attempted rape

© The Author(s) 2017 83
S. Sharot, *Love and Marriage Across Social Classes in American Cinema*,
DOI 10.1007/978-3-319-41799-8_4

and 68 films that included rape. The portrayal of the female as victim was also pronounced in the white slavery films that aroused considerable controversy in 1913 and 1914, just prior to the sharp increase in cross-class romance films. White slavery, the forcible abduction and sale into prostitution of innocent women, became a widespread concern in the early 1910s and many objected to its depiction in the films *Traffic in Souls* and *The Inside of the White Slave Traffic*, both released in 1913, which attracted large audiences. Lee Grieveson compares the quasi-documentary approach of *The Inside of the White Slave Traffic* with the "fictional indulgence" of *Traffic in Souls*, which shifted from a quasi-documentary opening into a melodrama of abduction by villains and rescue by the police. Grieveson writes that the National Board of Censorship was troubled by the "excessive realism" of *The Inside of the White Slave Traffic* and preferred "controversial subjects to be enfolded within a melodramatic or self-enclosed fictional world" as was the case in *Traffic in Souls*.[2] The white slave films that were made during the next few years followed the melodramatic formula. In *The House of Bondage* (1914), the white slave traffic provided the backdrop to the classic plot of seduction of an innocent girl followed by her downward path and tragic end.[3] Although a few additional white slave films were made in the following years, the furor had passed its peak and the mainstream industry concluded that the bans and calls for censorship made these films too troublesome to produce.

The theme of the working-class young woman as a victim of sexual exploitation continued in some cross-class romance films. A happy ending was becoming almost obligatory in American-made films, and although the seduction plot that ends with the heroine's death was becoming rare, it was played out once more in *Her Hour* (World Film, 1917). Rita, a department store saleswoman, is fired after she rejects the advances of a floor walker, but she submits to her new employer, a prominent lawyer, who casts her off after making her pregnant. At the end of the film, Rita dies of heart failure after she shields her daughter's name by declaring that she is not the girl's real mother.[4] Other films in which the heroine is a victim of seduction end happily. Following her seduction and abandonment by a city man, the country girl in *The Innocent Sinner* (Fox, 1917) is rescued from a life of shame and wins the love of a doctor who overcomes her fears that he will scorn her because of her past.[5] In *Playthings* (Bluebird, 1918), Marjorie, a shop girl, refuses an offer of marriage from John, a young lawyer, because of her shame over her affair with Gordon, her employer's son, whom she discovers was only using her as a plaything and leaves her with a baby who subsequently dies. The film ends with Gordon's death and John, now a successful attorney, forgiving and marrying Marjorie.[6] In *The Beautiful Lie* (Rolfe, 1917), Louise, a stenographer, attempts to overcome her status as a victim after Mortimer, her employer, tricks her into a mock marriage and subsequently abandons her. Despite her resolve to take all she can from men and give nothing in return, Louise falls in love with Paul, a protégé of her seducer, and unites with him after Mortimer is shot by another woman.[7]

Working-class heroines would sometimes take revenge on their seducer or would-be seducer who has done them wrong. The artist's model in *The Common* Law (Clara Kimball Young Film Corp., 1916) kills one painter when he tries to force himself upon her and marries another after his parents withdraw their disapproval of the model's lower-class background.[8] In *The Law's Injustice* (Lubin, 1916), Nina, a factory worker, spurns the advance of Morris, the factory owner. She prefers to go to jail accused of theft rather than yield to him; after serving her sentence, she exposes Morris, now a candidate for governor of the state, as a fraud.[9] In other films the wealthy seducer or would-be seducer is reformed through love and becomes a worthy partner of the virtuous heroine. The wealthy man in the two-reel *Viviana* (American, 1916) makes love to the poor working girl without any intension of marrying her but proposes to her after he discovers that his sister is having an affair and realizes that he is no better than his sister's lover.[10] The advances of the wealthy man toward a chorus girl in a taxi in *Broadway Love* (Bluebird, 1918) cause the girl to jump from the speeding car and suffer injuries. Repentant, and with his ideas on chorus girls revised, the wealthy man proposes marriage after some complications and misunderstandings. The reviewer for *Motion Picture News* wrote that this film "shows why some New York chorus girls have elegant apartments on Central Park West and why others live in hall rooms." However, the wealthy man discovers "that a girl can be of the chorus and still be capable of loving with the same degree of purity prevalent in the best regulated families."[11]

Another virtuous heroine, this time a stenographer, in *The Grain of Dust* (Crest Pictures, 1918) repulses the advances of her boss, a junior partner of a Wall Street firm, but after he saves her from an attempted suicide by drowning she realizes that his love is genuine and marries him.[12] Marjorie, the stenographer in *The Risky Road* (Universal, 1918), at first refuses the non-marital arrangement proposed by a prosperous broker and only after the loss of her job leaves her penniless and cold does she agree to accept an apartment and gifts from him. The agreement does not require her immediate sexual favors and Marjorie's despair over the appearance of being a kept woman is dispelled after the broker confesses his love and declares that he wants to marry her. One reviewer noted that the film was typical of the many stories that "lead the hero and heroine up to the door of a bedroom and then disclose the fact that it is locked and the key lost."[13] Another reviewer wrote that "there are two or three instances when you think, or rather feel, that the girl is just about to give in only to find that you have guessed wrongly."[14] The reviewer for *Variety* wrote that the film teaches stenographers the lesson that a girl should retain her virtue even when she is showered with jewels and given an apartment because "in the end the John will 'come through' with the marriage license."[15]

Working-class girls who resist sexual harassment or attacks are rewarded by marriage with wealthy men in cross-class romances. After the department store salesgirl in the one-reel *The Little Saleslady* (Edison, 1915) recovers from a blow on the head she received when repulsing a sexual attack, she is rewarded by a proposal of marriage from the owner of the store.[16] *Winifred the Shop Girl* (Vitagraph, 1916) has to ward off the unwelcome attentions of male customers, floorwalkers, salesmen and, in particular, the store superintendent from whose sexual attack she is saved by the owner's son, who proposes to her.[17] Wealthy men marry working-class girls after they have protected them from the sexual aggression of other men. In *Moral Courage* (Peerless, 1917), the son of the mill owner marries the mill girl after he protects her from the unwelcome advances of his father's male secretary, and the father removes his opposition to their marriage after the girl demonstrates her cleverness.[18] Yet another mill owner's son who protects a mill girl from sexual harassment, this time from a foreman of the mill, appears in *Whims of Society* (World, 1918). The mill owner disapproves of his son's relationship with the mill girl and intends to disown him, but before he can do so he is killed by a bomb planted by the ex-foreman. The son inherits and marries the mill girl.[19]

SEXUAL HARASSMENT IN SOCIETY

Like the maid servant readers of *Pamela* in the eighteenth century, the working-girl audiences of cross-class romance films knew that they had little chance of marrying their 'masters', but they were likely to be familiar, either through their own experiences or knowledge of their coworkers, with sexual exploitation. Investigations by governmental agencies and reform organizations in the first two decades of the twentieth century reported that working girls and women were subjected to widespread sexual harassment by employers, supervisors, and, in the retail and service sectors, by customers and clients. A report in 1911 for the Commissioner of Labor stated that the female occupations subject to the greatest "moral danger" were those in domestic service, hotel and restaurant waitresses, low-grade factory workers, nurses and "cheaper stenographic positions." Those who were particularly vulnerable were girls of 14 or 15, who were just out of school and received the lowest salaries. They were "unquestionably taken advantage of by their employers," and girls complained of employers who "were outrageous in their conduct."[20] A report of the National Consumer' League, published in 1911, states that saleswomen in department stores were "importuned, not only by men from without these establishments, but also, to the shame of the managements, by men employed within the stores."[21] Yet another investigation from 1911 reported that male customers whose propositions to salesgirls had been refused were known to complain to floor walkers that the girls had neglected their business and that the floor walkers would harass the girls to accept the invitations of customers.[22] In her account of prostitution in America between 1900 and 1918, Ruth Rosen writes that the sexual harassment that women frequently experienced at work may have led some women to the conclusion that outright prostitution was more profitable that prostituting oneself in order to obtain or retain a low-paying job.[23]

Widespread sexual harassment was part of a culture that accepted a wide range of aggression in male sexual behavior toward women. Evidence of this aggression is revealed in the records of court cases in which females, almost all working class, accused males of seduction. Most states had seduction laws and under the seduction statute in the state of New York a man could be persecuted for obtaining a woman's consent to sexual intercourse by promising to marry her and then failing to carry out his promise. In many cases, the women charging seduction would describe having been sexually assaulted; the acts of seduction had been accomplished as much by violence as by a promise of marriage. Most of the women, however, expressed a desire to marry the man that they accused rather than have him sent to prison. The voluntary entrance of women into marriage in such circumstances demonstrates that the boundary between consensual sex and coerced sex was blurred at that time. New understandings of sexual violence began to emerge in the 1920s and, from the mid-1930s seduction prosecutions almost disappeared as they were replaced by prosecutions of rape.[24]

WORKING-GIRLS AS SEXUAL AGENTS IN CROSS-CLASS ROMANCE FILMS

A large set of cross-class romance films portray the working-class heroine, not as a victim of sexual predators requiring the intervention of a wealthy man who will marry her, but as an agent who chooses to attempt to overcome her economic circumstances by using her sexual assets or allure. The goals that motivate these heroines are varied. A frequent goal is to improve their personal economic situation. *Everybody's Girl* (Vitagraph, 1918) shows that, although the limited income of working girls requires them to depend on men for their entertainments, the heroine, Florence, and her flat mate are taken to the theatre by chance acquaintances "without being made to pay too dearly for their fun." On a trip to Coney Island, Florence meets a young man who turns out to be the owner of the tenement in which she lives and, before the happy ending, the rich man has to be persuaded that Florence is not "everybody's girl."[25] Most heroines in cross-class romances successfully retain their virtue but the fact that many working girls were only able to meet essential economic needs by occasional prostitution was recognized in *Shoes* (Bluebird, 1916), which, significantly, was not a cross-class romance. A number of cross-class romance films portrayed the economic dilemma of working girls but, unlike the cross-class romance films, the heroine of *Shoes* sacrifices her virtue without being saved or compensated by marriage to a wealthy man.

Shoes, directed by one of the few female directors, Lois Weber, begins with a shot of sales women lining up to receive their pay in a department store. Eva, one of the workers, walks through the streets of the shopping district on her way home and stops to admire a pair of stylish shoes in a storefront window. The shoes in the window appear to be solely an item of fashion because, at this point, we are not aware that Eva has worn out the soles of her shoes by standing all day in the five-and-ten dime store. Eva reaches out for the boots and a close-up shows the window glass that separates her from the desired item. Eva's need for new footwear is made evident in scenes where she places insoles cut from cardboard boxes in her old shoes and begs her mother for money to buy new shoes. Her mother cannot spare the money because Eva's meager $5-a-week wages must support the entire family; her lazy father who makes no attempt to find work, her mother who earns very little by taking in laundry, and her three younger sisters.

Eva is surrounded by the consumer society at work and as she makes her way between work and home, but her wages and family circumstances do not allow her to participate in the consumer economy that her labor supports. Eva needs the shoes for work and she also wants to look fashionable like the young women she sees in the park. During her lunch break, Eva watches the middle- and upper-class men and women walking in the park, and her view of the well-dressed feet of rich girls, which we are shown in close-up, encourages her to imagine her own feet transformed by new shoes. Eva's consumer desire is accentuated by the example of Lil, a co-worker, who accepts gifts of jewelry and clothing from men in exchange for what we assume to be sexual favors. At first Eva repels the advances of Charlie, a Cabaret singer, but after catching cold from walking in the rain in her worn shoes, she agrees to accompany him to the morally suspect Blue Goose cabaret. The following day, she arrives home wearing the new shoes and falls weeping into her mother's lap. Her exchange of sex for the shoes is especially bitter when she learns that her father has found employment to support the family.

In two fantasy scenarios, which are shown prior to the final scene, Eva envisages futures in which she does not have to work. In one scenario she is supported by her father's earnings and is preparing for a domestic life at home with her future husband. In another scenario, which evokes the fantasy of cross-class romance films, she makes her society debut among tuxedo-clad admirers. The fantasy sequences imply that if traditional gender roles were upheld, Eva would not be placed in a position in which she is exploited both economically in her work and sexually in an economy of sexual favors in exchange for material benefits. On the one hand, the film can be read as a plea that working girls should receive fair wages so that they no longer have to submit to sexual exploitation. On the other hand, the film suggests two conservative messages: firstly, women ought to depend on the income of their fathers and husbands; secondly, it is the female's desire for consumer items that induce her to give sexual favors. These conservative messages are made more explicit in a cross-class romance film that Weber made a year later, *The Price of a Good Time* (1917). In this film, the desire of Linnie, the sales clerk, for the commodities on display in the store where she works induces her to submit to the attentions of Preston, the store owner's playboy son, who gives her money to buy new clothes and arranges six nights of luxurious pleasure. Although their relationship remains platonic, Linnie returns home in disgrace and, as she is unable to live with her dishonor, she commits suicide by throwing herself under Preston's car. Linnie's predicament is contrasted to that of another sales clerk whose marriage to a man from her own class assures her happiness[26] (Fig. 4.1).

A number of films presented cautionary tales of working-class women who sought to escape the grind of work and enjoy a comfortable life by taking the 'easiest way.' In *The Hard Road* (Victor Film Company, 1915), Myra, a stenographer, enjoys for a time the comfortable life of being the kept woman of Thorne, a rich broker. When Bess, Myra's sister, begs her to return home, Myra refuses and contrasts her life of luxury with her sister's poverty. Bess says, "It may not seem so now, but yours is the 'hard road' and mine the easy and happy one." After Thorne discards Myra in favor of a rich girl, Myra begins her descent and ends up as a prostitute. Six years later, Myra meets her happily married sister who takes her to her home, but the sister's husband refuses to let her stay with them because of their children. Myra stops at a mission where she meets her former lover, now a derelict, and they enter the mission together.[27] The theme of two sisters is repeated in *The Cup of Life* (Mutual, 1915); one sister marries happily with a man from her own class and the other becomes the mistress of a succession of wealthy man until her allure fades and her attempts to escape suffering through alcohol and drugs hasten her death.[28] *The Easiest Way* (Clara Kimball Young Film Corporation, 1917), based on a 1909 play, also ends with the death of the luxury-loving heroine, but in this film there is some compensation at her death bed, as the man she truly loves arrives in time to let her know that he forgives her. One reviewer wrote that the film portrayed "the life of temptation and bitter disillusion that

--------------------------------→

Fig. 4.1 *The Price of a Good Time* (Lois Weber Productions, 1917) is a lost film and these images are part of a photo spread on the film in *Moving Picture World*, December 29, 1917 (digitalized by Media History Digital Library). The caption of the top left image describes Linnie, a saleswoman in a department store, living in a "sordid home of poverty and unhappiness" and desiring "just a little of the pleasure and pretty clothes that other girls had." In the top right image, Preston, the son of the store owner, asks Linnie, "Did you ever have a good time." The bottom left image shows Linnie and Preston in his family's palatial home. She says, "I'll give anything to stay in this wonderful home just for one night." The bottom right image shows Linnie on her return home, disgraced before her mother and brother and soon to pay the price of a good time by committing suicide

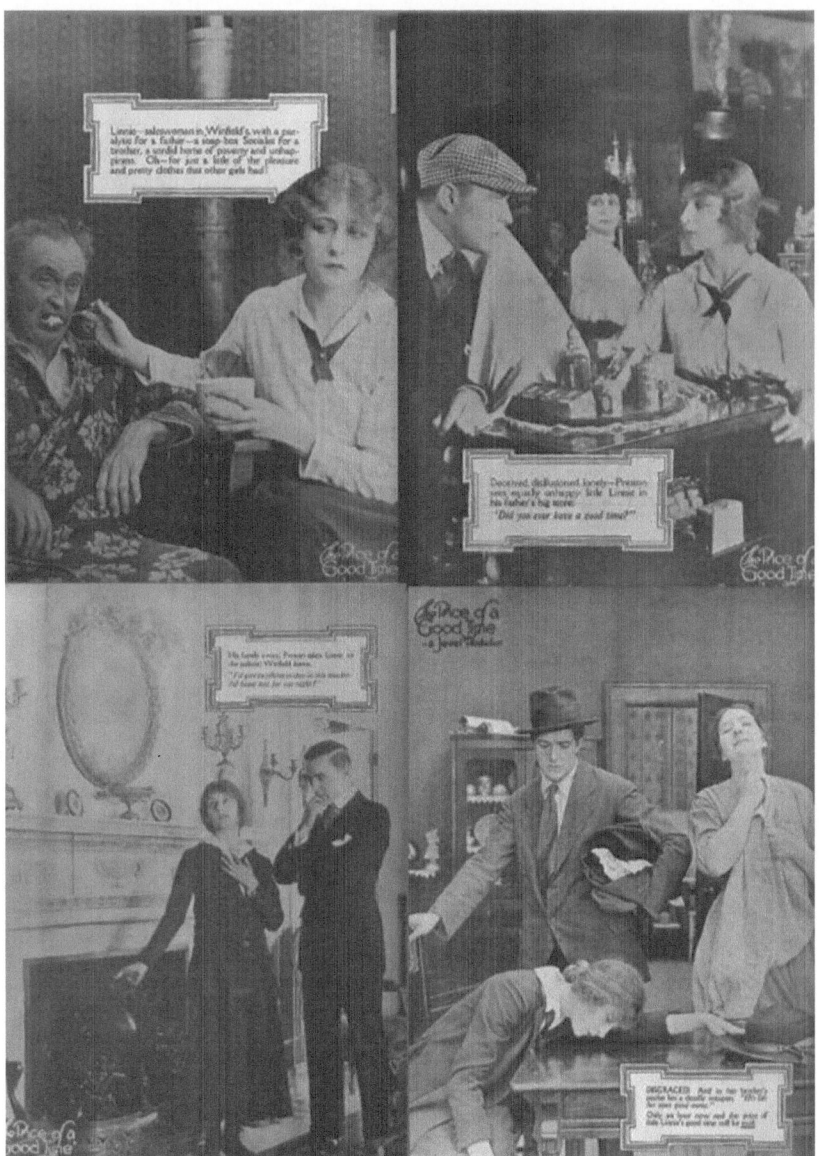

many women are forced to lead by the struggle for a livelihood." It was, however, the "weakness of character alone [that] wrecks the happiness" of the heroine.[29]

Other films of this type provided happier endings for their wayward heroines. The young working girl in *The Libertine* (Triumph, 1916) decides to commit suicide after her decision to break off her engagement with a man of her class and become the mistress of a wealthy man leads to her despondency. In this case, however, the story turns out to be a cautionary dream and the heroine quickly decides to marry her working-class true love.[30] In *A Soul Enslaved* (Universal, 1916), a man's recognition of his own double standard provides a happy ending for the factory girl who takes the 'easiest way' by becoming the mistress of a factory owner followed by another wealthy man. In an attempt to change her life, the heroine marries a man who is unaware of her past, but when the husband discovers that she had previously been a kept woman, he leaves her. The husband returns to the heroine after he recalls that in his college days he had seduced and abandoned a young woman who subsequently committed suicide. He realizes his hypocrisy in judging his wife by a higher standard than the one by which he had lived.[31]

A Soul Enslaved was directed by Cleo Madison who had also directed another cross-class romance, *Her Bitter Cup*. Madison was one of a number of female directors employed by Universal, which for a few years, from 1915 to 1919, led the studios in providing opportunities for women—most of whom had been script writers—to direct. Even in Universal, the films of female directors accounted for less than 10 % of its total output, but these years stand out in comparison with the almost total absence of female directors in the years that followed.[32] Two prominent female directors directed a number of cross-class romances: Ida May Park made *Fires of Rebellion* in 1917 and *The Model's Confession, Bread, Broadway Love* and *The Risky Road* in 1918; Lois Weber made *The Price of Good Time* in 1917, *Borrowed Clothes* in 1918, *Home* and *Forbidden* in 1919, and unlike most other female directors was to continue directing in the 1920s, directing *The Blot*, which included a cross-class romance, in 1921. The themes to be found in these films, which included the link between sexual exploitation and poverty and the disillusion that a working girl was likely to experience if she entered high society,[33] were not confined to cross-class romances directed by women, but the fact that the female directors wrote as well as directed their films prompts the question of the frequency of female script writers of the cross-class romances directed by men.

The relatively large proportion of female script writers during the silent period has led some writers to exaggerate their numbers. Anthony Slide reports that of the 5,189 films listed in the 1911–1920 volume of the American Film Institute Catalog, 1077, a little over 20 %, included credits for females involved in some aspect of the writing, which included original story, adaptation and inter-titles; 707 of the titles, or 13.6 %, were credited solely to female writers.[34] Of the 109 cross-class romances made in the period 1915–1919 for which I have the names of script writers, 35 of the films had female script writers but only 17 of the films were written solely by female script writers. Of the total number of script writers for these films, there were 47 credits for females and 125 credits for males. As the studio heads were reported to believe that romantic films were best written by women,[35] what is significant is not the somewhat larger proportion of women involved in writing cross-class romances compared with other films but the fact that males made up the majority of writers even in this romantic genre.

'TREATING' AND PLAYING THE 'SEX GAME' IN SOCIETY

Together with their depictions of fantasies of marriages with wealthy men, many cross-class romance films showed with some accuracy that, apart from direct harassment and sexual violence, working girls were under considerable economic constraints to exchange sexual favors for material compensations. The wages earned by working females were often inadequate for even their most basic needs and were certainly inadequate if they wanted to participate in the developing consumer culture and the commercialized entertainment that had undergone rapid expansion in the late nineteenth century and early twentieth century. The 60 % of working women who lived at home gave most of their earnings to their parents, and the increasing number of women who lived away from home had little or no money to spare after they had paid for their rent, food and other basic necessities. The 1911 Consumers' League investigation reported that department store saleswomen in particular were subject "to a temptation readily conceivable," especially in the "presence of some of the customers and their wealth and their freedom in buying—all the worldliness of the most moneyed city of the USA here perpetually passes before the eyes of Zettas in their $1.20 muslin waists so carefully scrubbed the midnight before, and of Alices who have had breakfasts for 10 cents.

Is it surprising that they should adopt the New York shop-window-display ideal of life manifested everywhere around them?"[36]

Working girls and women relied on men for luxury items, entertainment and sometimes necessities in an exchange of 'treating', which emerged as an explicitly named term in the 1890s. Treating involved both the economic 'treat' that women received from men and the sexual 'treat' that men received in return from women. Men paid for the entertainments and provided gifts and the girls reciprocated with sexual intimacy such as kissing, petting and, at times, intercourse. Those women who participated most fully in this form of exchange came to be known as 'charity girls', and like other women who treated on a less regular basis they made a clear distinction between accepting treats and accepting money, which was considered as prostitution. Women who participated in treating, including the charity girls, exercised more choice than prostitutes with respect to the men they favored and how far they were prepared to go with them. Treating occupied a kind of moral middle ground between, on the one hand, courting couples who had intercourse when their declared intention was marriage and, on the other hand, prostitution.[37]

Investigators emphasized the vulnerability of women, especially those who did not live at home and were unprotected by their families, but women were often able to exert considerable control in the sexual bartering, sometimes withholding sex from men who were insufficiently generous or attractive. A major site for working girls' negotiation of sexual favors was the dance hall. Most women would come to dance halls in twos and threes, unescorted by men, and would begin by dancing together. Men would walk up to a girl and ask for a dance without knowing her and, because men nearly always outnumbered girls at dance halls, the girls could afford to be choosy and to try to pick out the men with the most money. Some of the girls who entered an exchange of treating with their dance partners sought to outwit them and used various strategies, such as feigning illness, to receive benefits from the men without having to 'come across'. In taxi dance halls, which began in 1913, the men who purchased tickets to give to the taxi dancers for a dance would often seek favors from the taxi dancers beyond the dances. The taxi dancers gained considerable experience in these negotiations and invented various ways by which they could enjoy meals in restaurants and accept gifts without having to provide the sexual favors expected by the men.[38]

Frances Donovan, a participant observer, who worked for nine months as a waitress in various restaurants in Chicago in 1917–1918 found that some waitresses were particularly adept in what Donovan called the "sex game." One waitress told her that she always kept "two or three fellows on the string and I get all I can out of them. I never 'come across' unless I have to." Another girl told her that although she had gone out with men from the toughest places in the Loop she was still virtuous when she married. Donovan asked her how she managed it. She replied that she "always make them think that you intend to go the limit and then when it comes to the show down, give 'em the merry ha! ha! The damn fools still stand for it over and over again. Men are easy to string."[39]

One female occupation in which working girls were reputed to gain considerable economic benefits from the 'sex game' was the chorus line. Cabaret chorus girl revues made their appearance on a regular basis in 1915 and became an important staple of the entertainment provided by cafes and nightclubs.[40] Chorus girls or 'soubrettes' had in the last decades of the nineteenth century become associated with burlesque, a disreputable form of entertainment for working-class men. However, in the new type of revue represented by the Ziegfeld Follies, the chorus girl was made 'respectable' by combining sexual spectacle and bourgeois consumer culture. In place of the markers of working-class culture that prevailed in burlesque, chorus girls were presented as combining sensuality with the niceness of the middle-class girl next door. The elegance of their costumes, despite their often revealing nature, was a sign of their social status.[41] The choruses were open to a fairly restricted number of working girls, and the belief that chorus girls could advance themselves materially and even achieve marriage with wealthy men was reinforced by fictional portrayals on stage and film. Most chorus girls did not fulfill these dreams; the average career in the chorus lasted no longer than five years, when the girls were between the ages of 17 and 21, and while it lasted the work was hard with few opportunities for advancement beyond the chorus.[42]

By occasional prostitution, many unmarried working women sought to buy suitable clothes in which they might attract promising husbands. A 19-year-old Polish factory worker admitted to an investigator that she had had sexual relations with men at work for money or articles of clothing but that her ultimate goal was a respectable marriage that would bring economic and social rewards. A laundry worker told an investigator that she engaged in occasional prostitution because men do not look for wives in laundries.[43] One waitress explained to Donovan that the "Stock Exchange Restaurant is the place to work. There is where you meet the rich men. A girl I know married a fellow she met when she was working there and now she has a grand flat on the North Side where she entertains her waitress friends at afternoon tea." Donovan wrote that the "economic inefficiency" of the men in the waitresses' world meant that it was most unlikely that a waitress would marry a wealthy man and that their alternative was to engage in semi-prostitution.[44] Rosen writes that full-time prostitutes understood the limited options that a young woman faced in her desire to improve her status, and that they believed that by using the money they earned on their physical appearance they could improve their chances of finding a suitable husband.[45] Thus, whether they practiced treating or full-time prostitution, working women viewed their sexual behavior not just as a means to meet their immediate economic needs but also as a means of upward mobility.

The participation of large numbers of working girls in treating influenced the views and actions of middle-class female reformers who focused their attention on the sexual behavior of young girls from the working class. Reformers of the late nineteenth century viewed young working women who had 'gone astray' as innocent victims of predatory men, and they sought to help the young girls by persuading lawmakers to raise the age of consent in rape laws and to enact legislation designed to punish male seducers. The female reformers had little influence on the enforcement of the law and their views of young women as victims found little sympathy among police officers, judges and legal officials who were more inclined to view sexually active young women as delinquents who should be disciplined and punished. A new discourse that viewed young working class women as sexual opportunists emerged among female reformers in the early twentieth century, and although many continued to use the language of victimization, they established juvenile courts, detention centers and reformatories to monitor and regulate the sexuality of young women and girls. The intention of female reformers may have been to shield young girls from sexual exploitation but their actions often led to repressive measures, and the double standard of morality that punished young women more often and more severely than young men persisted.[46]

THE CROSS-CLASS ROMANCE AND CLASS CONFLICT

In some cross-class romances, through her relationship with a wealthy man, the working-class heroine seeks to improve the conditions of the working-class community of which she is a part. In *A Daughter of the People* (Dyreda, 1915), Dell, the heroine, is the daughter of a dyer who is thrown out of work, together with Dell's lover, when Stillman, the cotton manufacturer, closes his mills as part of his aim to corner the cotton market. When Dell pleads with Stillman to open his mills he agrees to do so on the condition that she marry him. Stillman arranges a mock marriage but he comes to love Dell. When the workers, including her father and former lover, turn their backs on her, Dell realizes that Stillman is her real love and returns to him.[47] Another heroine whose major concern is the welfare of her fellow workers is Mary, one of three sisters employed in a sweatshop in *The Eternal Grind* (Famous Players, 1916). Mary, played by Mary Pickford, is loved by one of the owner's sons who is mortally injured when the rotten floor of the sweatshop collapses. The doctor tells the owner that only the presence of Mary will save his son and Mary only responds to the father's pleas to come to his son's bedside after he agrees to her condition to build a new factory and pay his workers fair wages[48] (Fig. 4.2). In other films, discussed below, the cross-class romance was placed more explicitly and integrally into narratives of class conflict.

Fig. 4.2 Still from a lost film, *The Eternal Grind* (Famous Players, 1916), provides a realistic image of sweatshop conditions. Image courtesy of Marc Wanamaker/Bison Archives

Among the many cross-class romances, mostly feature length, made from 1915 to 1918, I found no less than 19 films in which conflict between employers and workers was a major element in the plots. These were, however, only a small proportion of the total number of films during this period that dealt with conflict between capital and labor. Steven Ross found 274 labor–capital films made between 1905 and 1917.[49] Another classification provided by Michael Shull found that between 1909 and 1917, at least 250 films (shorts and features) dealt with socio-political themes; more than 150 films portrayed workers taking some form of direct action against capitalist employers, and at least 107 films highlighted labor turmoil resulting from work stoppages.[50] These categorizations do not distinguish between one- or two-reel films and features but there can be no doubt that a large proportion of the labor–capital films released before 1915 were of short length. The few short length labor–capital films that were cross-class romances represented a small proportion of these films. As noted, the number of cross-class romance films increased together with the rise in the number of feature-length films, and among these romance films, a significant number dealt with the labor–capital conflict. This proved to be an exceptional period because conflict between capital and labor almost disappeared from cross-class romance films after 1918. This trend paralleled, in part, the general downward trend in labor–capital films. Ross found 171 labor–capital films released between April 1917 and December 1922, and 48 released between 1923 and 1929.[51] Almost none of the labor–capital films of the 1920s were cross-class romances.

Of the labor–capital films made between 1905 and 1917, Ross found that most were either liberal (46 %), condemning irresponsible capitalists and calling for cooperation between capital and labor, or conservative (34 %), presenting the workers' activism in a negative light. Only 4 % were radical, criticizing capitalism as a system and promoting socialist or other radical solutions.[52] Of the films investigated by Shull that could be categorized in terms of their predominant discernible biases he found that 54 were anti-capital, 39 anti-labor, 49 urged some form of labor–capital cooperation, and nine films had a discernible pro-socialist bias.[53] From 1917, there was a decline in the range of economic and political ideologies represented in films. Ross writes that of the 171 labor–capital movies released between April 1917 and December 1922, 64 % were conservative, only 24 % were liberal, and not a single radical film was produced.[54] With the possible exception of *What Is to Be Done?* (1914), none of the cross-class romance films took a radical stance toward the labor–capital conflict. Most were liberal and a few were conservative. Where romance was included in radical labor–capital films, it was not cross-class romance and it was not offered as a solution to class conflict. One example is *From Dusk to Dawn* (Occidental, 1913), a five-reel film in which a working class romance between an iron molder and a laundress is mixed with a story of the success of workers' industrial and political action.[55]

CLASS CONFLICT IN AMERICA

The cross-class romance films that dealt with labor–capital conflict were responding, albeit from highly slanted ideological perspectives, to class conflict in American society. American society has commonly been portrayed as one in which classes are of relatively little importance, and when classes have been acknowledged in America, they have been described as having permeable boundaries and a weak consciousness. However, class conflict as measured by the participation of workers in strikes and the level of violence in industrial disputes was greater in the USA prior to 1923 than in most European countries. Strike activity reached one peak in 1904, dipped somewhat as employers intensified their offensive against labor, resurged after 1909 and reached a new height in 1919 when the greatest strike wave in American history saw the eventual participation of about one-fifth of American workers. The refusal of many employers to recognize unions and bargain with them, their use of strikebreakers and their readiness to use force to break strikes were the major factors that resulted in many fatalities. More than 90 % of the fatalities were workers; the vast majority of casualties were strikers and their sympathizers who were killed, in most cases, by agents of employers and by state authorities who supported the employers. American workers were more likely than European workers to take up arms against their enemies, including strikebreakers, but they were far less likely to inflict casualties than the forces arraigned against them. A general upward trend of strike-related violence lasted from 1895 through to 1914, abated during America's participation in World War I, reemerged for a short time after the War, and was uncommon during most of the 1920s.[56]

A number of strikes became famous during this period because of the number of workers involved and the brutality of the attempts to break them. Women and young girls made up a majority of strikers in the strikes of shirtwaist and cloak makers in New York in 1909 and 1910 and in the strike of over 20,000 textile workers in 1912 in the town of Lawrence,

Massachusetts. The attempts to break the strike in Lawrence included use of the local and state militia and police as well as mass arrests. Brutal police actions against women and children aroused national attention and after two months of struggle, the company capitulated, although the workers' gains were later lost. A particularly horrendous instance of violence against workers occurred in 1914 in the coal mining regions of Ludlow, Colorado. The state militia, called out at the bequest of the Colorado Fuel and Iron Company, a Rockefeller subsidiary, opened fire without provocation upon striking miners and killed five men and a boy. They next burned the strikers' families out of their makeshift homes, killing 11 children and two women who perished in the flames.

It has been argued that the absence of a feudal past in the USA meant that class boundaries were more permeable than in European countries where hierarchies of ascribed social statuses continued to be operative in the industrial, modern period. It can also be argued, however, that class conflict between capitalists and workers was fiercer and more violent in the USA because, without the constraints imposed on the bourgeoisie in European countries by still powerful aristocracies and strong states, American capitalists were able to act more ruthlessly against the attempts by workers to organize unions and improve their wages and conditions. Uninhibited by the need for alliances with aristocrats or by the restrictions of government, American capitalists espoused their belief in the virtues of free enterprise unimpeded by organizations of workers and they reacted with particular vehemence when unions sought to interfere in the management of their companies.[57]

Cross-Class Romance as a Solution to Class Conflict

Class conflict was dramatically portrayed in cross-class romance films made between 1915 and 1918, and it was solved or neutralized by the cross-class romance. The portrayal of the deplorable conditions in which workers worked and lived would appear to justify their strikes and other actions against their employers, but cross-class romance proved a solution to the conflict because the problem was presented as one that lay with particular capitalists rather than with capitalism as a system. Once the bad capitalist was reformed through love, or was replaced by a good son or daughter who was in a cross-class romance, a just peace was attained in the relationships of employers and workers.

The employers who were blamed for industrial unrest in the cross-class romance films varied in their culpability; some were greedy or uncompromising while others were unaware of the conditions of their workers or were unaware that their managers were oppressing the workers. If the capitalist epitomized greed or was unredeemable, his punishment was death. This was the case of John D. Maximillian, commonly known as "Croesus," the enormously wealthy and powerful capitalist in *Money* (United Keanograph, 1915), a film whose plot is set in 1921. Croesus, assisted by his despicable junior partner, Livingstone, heads an industrial empire and has gained control of financial markets, the wheat market and public utilities. His refusal to pay his workers a living wage provokes a strike in his steel factories and Croesus shows his contempt for the workers by giving an extravagant banquet in his mansion. The cross-class romantic element is provided by Croesus' daughter, Ruth, who falls in love with George Crosby, a foreman whose dismissal she prevents after he defends Hope, a stenographer, from the sexual advances of Livingstone. Ruth has only recently learned of her father's nefarious activities and when she leaves his banquet in disgust she is followed by an intoxicated Livingstone who assaults her just as the strikers break into the mansion. George rescues Ruth and succeeds in persuading the workers to leave the mansion. After a number of further melodramatic turns in the plot, George overcomes Livingstone in a fight on a sinking vessel and Livingstone drowns. A lighting storm destroys Croesus' mansion and he is killed by a falling column. As his heir, Ruth introduces justice for the workers and she steps aside as Hope marries George, whom Ruth has made manager of the steel works.[58]

Death is the penalty imposed on Alford, the wealthy mill owner in *The Quality of Faith* (Mutual, 1916) who spurns a delegation of his workers when they petition him to rescind his proposed increase in their working hours. In this film, the cross-class romance between Louise, Alford's daughter, and Albert Richards, a minister who encourages the workers to strike, does not work out, in part because Louise is a pleasure-loving girl who breaks off their engagement in favor of a worthless society man but also because Albert falls in love with another woman. The other woman is Marta, an ex-factory worker whose ill-health has driven her to prostitution.[59] Yet another evil capitalist who dies for his sins is portrayed in *Cheating the Public* (Fox, 1918). John Dowling, factory owner and boss of Millvale, cuts the pay of his workers, who are shown living in miserable homes, and raises the food prices in his company's store. The workers strike and Dowling is backed up by the law when he shoots one of them as a "trespasser." The heroine, Mary Garvin, goes to Dowling to plead the workers' cause, and when he attacks her she shoots him. Mary is tried and condemned to death for killing Dowling, but just before the execution a foreman boasts that his bullet killed Dowling. With this information, Chester, Dowling's son, races to the governor's train to secure a pardon for Mary, and this is followed by their marriage and Chester's reforms for the workers. *Moving Picture World* advised exhibitors to advertise the film by making transparencies like those carried in political parades, with messages such as "don't cut our pay and raise food prices too."[60]

An exception to the formula that really bad capitalists are severely punished is the mine owner, Craighill, in *The Lords of High Decision* (Universal, 1916). Craighill not only underpays and overworks his workers, he also embezzles bank funds and attempts to ruin a small mine operator whose daughter, Jean, is loved by Wayne, Craighill's son. Jean tells Wayne that the gulf between them cannot be bridged and she marries a worker. Wayne sympathizes with the workers and, for a time, he is able to pacify them when they threaten a strike and come to kill his father. When there is no money to pay the workers, they proceed to blow up the mines. Oil spouts from one of the explosions and the value of the wrecked mines is greatly increased by the geysers of oil and natural gas. This provides a solution for both mine owner and workers, and as Jean's husband dies in the wreckage, Jean and Wayne can unite.[61] *The Golden Goal* (Vitagraph, 1918) is another film in which both cross-class romance and labor–capital conflict are tied up with an attempt by a bad capitalist to ruin a competitor. Richard Walton, a wealthy shipbuilder uses his daughter, Beatrice, to lure John Doran, a longshoreman and labor leader who is in love with her, to organize a strike of his competitor's workers. Doran agrees and calls a strike but, after he realizes his wrongdoing, he calls his men back to work, and he decides that Laura, a poor stenographer, is far better than the wealthy Beatrice.[62]

Many capitalists in cross-class romance films are not as bad as those in the aforementioned films, and they undergo a change of heart as a consequence of their cross-class romances or those of their sons or daughters. The reform of Andrew Hamilton, the owner of steel mills in *Love's Law* (Mutual, 1915), is accomplished by Sonia Sarinoff, an American-born Polish orphan who lives with her guardian, a mill worker who responds to a cut in wages by selling Sonia's precious violin. Hamilton buys the violin, recognizes Sonia's musical talents, and offers to finance a musical education in exchange for her sexual favors. Her response is to smash the violin and to return to the poverty of the mill village where she not only nurses workers through an epidemic brought about by the unsanitary conditions in Hamilton's mills, she also prevents a strike that would have ruined Hamilton. When Hamilton finds Sonia has succumbed to the illness, he realizes his injustices to her and to his workers, nurses her back to health and promises to improve the conditions of the workers as one of his wedding presents to her. *Moving Picture World* advised exhibitors to advertise the films as a drama that "makes clear the fight between oppressed and oppressors," as a "gripping love story woven into the prevailing problem of labor," and as a film that shows how "a good girl changes labor conditions in an oppressed community."[63]

The reform of the capitalist Van Nest in *The Bigger Man* (B.A. Rolfe, 1915) follows upon the romance of his daughter Janet with his construction chief, John Stoddard. Van Nest refuses to improve the wages and conditions of his workers and sends in the militia to crush their strike. He comes to an agreement with John to settle the strike on the condition that John refrains from seeing Janet, but after Janet leaves home to help poor families and Van Nest discovers the consequences of her good deeds, he softens and agrees to her marriage with John. The film begins with a prologue showing the relationship between capital and labor throughout history and it ends with an epilogue showing blindfolded Justice saying to fat Capital and burly Labor, "Why quarrel? You are worthless without the other."[64] The reviewer for *Variety* wrote that the film was aimed at workers but that it would be some time before the film reached them in their "nickel houses." As the "better houses" would probably be only interested in the romance, he suggested that film-makers "might as well lay off the labor matter, or give it a very long rest."[65]

In some films, a capitalist father would remove his opposition to his child's relationship with a poor or working class person after that person rescues him from workers who threaten his life, as in *The Spender* (Pathe Exchange, 1915)[66] and *The Right Direction* (Pallas, 1916).[67] The rescue of a capitalist from workers to enable a cross-class marriage is made possible by a worker who sacrifices himself in *The Song of the Wage Slave* (Popular Plays and Players, 1915). Dawson, a rich pulp-mill owner, forbids his son, Frank, to marry Mildred, a foreman's daughter who carries Frank's child. Ned, a mill worker "wage slave" offers to marry Mildred and, for the sake of her child, she agrees. The elder Dawson dies and Mildred believes that she is free to marry Frank after Ned is shot in a barroom brawl and believed dead. In fact, Ned recovers, changes his name and becomes a labor leader.

Discontented workers plant a bomb in Frank's house and it explodes in Ned's hands when he recovers the bomb from the house. Ned's sacrificial death not only removes the obstacle to the cross-class marriage between Mildred and Frank, it also advances the interests of the workers as Frank agrees to Ned's dying request to improve their conditions.[68]

Some capitalists are reformed when they experience love while disguised as workers in their own factories, as in *Fires of Youth* (Thanhouser, 1917)[69] and *A Little Sister of Everybody* (Anderson-Brunton, 1918).[70] In *Those Who Toil* (Lubin, 1916), it is John Jameson, the son of the millionaire owner of an oil field, who poses as a worker in order to investigate conditions. John falls in love with Jane, who had previously tried to kill his father after her father was seriously injured at work and had his pay stopped. Jane is a leader of a group of strikers who intend to set fire to the wells, but after John confesses his identity she pleads with the workers to hold off from violence. The workers accuse her of treachery and, led by a worker who is secretly in love with Jane and jealous of John, they set fire to the wells and battle the police. Jane risks her life to save John, who eventually persuades the workers that he will act on their behalf and gain concessions from his father. Once again, a film ends with the promise of reforms for the workers and with a cross-class couple who are united. The exteriors of the film were shot in oil fields in Pennsylvania and contemporary reviewers commented favorably on the large scale of the settings and the mob scenes in which strikers burn the oil works. The reviewer for *Motion Picture World* wrote that the story of a lowly born girl who is the central figure in the struggle between capital and labor was a favorite theme with stage and screen fiction and that "the physical combat which takes place when the rebellious workmen attempt to enforce their demands by an attack upon the property and life of their oppressor, never fails to furnish a 'big scene' of sufficient violent action and dramatic power."[71]

Another cross-class romance film that was praised by contemporary reviewers for its realistic portrayal of the conflict between capital and labor was *The Blacklist* (Jessie L. Lasky, 1916). The title of the film referred to the practice of companies to list the names of workers who refused to submit to company rules or who protested against the conditions of work. Once on the blacklist, these workers could not hope to secure employment. The scenes of violence were based on the massacre of miners and their families in Ludlow, Colorado, in 1914. Marion Fairfax, who wrote the script together with the director William C. de Mille, was able to draw on her personal observation and knowledge because she had gone to Colorado during the strike in order to write a series of articles.[72] The film depicts a miners' strike following the refusal of the president of the mining company, Warren Harcourt, to meet the miners' demands. The superintendent of the mines orders the striking miners to be evicted from the company's property and the strikers take refuge in the hills. After one of the mine guards is killed, strike-breakers surround the camp of evicted miners and attack it with rifles and a machine gun, in violation of Harcourt's orders. Men, women and children are shot down. The residents of the camp hold Harcourt responsible and they draw lots in order to select one of them to shoot him. Vera Marff, the schoolmistress of the workers' children draws the fatal lot and, even though she and Harcourt have fallen in love with each other, she goes to his office to kill him. She informs him that there are two bullets in her gun—one for him and the other for herself—but she only wounds him and, in the ensuing struggle, the other shot causes no damage. Harcourt recovers from the wound, grants the miner's demands and announces that he will run the mine in cooperation with Vera, his wife.[73] Needless to say, although the massacre in the film was based upon the massacre at Ludlow, the outcome in the film of industrial reform and peace brought about by cross-class romance had no relationship to the outcome at Ludlow.

The reviewer of the trade paper *Motography* wrote that the film dealt with the struggle between capital and labor "in a manner that is both intelligent and convincing. Perhaps we have never seen capital and labor fight their battles on the screen so realistically."[74] *Motion Picture News* reported that socialist and labor publications had given prominence to the film and that some labor leaders had given the film their unqualified endorsement.[75] It was also reported that the film had broken a house record at the Strand Theater in New York.[76] The *Motography* reviewer wrote that "the conditions which cause the workers to grumble about slavery and oppression are depicted convincingly," but the reviewer also observed that the story "really subordinates the labor strife to the romance of the capitalist and the daughter of one of the workers."[77] In general, the films of this period that wove together cross-class romance and conflict between capital and labor are characterized by a number of realistic portrayals of the conditions of workers and the violent conflicts of capital and labor, together with sensationalist melodramatic plots and utterly unrealistic solutions through cross-class romance.

The dilemma of the heroines in *Those Who Toil* and *The Blacklist*, in terms of their support for the workers' struggle and their love of the capitalist, is taken to an even more melodramatic height in *Her Bitter Cup* (Universal, 1915). Cleo Madison, the writer and director of the film, plays the heroine, Rethna, who works in a factory in which harsh treatment and unsatisfactory conditions prevail. When one of the female workers faints, Rethna and the foreman take the girl to the office of the factory owner, Henry Burke, and Rethna begs him to give the workers more sun and air. Burke refuses and discharges Rethna for her impertinence. Rethna takes revenge on Burke by manipulating his two sons who fall in love with her; the spendthrift Harry and the successful lawyer Walter, whom she marries and finally loves. She uses the money and jewels she receives from the sons in order to advance the workers' struggle with their father, but when Burke is attacked by his workers and his office catches fire just as he has a heart attack, Rethna helps Walter to save him. Some highly melodramatic scenes follow: an insanely jealous and doped Harry begins to crucify a passive Rethna by nailing her hands and feet to a door before realizing the horror of his action and retreating. The film ends with the father admitting that he had been wrong, and with Rethna and Walter recognizing their love for each other and deciding to bury the past. Based on a synopsis of this lost film, Mark Garrett Cooper argues that it "depicts improper sexual relations as the logical extension of poverty and labor exploitation,"[78] but like other films discussed here, the theme of class exploitation and conflict tend to be overwhelmed by the sensationalist melodrama.[79]

Films such as *The Blacklist* and *Her Bitter Cup* are designated by Ross as liberal with respect to the labor–capital conflict. Although the genuine economic and physical sufferings of workers are portrayed as just cause for their protests, they are unable by themselves to channel their frustrations in an effective, non-violent manner.[80] It is a change in heart of the capitalist, often prompted by a cross-class romance, rather than the collective action of workers that provides the solution to the conflict.[81] Cross-class romance films did not include radical interpretations of the labor–capital conflict and liberal versions of labor–capital conflict in cross-class romance films disappeared from the screen after 1918. I did not find labor–capital conflict in any of the cross-class romance films made in 1919 and the only one I found in 1920, *The Face at Your Window* (Fox), took a conservative stance toward the labor–capital issue.[82] According to *Exhibitors Herald*, the title of the film referred to "the spirit of unrest threatening industrial security and domestic harmony in America." The trade journal recognized the film as "anti-Bolshevik propaganda" and recommended it because a film "which in any way seeks to soothe the existing spirit of industrial unrest is worth the world's attention."[83] It is worthy of note that even this conservative film, in which labor unrest is overcome by a call to patriotism supported by a cross-class romance, has its bad capitalist. This was the last cross-class romance film in which conflict between capital and labor played a prominent part. The cross-class romance films of the 1920s dealt with issues of consumerism rather than issues of production.

FROM CONFLICT TO ROMANCE

Ross associates the sharp drop in the number of films portraying conflict between labor and capital after World War I to the increase in films that provided "cross-class fantasies of luxury, comfort, and consumption." Not only were films shown in movie palaces that brought the classes together under one roof, they presented "conservative visions ... that emphasized love and harmony among the classes." Whereas many films prior to the war had recognized conflict between the classes, the post-war films removed class identity from "the conflictual world of production" and placed it in "the more alluring world of consumption" where "problems, both personal and society, could be solved by love." It was love rather than class that was real and "true love was strong enough to break down all class barriers."[84] Ross possibly understates the importance of cross-class romances in the labor–capital films of the transitional period; they were no less fantasies than the cross-class romances, albeit located in different contexts, of the 1920s. There is no doubt, however, that labor–capital conflict disappeared from cross-class romance films after 1918. Why did this happen?

One reason was that the 1920s was a relatively peaceful period of industrial relations. The strike wave in 1919 was the largest in American history with the eventual participation of more than 4 million workers, but the breaking of the harshly fought strike of steel workers, which involved 22 deaths and hundreds of injuries, was a benchmark in ending the workers' wartime gains and the upsurge in unionization. Union membership fell from its peak of 5 million in 1920 to 3.5 million in 1924 and stayed at about that level for the rest of the decade. Strike activity dropped considerably from 1923 and by the end of the decade had reached an all-time low.[85] The conservative trend in the USA was reflected in the decline of the Socialist Party of America (SPA). First organized as the Social Democratic Party in 1898, the votes for its presidential candidates increased from less than 100,000 in 1900 to almost 900,000, or about 6 %, of the popular vote in 1912. By 1912, the Party had made significant gains in local elections; some 1,200 of its candidates had been elected as local officials, 33 had been elected as state legislators, and the Party controlled municipal governments in a number of cities. In that same year, the Party's delegates made up nearly one third of the national convention of the American Federation of Labor (AFL), and its candidate for the presidency of the AFL secured one third of the votes against the incumbent. Unlike the European Socialist parties, however, the SPA declined rather than grew after World War I. The Party's membership reached a peak in 1919 with over 100,000 members, dropped to 13,000 in 1921, and was less than 8,000 in 1926, by which time it had become an organization of intellectuals rather than a party of industrial workers. The Party's opposition to America's intervention in World War I was met by intense political repression, which, together with internal schisms, effectively destroyed its organization.[86]

Two events in 1917 contributed to the conservative trend in the USA: the entrance of America into World War I and the Russian Revolution. Soon after declaring America at war, President Wilson established the CPI (Committee on Public Information) to "sell the war to the American public," and the CPI became the major agency for putting pressure on American filmmakers to promote harmonious representations of class relations. The granting of licenses for film exports by the CPI was an important power resource because the sale of American films abroad had vastly increased as the film industries and film exports of the European nations had been dealt a blow by the war. Distribution within the USA was also subject to political pressures as local and state censors banned films they deemed unpatriotic. The film companies, concerned above all with securing the widest distribution of their films, acceded to these pressures and refrained from representing American society in a negative light, including the portrayal of class conflict.

Political pressures did not end with the war. The Russian Revolution, together with increased unionization, strikes and labor militancy, gave rise to a 'Red Scare' from 1918 through to 1920 when there were mass arrests and deportations of communists, socialists and members of the IWW (Industrial Workers of the World). Whereas, prior to 1917, some films had portrayed foreign radicals sympathetically as striving for the kind of freedom purportedly prevalent in America, after the Russian Revolution, all revolutionaries were portrayed negatively. The representation of American radicals also changed from the varied and sometimes ambivalent portrayals in the pre-war films to unvaried portrayals of radicals as enemy agents, crazed bomb-throwing anarchists and, in their female form, as vampiric creatures who converted their male victims into communist zombies. Class conflict was no longer portrayed as having a justifiable basis; destructive agitators were the true cause of social discord.[87] Sympathetic protagonists in cross-class romances who supported and sometimes led the workers' struggle disappeared from the screen.

Structural changes in the film industry account for its general responsiveness to the political pressures. The large number and variety of geographically scattered producers, distributors and exhibitors of the pre-war era were being replaced by a few large companies that were extending their activities to include all three branches of the industry. As initial capital requirements grew, fewer new companies entered the business, and many of the older companies found that they were unable to cover the production costs of a film that rose from a few hundred dollars for mostly one-reelers in 1908 to between 10 and 20 thousand dollars for the increasing number of feature films in 1914–1915. Far more elaborate production procedures involved specialized personnel and a complex division of labor. Salaries increased—especially the salaries of the major actors and actresses—as the star system developed. The expansion of distribution on a national basis involved greater costs of more prints, exchanges and advertising. The emerging larger companies brought out the small companies and moved toward vertical integration of the three branches.[88]

The new type of film industry was to be denoted by the term 'Hollywood'. As a geographical entity, Hollywood was the name of a rural suburb of Los Angeles, annexed to the city in 1910. The first Hollywood studio was established in 1911; by May 1911, ten motion picture companies had set up operations within the Los Angeles area, including Hollywood. Prior to World War I, Southern California was a comparatively minor production site among many, and in 1914, the name Hollywood still meant nothing to most Americans. Southern California attracted film companies because of its good all-year-round weather, its varied landscapes, low-cost real estate and cheap labor. In 1915, the Los Angeles studios employed over 15,000 people and were producing between two-thirds and three-quarters of all American films, but only after World War I did 'Hollywood' come to be used as a generic term for American movies.[89]

Changes in production were accompanied by changes in exhibition. Efforts to shed the low class image of the nickelodeon began in New York as early as 1908 with the construction of the Unique on 14th Street, seating about 1,200.[90] A social hierarchy of movie theaters was evident by

1914; many of the cheaper theaters continued to show programs of one- and two-reel films, and the more prestigious theaters screened feature films. The more prestigious film theaters with their comfortable seating, large halls, plush foyers, restrooms and uniformed ushers resembled legitimate playhouses rather than nickelodeons.[91] Movie-going among the urban middle classes had not been uncommon even during the nickelodeon period, but it was only in the post-World War I period that movie-going became a regular part of their lives.[92] The picture palaces drew in the middle classes without the industry losing its working class audience, many of whom continued to frequent their neighborhood film theaters.

Many of the new movie palaces were owned and operated by the major production companies, which also distributed their films. A significant step in the transition to concentration and vertical integration was taken in 1914 when agreements were signed between Paramount Pictures Corporation, a newly formed distribution company, and the production companies of Adolph Zukor, the Famous Players Film Company, and Jesse L. Lasky, Feature Play Company. The companies of Zukor and Lasky merged in 1916, and in 1917 they were joined by twelve other production companies. The company then merged with the Paramount distribution firm; in 1919, it started to buy cinemas, and by 1921, it had acquired 303 theaters. Other companies soon followed suit. As early as 1912, William Fox had extended his chain of theaters and a film exchange into production, and in 1915, he founded the vertically integrated company, Fox Film Foundation. In 1917, a group of exhibitors formed the First National Company. which added production to its exhibition and distribution arms.[93] These vertically integrated companies continued to make cross-class romance films, but large corporations catering to a heterogeneous class audience were not inclined to weave the romance with labor–capital conflict.

NOTES

1. Mary E. Odem, *Delinquent Daughters: Protecting and Policing Adolescent Female Sexuality in the United States, 1885–1920* (Chapel Hill: University of North Carolina Press, 1995), 62.
2. Lee Grieveson, *Policing Cinema: Movies and Censorship in Early-Twentieth-Century America* (Berkeley: University of California Press, 2004), 158–191, quote 183.
3. AFI online catalog; *Motion Picture News* (henceforth MPN), January 17 1914, 25; *Motion Picture World* (henceforth MPW), January 17 1914, 276.

4. MPW, December 1 1917, 1334.
5. MPW, August 11 1917, 953.
6. AFI online catalog.
7. MPW, May 26 1917, 1340.
8. AFI online catalog.
9. MPW, January 22 1916, 621.
10. Motography, January 15 1916, 135.
11. MPN, February 2 1918, 736.
12. MPN, February 9 1918, 887.
13. MPN, April 20 1918, 2421.
14. MPN, April 20 1918, 2354.
15. *Variety*, April 12 1918, 42.
16. MPW, October 16 1915, 499.
17. MPW, July 1 1916, 50; Motography, July 8 1916, 96.
18. MPN, May 19 1917, 3160; MPW, May 19 1917, 1140.
19. *Variety*, February 8 1918, 43; MPW, February 23 1918, 1136. Other examples of this type include *Help Wanted* (Hobart Bosworth, 1918), MPN, May 1, 1915, 55, and *Bread* (Universal, 1918), MPW, August 2 1918, 1160, discussed in, Mark Garrett Cooper, *Universal Women: Filmmaking and Institutional Change in Early Hollywood* (Urbana: University of Illinois Press, 2010), 160–163.
20. Jeannette Eaton and Berta M. Stevens, *Commercial Work and Training for Girls* (New York: The Macmillan Company, 1915), 245, 247.
21. Sue Ainsley Clark and Edith Wyatt, *Making Both Ends Meet: The Income and Outlay of New York Working Girls* (New York: Macmillan, 1911).
22. Chicago Vice Commission, *A Study of Existing Conditions with Recommendations* (Chicago: Gunthorp-Warren Printing Company, 1911), 207–209.
23. Ruth Rosen, *The Lost Sisterhood: Prostitution in America, 1900–1918* (Baltimore, MD: Johns Hopkins University Press, 1982), 154.
24. Stephen Robertson, "Seduction, Sexual Violence, and Marriage in New York City, 1886–1955," *Law and History Review* 24.2 (2006): 331–373.
25. MPW, November 2 1918, 622.
26. Shelley Stamp, "Lois Weber, Progressive Cinema, and the Fate of The Work-a-Day Girls in Shoes," *Camera Obscura* 19.2 (2004): 140–169; Shelley Stamp, *Lois Weber in Early Hollywood* (Oakland: University of California Press, 2015), 101–117; Constance Balides, "Making Ends Meet: 'Welfare Films' and the Politics of Consumption during the Progressive Era," in Jennifer M. Bean, Diane Negra, eds., *A Feminist Reader in Early Cinema* (Durham, NC: Duke University Press, 2002) 166–194; Cooper, *Universal Women*, 156, 158.

27. MPW, February 27 1915, 1340.
28. MPW, May 1 1915, 740, 806; Balides, "Making Ends Meet."
29. MPW, April 28 1917, 635.
30. MPW, November 18 1916, 1001–1002; Variety, November 10 1916, 25.
31. MPN, January 22 1916, 393; Cooper, Universal Women, 146.
32. Mark Garrett Cooper, "Studio History Revisited: The Case of the Universal Women," Quarterly Review of Film and Video 25 (2008): 17. On the rise and decline of female directors at Universal see, Cooper, Universal Women. On female directors at Universal and other studios during this period see, Keren Ward Mahar, Women Filmmakers in Early Hollywood (Baltimore: John Hopkins University Press, 2006).
33. Cooper, Universal Women, 146–163.
34. Anthony Slide, "Early Women Filmmakers: The Real Numbers," Film History 24.1 (2012): 114–115.
35. Donna R. Casella, "Feminism and the Female Author: The Not So Silent Career of the Woman Scenarist in Hollywood, 1896–1930," Quarterly Review of Film and Video 23.3 (2006): 223.
36. Clark and Wyatt, Making Both Ends Meet.
37. Elizabeth Alice Clement, Love For Sale: Courting, Treating, and Prostitution in New York City, 1900–1945 (Chapel Hill: University of North Carolina Press, 2006); Kathy Peiss, "Charity Girls and City Pleasures," OAH Magazine of History 18.4 (2004): 14–16.
38. Randy D. McBee, Dance Hall Days: Intimacy and Leisure Among Working-Class Immigrants in the United States (New York: New York University Press, 2000), 6, 86–95, 108–114. See also, Paul Goalby Cressey, The Taxi-Dance Hall: A Sociological Study in Commercialized Recreation and City Life (Chicago: University of Chicago Press, 2008 [1932]). This study was based on an investigation that Cressey made of taxi-dance halls in 1925.
39. Frances Donovan, The Woman Who Waits (Boston: Gorham Press, 1920), 213.
40. Lewis A. Erenberg, Steppin' Out: New York Nightlife and the Transformation of American Culture, 1890–1930 (Chicago: University of Chicago Press, 1981), 206.
41. Robert C. Allen, Horrible Prettiness: Burlesque and American Culture (Chapel Hill: University of North Carolina Press, 1991), 245–246; Erenberg, Steppin' Out, 214.
42. Erenberg, Steppin' Out, 222–224.
43. Rosen, The Lost Sisterhood, 158.
44. Donovan, The Woman Who Waits, 219–220.
45. Rosen, The Lost Sisterhood, 158–159.
46. Odem, Delinquent Daughters; Ruth M. Alexander, The Girl Problem: Female Sexual Delinquency in New York, 1900–1930 (Ithaca, NY: Cornell

University Press, 1995); Joanne J. Meyerowitz, *Women Adrift: Independent Wage Earners in Chicago, 1880–1930* (Chicago: University of Chicago Press, 1988).

47. *Motography*, February 20 1915, 307; MPW, February 20 1915, 1200.
48. MPW, April 22 1916, 642; *Motography*, April 22 1916, 941.
49. Steven J. Ross, *Working-Class Hollywood: Silent Film and the Shaping of Class in America* (Princeton: Princeton University Press, 1998), 57.
50. Michael Slade Shull, *Radicalism in American Silent Films, 1909–1929: A Filmography and History* (Jefferson, North Carolina: McFarland & Company, 2000), 7, 24.
51. Ross, *Working-Class Hollywood*, 116.
52. Ross, *Working-Class Hollywood*, 57.
53. Shull, *Radicalism in American Silent Films*, 24, 27, 43, 54. Shull's categories need some clarification. What he calls anti-capital films were more often anti-capitalists rather than anti-capitalism because the blame for the deprivations and plight of workers was placed on individual capitalists rather than on capitalism as a system. Although few films were explicitly pro-capital or anti-socialism, the assumption underlining most films was that capitalism rather than socialism was the appropriate social order.
54. Ross, *Working-Class Hollywood*, 116.
55. Ross, *Working-Class Hollywood*, 95–98; Shull, *Radicalism in American Silent Films*, 55–56.
56. Paul F. Lipold and Larry W. Isaac, "Striking Deaths: Lethal Contestation and the 'Exceptional' Character of the American Labor Movement, 1870–1970," *International Review of Social History* 54.2 (2009): 167–205.
57. Sanford M. Jacoby, *American Exceptionalism Revisited: The Importance of Management* (Los Angeles: Institute of Industrial Relations, UCLA, 1987), 11–13.
58. MPW, February 6, 1915, 833, 892; MPN, February 13, 1915, 267. *Money* is the only cross-class romance film discussed here that Ross designates as radical. Ross, *Working-Class Hollywood*, 70, 72. However, I find no evidence that this film offered an unmitigated critique of capitalism or espoused socialism. As in other films designated by Ross as liberal the problem is individual capitalists and the solution is their replacement by good capitalists.
59. MPW, May 6, 1916; MPN, March 25, 1916, 1176; *Motography*, May 13, 1916, 1112.
60. MPW, February 12, 1918, 684, 717.
61. MPN, February 19 1916, 1024; MPW, March 11 1916, 1701.
62. MPN, June 1, 1918, 3307; MPW, June 1, 1918, 1330.
63. MPW, September 7, 1918, 1465.

64. MPW, October 2, 1915, 89.
65. *Variety*, October 8, 1915, 23.
66. MPW, October 2, 1915, 92; *Motography*, October 9, 1915, 752.
67. MPW, December 30, 1916, 1449.
68. MPW, October 2, 1915, 78; *Motography*, October 9, 1915, 748.
69. A shortened version of this film can be seen on a DVD of *The Thanhouser Collection*, volume 6, and on YouTube.
70. AFI online catalog; MPW, June 29, 1918, 1891.
71. MPW, July 1, 1916, 103, 148, 150; MPN, July 1, 1916, 4084; *Motography*, July 1, 1916, 42; *Variety*, June 23, 1916, 21.
72. MPN, February 19, 1916, 989.
73. MPN, March 4, 1916, 1319; *Variety*, February 18, 1916, 21.
74. *Motography*, March 4, 1916, 532.
75. MPW, March 18, 1916, 1859.
76. *Motography*, March 25, 1916, 727.
77. *Motography*, March 4, 1916, 532.
78. Cooper, *Universal Women*, 148.
79. The scenario for *Her Bitter Cup* was filed with the Library of Congress and can be assessed in the profile of Cleo Madison in the Women's Film Pioneers Project (wfpp.cdrs.columbia.edu/pioneer/ccp-cleo-madison/). The synopses of the film in the trade press differ in some details from the scenario. MPN, April 6, 1916, 2062; MPW, April 29, 1916, 855–856. One of the reviews indicates that Harry's attempted crucifixion of Rethna was in his dream, but this is not the case in the scenario.
80. Ross, *Working-Class Hollywood*, 73–75.
81. Although Ross suggests that capital-labor films in which the "poor heroine marries the wealthy guy" are conservative (74), a number of films he mentions in which this occurs he designates as liberal.
82. According to Ross, in conservative capital-labor films strikes are led by agitators, often foreign-born, who stir up easily-persuaded workers into a frenzy of violent action. Ross, *Working-Class Hollywood*, 63–64.
83. *Exhibitors Herald*, December 11 1920, 80.
84. Ross, *Working-Class Hollywood*, 175, 195, 199, 335–36. Ross may have overestimated the number of cross-class romance films because he appears to include in "cross-class fantasy" all the films categorized by the American Film Institute catalog as "society" films, most of which dealt with the doings among the wealthy or 'leisured' class and did not deal or focus on the relationships, romantic or otherwise, between different classes.
85. Michael Mann, *The Sources of Social Power, Vol. 2: The Rise of Class and Nation-States, 1760–1914* (Cambridge: Cambridge University Press, 1993), 632–33, 644–4; Richard Franklin Bensel, *The Political Economy of American Industrialization, 1877–1900* (Cambridge: Cambridge University Press,

2000), 14; Robert Justin Goldstein, "Political Repression of the American Labor Movement During Its Formative Years—A Comparative Perspective," *Labor History* 51.2 (2010): 271–293; David Montgomery, *Workers' Control in America: Studies in the History of Work, Technology, and Labor Struggles* (Cambridge: Cambridge University Press, 1979), 6–7; David M. Gordon, Richard Edwards, Michael Reich, *Segmented Work, Divided Workers: The Historical Transformation of Labor in the United States* (Cambridge: Cambridge University Press, 1982), 122, 153, 156; Chip Rhodes, *Structures of the Jazz Age: Mass Culture, Progressive Education, and Racial Disclosures in American Modernism* (London: Verso, 1998), 99–100.

86. Mike Davis, *Prisoners of the American Dream: Politics and Economy in the History of the U.S. Working Class* (London: Verso, 1986), 47–48; Gordon, Edwards, Reich, *Segmented Work, Divided Workers,* 160–161; John Whiteclay Chambers II, *The Tyranny of Change: America in the Progressive Era 1900–1917* (NY: St. Martin's Press, 1980), 24, 66; Jurgen Kocka, *White Collar Workers in America 1890–1940: A Social-Political History in International Perspective* (London: Sage, 1980), 51–52; Aristide R. Zolberg, "How Many Exceptionalisms?" in Ira Katznelson and Aristide R. Zolberg, eds., *Working-Class Formation, Nineteenth-Century Patterns in Western Europe and the United States* (Princeton NJ: Princeton University Press, 1986), 427; Ellis W. Hawley, *The Great War and the Search for a Modern Order: A History of the American People and Their Institutions 1917–1933* (New York: St. Martin's Press, 1992), 108; Robert Justin Goldstein, *Political Repression in Modern America: From 1870 to 1976* (Urbana: University of Illinois Press, 1978), 552; Robin Archer, *Why Is There No Labor Party in the United States?* (Princeton, NJ: Princeton University Press, 2007), 238; Howard Kimeldorf and Judith Stepan-Norris, "Historical Studies of Labor Movements in the United States," *Annual Review of Sociology* 18 (1992): 505.

87. Shull, *Radicalism in American Silent Films, 1909–1929,* 71–109; Ross, *Working-Class Hollywood,* 125–127.

88. Janet Wasko, *Movies and Money: Financing the American Film Industry* (Norwood, NJ: Ablex Publishing Corporation, 1982), 9, 22; Lary May, *Screening Out the Past: The Birth of Mass Culture and the Motion Picture Industry* (New York: Oxford University Press, 1980), 168, 177.

89. Steven J. Ross, "How Hollywood Became Hollywood: Money, Politics, and Movies," in Tom Sitton and William Deverell, eds., *Metropolis in the Making, Los Angeles in the 1920s* (Berkeley: University of California Press, 2001), 255–276.

90. Kathy Peiss, *Cheap Amusements: Working Women and Leisure in Turn-of-the Century New York* (Philadelphia: Temple University Press, 1986), 160.

91. Russell Merritt, "Nickelodeon Theaters, 1905–1914: Building an Audience for the Movies," in Tino Balio, ed., *The American Film Industry* (Madison: University of Wisconsin Press, 1976), 97–101; David Nasaw, *Going Out: The Rise and Fall of Public Amusements* (Cambridge, MA: Harvard University Press, 1993), 202; Eileen Bowser, *The Transformation of Cinema 1907–1915* (New York: Charles Scribner's Sons, 1990), 125–6.
92. Ross, *Working-Class Hollywood*, xiii, 175.
93. Douglas Gomery, *Shared Pleasures: A History of Movie Presentation in the United States* (London: British Film Institute, 1992), 34–43; Wasko, *Movies and Money*, 18–22; Tino Balio, "Struggles For Control," in Balio, ed., *The American Film Industry*, 117–122.

BIBLIOGRAPHY

Alexander, Ruth M. *The Girl Problem: Female Sexual Delinquency in New York, 1900–1930*. Ithaca, NY: Cornell University Press, 1995.

Allen, Robert C. *Horrible Prettiness: Burlesque and American Culture*. Chapel Hill: University of North Carolina Press, 1991.

Archer, Robin. *Why Is There No Labor Party in the United States?* Princeton, NJ: Princeton University Press, 2007.

Balides, Constance. "Making Ends Meet: 'Welfare Films' and the Politics of Consumption during the Progressive Era," in Jennifer M. Bean, Diane Negra, eds. *A Feminist Reader in Early Cinema*. Durham, NC: Duke University Press, 2002, 166–194.

Balio, Tino. "Struggles For Control," in Tino Balio, ed. *The American Film Industry*. Madison: University of Wisconsin Press, 1976, 117–122.

Bensel, Richard Franklin. *The Political Economy of American Industrialization, 1877–1900*. Cambridge: Cambridge University Press, 2000.

Bowser, Eileen. *The Transformation of Cinema 1907–1915*. New York: Charles Scribner's Sons, 1990.

Casella, Donna R. "Feminism and the Female Author: The Not So Silent Career of the Woman Scenarist in Hollywood, 1896–1930," *Quarterly Review of Film and Video* 23.3 (2006): 217–235.

Chambers II, John Whiteclay. *The Tyranny of Change: America in the Progressive Era 1900–1917*. New York: St. Martin's Press, 1980.

Chicago Vice Commission. *A Study of Existing Conditions with Recommendations*. Chicago: Gunthorp-Warren Printing Company, 1911.

Clark, Sue Ainslie. and Edith Wyatt. *Making Both Ends Meet: The Income and Outlay of New York Working Girls*. New York: The Macmillan Company, 1911.

Clement, Elizabeth Alice. *Love For Sale: Courting, Treating, and Prostitution in New York City, 1900–1945*. Chapel Hill: University of North Carolina Press, 2006.

Cooper, Mark Garrett. "Studio History Revisited: The Case of the Universal Women," *Quarterly Review of Film and Video* 25.1 (2008): 16–26.

———. *Universal Women: Filmmaking and Institutional Change in Early Hollywood*. Urbana: University of Illinois Press, 2010.

Cressey, Paul Goalby. *The Taxi-Dance Hall: A Sociological Study in Commercialized Recreation and City Life*. Chicago: University of Chicago Press, 2008 [1932].

Davis, Mike. *Prisoners of the American Dream: Politics and Economy in the History of the U.S. Working Class*. London: Verso, 1986.

Donovan, Frances. *The Woman Who Waits*. Boston: Gorham Press, 1920.

Eaton, Jeannette. and Berta M. Stevens. *Commercial Work and Training for Girls*. New York: The Macmillan Company, 1915.

Erenberg, Lewis A. *Steppin' Out: New York Nightlife and the Transformation of American Culture, 1890–1930*. Chicago: University of Chicago Press, 1981.

Goldstein, Robert Justin. *Political Repression in Modern America: From 1870 to 1976*. Urbana: University of Illinois Press, 1978.

———. "Political Repression of the American Labor Movement During Its Formative Years—A Comparative Perspective," *Labor History* 51.2 (2010): 271–293.

Gomery, Douglas. *Shared Pleasures: A History of Movie Presentation in the United States*. London: British Film Institute, 1992.

Gordon, David M., Richard Edwards. and Michael Reich. *Segmented Work, Divided Workers: The Historical Transformation of Labor in the United States*. Cambridge: Cambridge University Press, 1982.

Grieveson, Lee. *Policing Cinema: Movies and Censorship in Early-Twentieth-Century America*. Berkeley: University of California Press, 2004.

Hawley, Ellis W. *The Great War and the Search for a Modern Order: A History of the American People and Their Institutions 1917–1933*. New York: St. Martin's Press, 1992.

Jacoby, Sanford M. *American Exceptionalism Revisited: The Importance of Management*. Los Angeles: Institute of Industrial Relations, UCLA, 1987.

Kimeldorf, Howard. and Judith Stepan-Norris. "Historical Studies of Labor Movements in the United States," *Annual Review of Sociology* 18 (1992): 495–517.

Kocka, Jurgen. *White Collar Workers in America 1890–1940: A Social-Political History in International Perspective*. London: Sage, 1980.

Lipold, Paul L. and Larry W. Isaac. "Striking Deaths: Lethal Contestation and the 'Exceptional' Character of the American Labor Movement, 1870–1970," *International Review of Social History* 54.2 (2009): 167–205.

Mahar, Keren Ward. *Women Filmmakers in Early Hollywood*. Baltimore: John Hopkins University Press, 2006.

Mann, Michael. *The Sources of Social Power, Vol. 2: The Rise of Class and Nation-States, 1760–1914*. Cambridge: Cambridge University Press, 1993.

May, Lary. *Screening Out the Past: The Birth of Mass Culture and the Motion Picture Industry*. New York: Oxford University Press, 1980.

McBee, Randy D. *Dance Hall Days: Intimacy and Leisure Among Working-Class Immigrants in the United States*. New York: New York University Press, 2000.

Merritt, Russell. "Nickelodeon Theaters, 1905–1914: Building an Audience for the Movies," in Tino Balio, ed. *The American Film Industry*. Madison: University of Wisconsin Press, 1976, 97–101.

Meyerowitz, Joanne J. *Women Adrift: Independent Wage Earners in Chicago, 1880–1930*. Chicago: University of Chicago Press, 1988.

Montgomery, David. *Workers' Control in America: Studies in the History of Work, Technology, and Labor Struggles*. Cambridge: Cambridge University Press, 1979.

Nasaw, David. *Going Out: The Rise and Fall of Public Amusements*. Cambridge, MA: Harvard University Press, 1993.

Odem, Mary E. *Delinquent Daughters: Protecting and Policing Adolescent Female Sexuality in the United States, 1885–1920*. Chapel Hill: University of North Carolina Press, 1995.

Peiss, Kathy. *Cheap Amusements: Working Women and Leisure in Turn-of-the-Century New York*. Philadelphia: Temple University Press, 1986.

———. "Charity Girls and City Pleasures," *OAH Magazine of History* 18.4 (2004): 14–16.

Rhodes, Chip. *Structures of the Jazz Age: Mass Culture, Progressive Education, and Racial Disclosures in American Modernism*. London: Verso, 1998.

Robertson, Stephen. "Seduction, Sexual Violence, and Marriage in New York City, 1886–1955," *Law and History Review* 24.2 (2006): 331–373.

Rosen, Ruth. *The Lost Sisterhood: Prostitution in America, 1900–1918*. Baltimore, MD: Johns Hopkins University Press, 1982.

Ross, Steven J. *Working-Class Hollywood: Silent Film and the Shaping of Class in America*. Princeton: Princeton University Press, 1998.

———. "How Hollywood Became Hollywood: Money, Politics, and Movies," in Tom Sitton and William Deverell, eds., *Metropolis in the Making, Los Angeles in the 1920s*. Berkeley: University of California Press, 2001, 255–276.

Shull, Michel Slade. *Radicalism in American Silent Films, 1909–1929: A Filmography and History*. Jefferson, NC: McFarland & Company, 2000.

Slide, Anthony. "Early Women Filmmakers: The Real Numbers," *Film History* 24.1 (2012): 114–121.

Stamp, Shelly. "Lois Weber, Progressive Cinema, and the Fate of the Work-a-Day Girls in Shoes," *Camera Obscura* 19.2 (2004): 140–169.

———. *Lois Weber in Early Hollywood*. Oakland: University of California Press, 2015.

Wasko, Janet. *Movies and Money: Financing the American Film Industry.* Norwood, NJ: Ablex Publishing Corporation, 1982.

Zolberg, Aristide R. "How Many Exceptionalisms?" in Ira Katznelson and Aristide R. Zolberg, eds. *Working-Class Formation, Nineteenth-Century Patterns in Western Europe and the United States.*, Princeton, NJ: Princeton University Press, 1986.

CHAPTER 5

Consumerism and Ethnicity

CONTINUITY AND CHANGE IN THE CROSS-CLASS ROMANCE FILM

The popularity of the cross-class romance film that began with the rise of the feature-length film around 1915 continued in the 1920s. Although the numbers of cross-class romance films dropped somewhat from the 115 that I found during the peak years 1915–1919, I found 99 of them from 1920 to 1928. The basic patterns did not change: in 80 of the films the wealthy protagonist was male; in 16 of the films the wealthy protagonist was female; and there were three films with two cross-class romances, one between a rich man and poor girl and another between a rich girl and poor man. In 82 of the films the cross-class romance was successful, usually ending in marriage or the promise of marriage. Only one of the 99 films was directed by a woman (Lois Weber), and although female script writers were credited in 61 films only 16 films were written exclusively by women. Of the total number of script-writing credits, 91 were female and 156 were male.

One significant change with respect to genre, which reflected wider cultural changes as the decade progressed, was the increase in the number of cross-class romance comedies and the decline in the number of dramas. The number of comedies gradually increased in the first half of the decade, and between 1926 and 1929, there were more cross-class romance comedies than dramas. Of the cross-class romance films released in 1928,

© The Author(s) 2017
S. Sharot, *Love and Marriage Across Social Classes in American Cinema*,
DOI 10.1007/978-3-319-41799-8_5

I found only one drama and seven comedies. This trend would come to be reversed in the early 1930s.

The themes common in the cross-class romance films from 1915 to 1919 continued to be common in the 1920s but, as the number of comedies increased and the number of dramas declined, certain themes became uncommon. One theme that became rare was that of the seduction and abandonment of a victimized poor girl by a predatory wealthy man.[1]

D.W. Griffith revived this plot in *Way Down East* (D.W. Griffith Productions, 1920), and although some critics had little sympathy for the plot, which they saw as an outmoded melodrama, they praised Griffith for making it into an absorbing entertainment.[2] Similar reservations about the melodramatic nature of Griffith's source material were made of *The White Rose* (D. W. Griffith Productions, 1923) in which a theology student and son of a wealthy southern plantation family first abandons and finally marries the cigar stand girl he had made pregnant. Whereas critics acknowledged that Griffith could make melodramatic "hokum" into acceptable entertainment[3] they were less tolerant of other film makers who made what the critics regarded as outmoded melodrama. The reviewer for *Variety* criticized *The Top of New York* (Paramount, 1922) as a "crude and old fashioned affair" in which a poor working girl struggles against "the dishonorable plotting of her rich employer, trying to remain straight under the temptation of his offered luxury." The reviewer wrote: "All the paraphernalia of the melodrama of a generation ago is present ... We do not take our heroines any more as altogether, inhumanly good and our villains as unqualifiedly viciously worthless. We prefer some semblance of shading between good and bad such as everyday experience has taught us is the stage of the world."[4] Although there were probably few films released in 1922 in which there was much shading of good and bad of protagonists, there is no doubt that the portrayal of the sexual harassment and exploitation of working class girls was becoming rare on the screen. It is doubtful whether this reflected any decline of sexual harassment in society, but the trend toward freer sexual mores may have made the portrayal of attacks on the virtue of heroines appear outmoded.

When heroines in cross-class romances of the 1920s had to defend their virtue, this was rarely grounded in the settings of exploitation that had been common in the cross-class romance films up to 1918. The shop-girl who receives a mysterious legacy of 1 million dollars in *Joanna* (Edwin Carewe Productions, 1925) defends herself with a shoe against a man who has made a wager with the bank president who provided the legacy that a working girl who has the means to enjoy a life of luxury will also lose her virtue. By way of contrast, sexual exploitation within a realistic setting was portrayed in *The Passaic Textile Strike* (International Workers' Aid, 1926), one of the very few features made by labor movements during the 1920s. The film, which included an acted "Prologue" and documentary material, was made while the actual strike in the wool mills of Passaic and nearby New Jersey cities was still ongoing. The acted part tells of a Polish family who, in the words of an intertitle, "come to America, the Land of Promise, only to find industrial oppression and bitter struggle." After a cut in the father's wages, the parents reluctantly decide that their 14-year-old daughter has to leave school and go to work in order that the family will have enough food to survive. The daughter is sexually exploited by the mill boss, presented as a smartly dressed, fat, cigar-smoking lecher, who later fires her after he finds her a nuisance. The father works overtime to make up for the loss of the daughter's wage but be becomes ill from overwork and dies. The film ends with the mother going to work as the sole breadwinner and the workers' decision to form a union. The melodrama of the Prologue conveys economic and sexual exploitation, there is no happy resolution, and its makers distinguished it from Hollywood melodrama in an intertitle: "The incidents are just the common facts of the textile workers' lives, empty perhaps of those flaming passions seen so often on the screen, but full of the actual tragedy of deadening labor and despairing struggle"[5] (Fig. 5.1).

One change in cross-class romance films was the milieu in which the romance was conducted and the occupations of the romantic couple. Together with the decline of the theme of class conflict, the factory was no

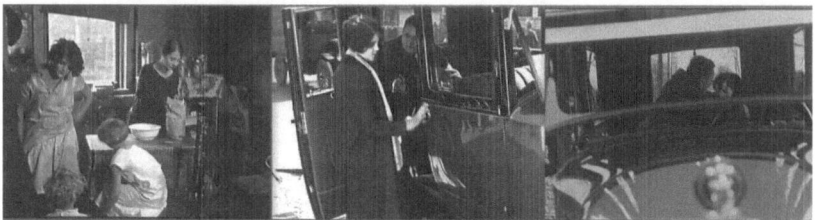

Fig. 5.1 Frames from *The Passaic Textile Strike* (International Workers' Aid, 1926): The tenement home of the fourteen year old working daughter shown with her mother and sisters; the "big boss" invites the daughter into his car; once out of town, he sexually assaults her

longer a context for cross-class romance, and the factory or mill girl and the factory owner or his son no longer appeared in cross-class romance. Apart from the anti-communist film *The Face at Your Window* (Fox, 1920), the only cross-class romance film that I found between a factory worker and a factory owner in the 1920s was *First Love* (Realart, 1921), and in this film the factory girl changes her occupation to that of a waitress. The most prominent milieu for the cross-class romance in the 1920s were the department store, the theatre or cabaret, and the office. Between 1915 and 1919, there were almost as many shop girls as factory girls in cross-class romance films, but whereas in the 1920s the factory girl disappeared, the shop girl working in a department store remained a prominent protagonist and was an especially popular role played by prominent stars such as Mary Pickford and Clara Bow in the late 1920s[6] (Fig. 5.2). Saleswomen were paid less than clerical workers and they worked long hours in difficult work conditions, often under a rigid discipline,[7] but such factors were largely ignored by films in which the department stores were

Fig. 5.2 Still of Clara Bow in *It* (Famous-Players Lasky, 1927), a department store sales girl wooing her boss, the owner of the store. His apparent indifference at this point in a result of his mistaken belief that she is an unmarried mother. Image courtesy of Jerry Murbach, http://www.doctormacro.com/

used as locations of consumerism and romance. As poor working girls located at the center of consumer culture, the salesgirl provided an ideal screen role for the stars to represent a working-class New Woman who transcended the barriers of class. In real department stores, managers were trying through training and discipline to erase the signs of their salesgirls' working-class origins and to apply the veneer of middle-class culture.[8] In film department stores, the star in the role of the salesgirl showed that, as a New Woman, the girl with a working-class background could win the upper-class man by remaining her 'natural' self.

One female occupation that was rare in the cross-class romance films of 1915–1919 and became as popular as the shop girl in the 1920s was the chorus or showgirl. In addition to the shop girls and chorus girls, there were stenographers, secretaries, and the occasional maid, waitress and manicurist. The wealthy male protagonists included financiers, lawyers, artists and department store owners, but often they were simply sons of wealthy families living a life of leisure or with no clearly defined occupation. The changes in the occupations of the romantic protagonists as well as other changes in the cross-class romances relate to the socio-economic and cultural changes in the 1920s, and, in particular, to the surge in consumerism.

CONSUMERISM AND GENDER

The consumer society did not begin in the 1920s. Its origins have been traced back to the eighteenth century, and it advanced significantly in the late nineteenth and early twentieth century. The pushing back into history of the origins and development of consumerism does not undermine the significance of the changes in the 1920s. This decade is viewed by some historians as the decade in which there was a clear shift from a producer to a consumer economy, when new social norms of consumption became pervasive, and when the consolidation of mass merchandising marked the decisive advent of the modern consumer society.[9]

An important segment of the new consuming public was those who worked in occupations that dealt with the distribution, selling and consumption of goods, but although these expanding occupations involved changes in the class structure, it would be a mistake to view consumerism as a process that encompassed the entire class structure. A large proportion of working-class families experienced some improvement in their living standards during the 1920s, but the majority was still not earning sufficiently to make them consumers much beyond subsistence levels,[10] and the advances in consumerism of the higher income strata could only increase feelings among the working class of their subordinate class status.[11]

The changes in the occupational structure were particularly evident among women. By 1920, a third of women wage earners were in clerical and sales work, and whereas in 1900 less than a quarter of all clerical and kindred workers were women, by 1930 over half were women.[12] By 1930, almost 2 million women were employed as secretaries, typists and file clerks and another 70,000 women were employed as saleswomen.[13] Gender was one of the most significant factors that shaped consumer demand and because, from the late nineteenth century, the consumer was frequently represented as a woman[14] the heightened consumerism of the 1920s was bound to focus on the interlinked discourses of consumerism and the sexuality of women.[15]

The New Woman type that most closely signaled the relationship between consumerism and women's emancipation in appearance and behavior was the flapper. An invention of the 1910s, the flapper became a symbol of the Jazz Age 1920s and a focus of the period's discourse on manners and morals. With her short hair, use of cosmetics, smoking, short skirts, and flamboyant dancing, the flapper was seen to personify a lifestyle condemned by conservatives as undermining morality and religion.[16] Most observers, however, did not perceive flappers as overpowering men; she was soft and romantic, and although she viewed her paid work as a sign of her independence, she did not seek a career that would require her to forgo marriage.[17]

The flapper and the general shift from sexual reticence to sexual expressiveness were associated with the middle, especially upper-middle, class. However, the wage-earning women who lived apart from their families appear to have been a vanguard in the changes of sexual standards. The pre-World War I reformers' discourse of innocent, helpless wage-earning women in an evil environment was replaced after the war by one of resourceful women who had freed themselves from the constraints of their families, succeeded in supporting themselves on low wages, and sought amusements in the new forms of commercialized entertainment, including the movies. In some respects, young flappers from the middle class imitated working-class girls who lived on their own or with their peers and socialized freely with men.[18] Many working-class girls in turn adopted the flapper image, which for them was an expression of class aspiration as much as a statement of personal freedom. Stylish clothes and the use of cosmetics were presented by the new forms of advertising as a means of empowerment and self-improvement, and they were simply necessary for women who wished to obtain employment in offices or as sales clerks in department stores. Advertisements addressed to women also emphasized the importance of their appearance in order to attract a husband and then secure his devotion and fidelity. As one advertisement for night cream put it, life-long marriage and security were "beauty's reward."[19]

The identification of many women in white-collar work as middle class was encouraged by mass production and the increased standardization of clothes that had partially democratized fashions and made it difficult, according to contemporary observers, to distinguish affluent middle-class women from secretaries or saleswomen. However, the chances for white-collar girls to achieve a middle-class income and style of life were small and they had good reason to believe that they could only realize their middle-class aspirations, if at all, through marriage. Most unmarried white-collar women from all classes said that they preferred marriage over a career and regarded their work as a temporary state in their lives prior to marriage. The critique of marriage, which had been common among feminists prior to World War I, was rarely heard after the war as it was undermined by the proponents of 'companionate marriage'. More women were getting married, they were marrying younger, and it was entirely rational for them to perceive that their opportunities for socio-economic mobility were largely dependent on the men they married.[20]

If marriage with the appropriate male held out the promise that a woman would enjoy the benefits, hopefully on a permanent basis, of the consumer society, the romance prior to marriage had to be linked integrally with consumerism. The diffusion throughout the class structure of the disinterested ideal of romantic love meant that love was now ideally free of economic considerations, but its pursuit was conducted within and through the conditions and means provided by the consumer society. More particularly, it was conducted through the new institution of dating that was intimately tied to consumerism, and it is noteworthy that movie theatres were a major site for dates. It is a reasonable assumption that the rise of dating and the importance of cinemas for dates encouraged the emphasis of Hollywood on romantic storylines, particularly stories that focused on a couples' courtship rather than marriage. Young women who provided a key audience for romantic films would find, in many of these films, situations that were relevant to their dilemma of what they had to give in return for being invited on a date. Cross-class romance films, in particular, addressed the interrelations and negotiations involved between romance and material considerations.

Although dating provided greater opportunities for class mingling, the commodities and forms of entertainment consumed in dating were largely determined by access to wealth and leisure time. Women required resources to make themselves attractive through clothes and beauty products, but the customary practice of 'treating' a woman meant that the costs of dating fell most heavily on the man. The costs of theater and movie tickets, flowers, chocolates, taxi-rides, items that had become central to the seduction process, meant that many lower income men were disadvantaged in the new economy of love. If a woman entered a romance with a man from a higher class than herself, it was advantageous for her to be conversant with the rituals of consumption. Help in such matters was provided by etiquette books that provided advice on the appropriate behavior in such settings as expensive restaurants and hotels.[21] Help was also provided by cross-class romance films that set forth the opportunities and obstacles that the poorer protagonist (most often a female) faced in her romance with the wealthier protagonist.

THE CROSS-CLASS ROMANCE NARRATIVES

When love and material considerations were in direct conflict in a cross-class romance, love took precedence. The shop girl in *Weavers of Destiny* (Edward Warren Productions, 1917) and the chorus girl in *Pettigrew's Girl* (Famous Players-Lasky, 1919) break off their relationships with millionaires after they decide that their true love is a man from their own class.[22] *Pettigrew's Girl* tells the millionaire that his money had been his main appeal, and the catch line proposed by a trade paper was, "She chose a man in a million instead of a man with a million."[23] The chorus girl in *Rouge and Riches* (Universal, 1920) warns her millionaire that she is marrying him for his money, but she finally realizes that her true love is her dancing partner. The girl employed in the classified ads department in *Classified* (Corinne Griffith Productions, 1925) loves wearing beautiful clothes and riding in expensive cars but she turns down the rich man who can provide these luxuries for a car mechanic. The wealthy man who attempts to refine the rough manner of the discharged salesgirl who gets a job in the chorus in *Becky* (Cosmopolitan, 1927) is finally rejected by her in favor of her humble boyfriend.

In some cases it is disillusionment with the mores of high society that lead the heroine back to their old sweethearts from their class of origin. The daughter of a plumber in *Home* (Lois Weber Productions, 1919) who visits her wealthy classmate's country residence where she hopes to find a rich husband discovers that the wealthy guest to whom she almost succumbs is conducting an affair with her friend's stepmother. The department store clerk in *The Triflers* (Universal, 1920) returns to her poor but honest boyfriend after she discovers the shallowness of socialites during a splurge vacation in a fashionable hotel. The female clerk in *The Loves of Letty* (Goldwyn, 1920) settles for a poor photographer after she rejects two wealthy men; one because of his boorishness and another because he believes that there is one morality for his class and another morality for hers. The poor protagonist in *Their Hour* (Tiffany-Stahl, 1928) is male, a shipping clerk, and after he is seduced by a spoiled socialite he returns to the girl from his own class who forgives him. *Rich But Honest* (Fox, 1927) confounds the usual expectations as it is the poor mechanic who turns out to be a cad and the wealthy man who turns out to have honorable intentions toward the shop girl who has become a dancer.

A suggestion that suitable marriage partners are best found within one's own class was contained in narratives in which one or both characters take on the identity of, or are mistaken as from, another class, only to find that they are, in fact, from the same class. The rich girl in *Fair Enough* (American Films, 1918) falls in love with a policeman who turns out to be a millionaire who took the job because he was tired of wasting his life. The female and male department store workers in *Young Romance* (Lasky, 1915) pose as wealthy persons in a seaside resort, they part when each feels they are unequal to the other in class, and they find happiness when they discover each other's true identity.[24] In the one-reel comedy *The Double Deception* (Majestic, 1915), two wealthy young people on vacation fall in love when they are posing as working class—the girl as a dairy maid and the young man as a clerk.[25] This theme is repeated in another one-reel film, *Mixed Matrimony* (Nester, 1917), in which a wealthy man changes places with his valet and the heiress changes places with her maid. They elope, marry, and then reveal their real identities.[26] The double class disguise variation was played out again in the five-reel *The Duchess of Doubt* (Metro Pictures, 1917), in which a maid poses as a duchess and falls for a ribbon clerk who turns out to be the son of the department store owner.

Whereas a double class disguise was used as a plot contrivance for an intra-class romance, the class disguise of just one of the protagonists more frequently transformed what was supposedly an intra-class romance into a cross-class romance. The chauffeur in *The Square Deceiver* (Yorke film, 1917) is really a rich man, although in this film the poor girl he courts inherits a fortune. The department store girl *Maggie Pepper* (Paramount, 1919) mistakes the young owner of the store as a job seeker,[27] and the department store girl in *The Final Close-Up* (Paramount, 1919) is wooed by a cub reporter who, in fact, is a millionaire.[28] As we have seen, factory owners or their sons posed as laborers in their own factories to discover why the workers were threatening to strike and would fall in love with a female factory worker, as in *A Little Sister of Everybody* (Anderson-Brunton, 1918). Even a millionaire owner of tenements would pose as working class when he falls in love with one of his poor tenants, as in *A Rich Man's Plaything* (Fox, 1917).[29] It is the wealthy male who is most prone to pose as a poor person, but in *The Fair Cheat* (F.B.O., 1923) it is the daughter of a wealthy man in love with a poor clerk in her father's employ who poses as a poor girl and supports herself by getting a job in the chorus line.

One trade reviewer of *The Final Close*-Up wrote: "Once more the tired shop girl who meets the young millionaire masking as a plain ordinary man."[30] The familiarity of the class disguise plot contrivance did not prevent it from being used in films of the 1920s. Poor heroines continued to be rewarded for their goodness, virtue, constancy, and disinterest in wealth by discovering that their supposedly poor sweethearts are really millionaires. *Subway Susie* (Al Rockett Productions, 1926), a salesgirl, postpones her wedding with a subway guard when her firm promotes her to the position of buyer and asks her to sail to Paris. After Susie misses her boat because of a stalled train, the subway guard reveals that his father is president of the subway, and Susie agrees to journey to Paris for a honeymoon rather than as a buyer. *Miss Nobody* (First National, 1926), a former heiress, now penniless, falls in love with a hobo who is revealed to be a famous, wealthy author who has donned rags in search of inspiration. In *Bertha, the Sewing Machine Girl* (Fox, 1926), the sewing-machine girl who finds new employment as a telephone girl discovers that the assistant shipping clerk is the owner of the company; in *Home James* (Universal, 1928), the departmental store clerk mistakes the son of the storeowner for a chauffeur; in *Orchids and Ermine* (First National, 1927), the hotel telephone receptionist mistakes the wealthy young oilman for his valet; and in *My Best Girl* (Mary Pickford Company, 1927), the department storeroom girl discovers that her sweetheart and co-worker in the storeroom is the son of the store's owner.

It was rare for a cross-class couple to end up poor, but this did happen occasionally. The wealthy Bob Van Dyke who catches and then releases Jenny who planned to burglarize his home in *The Ragamuffin* (Jesse L. Lasky, 1916) subsequently loses his money. It is Jenny who prevents him from committing a robbery, convinces him to get a job, and then make plans for their marriage.[31] The department store salesgirl in *Her Great Chance* (Select Pictures, 1918) accepts the millionaire's son's proposal of marriage only after he is disinherited.[32] Forsaking wealth was also the theme of *The Girl Who Wouldn't Work* (Shulberg, 1925) in which a rich philanderer spends his entire fortune in obtaining the acquittal of the girl's father from a charge of murder. These, however, were exceptions, and a frequent dilemma for the cross-class romantic film in its representation of the lower-class character was to sustain the character's disinterestness in love when it was evident that she was to receive enormous rewards if that love was reciprocated. A common solution through various plot contrivances, such as ignorance of the wealth of the love object, was to present the character's disinterestness in love as sufficient justification for the enormous rewards she was to receive.

The major obstacles to the cross-class romance were the class-motivated opposition of the wealthy protagonist's family and social circle, and the class-derived cultural differences of the romantic couple. Opposition from the rich family to the union was a major plot component in many of the cross-class romance films (e.g., *Flirting with Fate*, Fine Arts, 1916; *Peggy Leads the Way*, American Film, 1917; *Fuss and Feathers*, Ince, 1918; *Simple Souls*, Hampton-Pathe, 1920; *Out of the Chorus*, Realert, 1921; and *The Best People*, Famous Players-Lasky, 1925). Most often, the rich family relents and accepts the romance or marriage after their discovery of the heroine's noble character, as in *A Daughter of the Sea* (Equitable, 1915), *Jenny Be Good* (Realart Pictures, 1920), *The Misfit Wife* (Metro Pictures, 1920), and *Broadway Lady* (R-C Pictures, 1925); or after they realize the unhappiness they have caused, as in *East Side-West Side* (Principal Pictures, 1923); or after they discover that the girl is actually the lost daughter of a wealthy family, as in *The Gulf Between* (Technicolor, 1917).

It was exceptional for the wealthy family to break up the romance of their child with the poor protagonist and this would only occur if the wealthy protagonist lacked moral fiber. The son of a millionaire who marries a telephone operator named Eleanor in *The Divorce Trap* (Fox, 1919) is disinherited by his father and he falls in with evil associates who attempt to provide grounds for divorce by framing Eleanor for infidelity. Eleanor finds happiness with a former suitor, a lawyer, who helps to vindicate her honor. Most wealthy protagonists were made of sterner stuff and would remain true to their loved one even if it meant giving up their wealth. In *Poor Relations* (Brentwood, 1919), following his mother's humiliation of his wife, the son leaves to live with his wife and her poor relations in the country. In *Beckoning Roads* (B.B. Features, 1919), the son of a wealthy financier reunites with his wife, the adopted daughter of a farmer, after he renounces his father whose phony stock deal was responsible for the suicide of the farmer.

The opposition of the rich family could lead the romantic protagonists into serious predicaments from which one of them would save the other. The wealthy financier whose son Hal marries the shop-girl Evelyn in *The Moral Decline* (World Film Corporation, 1919) tries unsuccessfully to pay Evelyn to divorce his son, but succeeds in convincing his son to leave her for a year to test the strength of their love. Hal is shanghaied by sailors and Evelyn becomes a dancer in a disreputable café in order to raise money for an operation to save their baby's life. Hal arrives in time to defend Evelyn from a raid by the police and Vice Society, led by Hal's mother, on the café where Evelyn works. He begs forgiveness and they reunite. The son of the wealthy family in *The Price of Pleasure* (Universal, 1925) saves the shop girl who has become a dancer in a cabaret, both from the legal chicanery of his family and the unwelcome advances of her dancing partner.

The disinterestness of the heroine's love is frequently compared with other women who, if they are from the lower class, desire the wealthy man for his money or, if they are from his own class, perceive the man as an appropriate class partner, as in *The Gilded Dream* (Universal, 1920) and *In a Moment of Temptation* (R-C Pictures, 1927). A common obstacle to the cross-class romance or marriage is false accusations, often made by another woman or by the wealthy protagonist's family that lead to misunderstanding with respect to the qualities or actions of the working-class character, such as involvement in a crime or sexual immorality. In *Pearls of Temptation* (Balboa, 1915), *The Smart Sex* (Universal, 1921) and *In a Moment of Temptation*, the heroines are accused of robbery; in *Everybody's Girl* (Vitagraph, 1918), the tenement girl's morality is suspect because her entertainments are paid for by chance acquaintances; in *Rouged Lips* (Metro, 1923), the wealthy man suspects the chorus girl of unfaithfulness because he does not realize that the pearls she is wearing are imitation; and in *It* (Famous Players-Paramount, 1927), the department store girl is mistakenly believed to be an unmarried mother (Fig. 5.2). Once the truth comes out, the couple can unite. When the heroine is rich and the hero poor, the opposition of the girl's family can be overcome after the hero proves himself worthy: in *The Traffic Cop* (Robertson-Cole, 1926), the hero rescues the family from danger, and in *Romance Road* (Granada, 1925), the garage worker receives the blessing of the girl's family after he becomes wealthy from his invention. A working man's rapid rise to wealth was also the means to reward his working-class sweetheart after she had become involved with far less worthy wealthy men, as in *Manhandled* (Famous Players, 1924).

The difference in class cultures is a frequent obstacle to the cross-class romance and in a few films it proved insurmountable. This was the case in Cecil B. DeMill's comic drama *Saturday Night* (Famous Players-Lasky, 1922), which begins with an intertitle that prepares the audience to expect a film that departs from the conventional end of a cross-class romance: "Most stories stop where the real drama of Life begins. We are not told how CINDERELLA—who didn't know Oysters from Caviar—managed the Palace Banquets as MRS. PRINCE CHARMING." The intertitle warns that, "we don't always 'live happily ever after'." Additional intertitles clarify that the two working-class protagonists, Shamrock the laundress and Tom the chauffeur, are frustrated by their inability to afford the good things of life, and that the two wealthy protagonists, Iris and Dick, are bored with their privileged lifestyles and the potential spouses from their class. Comic circumstances lead to romantic encounters between Shamrock and Dick, who marries her and brings her back to the family mansion, much to the consternation of his mother and sister. Dick's snooty sister remarks to him: "Isn't it nice that your wife chews gum? She'll be sure to stick to you." Shamrock counters: "Ain't it awful that your sister smokes." Whereas smoking in company had become respectable among the upper strata, among the working class it was understood to denote a 'lose woman'.

Iris marries Tom, her chauffeur, after he saves her life. As her uncle, upon whom she is financially dependent, cuts off her allowance, she becomes financially dependent on Tom, who rents a small tenement apartment close to the noisy railway track. Iris looks with dismay at the apartment and at Tom after he takes off his smart chauffeur's uniform and puts on his shabby clothes. The class differences extend to cleanliness: when Dick's sister tells a maid to give Shamrock a bath, Shamrock responds that it is not Saturday night, and when Iris tells Tom that she has prepared a bath for him, he responds that, "it's only Tuesday!" This association between Saturday night and a weekly bath for the working class was taken up by some exhibitors who placed bath tubs in their lobby or in front of the theater,[33] but it aroused the ire of a reviewer for the labor press who wrote that, according to DeMille, "Workers stink and bathe only on Saturday night. Only the gentle-born are sweet and clean."[34]

DeMille emphasizes how the wives' inability to adjust to the class culture of their husbands causes considerable embarrassment. DeMille intercuts between a grand dinner given by Dick's family for their wealthy circle and Iris' attempt to cook a meal for Tom and two of his friends, another couple, who arrive unexpectedly and join them to eat. Shamrock drinks too much wine and falls asleep at the dinner table, resting her head on the shoulder of the guest sitting next to her. Iris' cooking makes the meat too tough to eat, and when Tom's friend dances with her in a rough manner she slaps him. Tom tells her that he is not going to have his wife insult his friends and he leaves with them. After further misadventures, the wives are adamant that the differences in tastes between them and their husbands make their marriages impossible. Iris tells Dick that "you can't bind the Woman you love with Peals and Limousines—when she wants Chewing Gum! Nor can I hold Tom with Poetry—when he's hungry for Pie!" Shamrock explains to Dick that she likes Tom "because he likes Gums and Hot-Dogs and Jazz! Just as you and Iris like High-Brow Operations, and Olives—and such!" After the protagonists have learnt the lesson that they should have chosen their partners in accord with class, an intertitle tells us that it is seven years later. Shamrock and Tom are married and enjoying Coney Island with their three children, and in Iris' wealthy home Dick suggests to her that it is about time they mended their engagement that was broken seven years ago. DeMille's message that peoples are more likely to be happy when they marry within their own class was no doubt a conservative one,[35] (Fig. 5.3) but one could argue that cross-class romances that end happily without extending the narrative beyond the marriage ceremony are conservative by default.

The failure of a cross-class marriage as a consequence of the cultural inadequacies of the lower-class character is a theme of *Stella Dallas* (Samuel Goldwyn, 1925), although the film (unlike the novel on which it was based) does not portray Stella as simply embodying the cultural defects of her class of origin.[36] Stella, a mill worker, succeeds in marrying a rich man, but she does not gain acceptance into the respectable upper-middle class she aspires to join because of her tastes, particularly in clothes, and her failure to appreciate the rules of decorum. Her husband divorces her

Fig. 5.3 The two advertisements for *Saturday Night* (Famous Players-Lasky, 1922) carry the message of the problems of cross-class marriage. The first shows the elegantly-dressed lady shackled to the gaudily-dressed, working-class male, and the second shows the embarrassing behavior of the working-class girl at a society dinner under the disapproving eye of her upper-class husband. *Source of images:* https://commons.wikimedia.org/

and marries again, and after their daughter learns the appropriate social behavior of her father's world, Stella understands that she is an impediment to her daughter's social success and marriage prospects. Stella passes her daughter into the care of her ex-husbands refined wife, and in the last scene she watches the marriage of her daughter from the street through a window. Although Stella is presented at the beginning of the film as a schemer with class ambitions, the failure of the cross-class romance is established early, and the major part of the narrative comes to focus on Stella's maternal sacrifice (Fig. 5.4).

The obstacle of the lower-class protagonist's lack of social graces is overcome when the 'uncultured' character learns the appropriate etiquette, as in *The Cave Man* (Vitagraph, 1915), *Fuss and Feathers* (Ince, 1918), *Impossible Susan* (Mutual, 1918), *Lonesome Corners* (Playgoers, 1922), and *The Teaser* (Universal, 1925). Etiquette is, on occasion, disregarded or minimized as an obstacle: in *Proud Flesh* (Metro-Goldwyn, 1925), a girl is repulsed by the manners of the family of the plumbing contractor she loves but decides that she cannot live without him. The millionaire in *Sunny Jane* (Balboa, 1917) is not pleased when the country girl he sent to be educated returns to ape the manners of a grand dame.

Fig. 5.4 Still from *Stella Dallas* (Samuel Goldwyn, 1925); the upper-middle-class Mrs. Dallas (Alice Joyce) having tea in her home with the working-class first Mrs. Dallas (Belle Bennett). Image courtesy of Derek Boothroyd

In *Fine Manners* (Paramount, 1926), the wealthy man realizes that it was a mistake to teach the chorus girl etiquette because it spoilt her vibrant personality.[37] Appropriate manners could be a problem, however, even if the character had money. The rich girl in *The Man Alone* (Motion Picture Utility, 1923) cancels her engagement to a gold mine owner after he demonstrates unacceptable manners for high society. She chooses instead the etiquette teacher who had been employed to teach the coarse mine owner.

Although the heroines from the working class often lacked etiquette, such as the use of the appropriate fork for the various dishes at dinner, they rarely lacked virtue. *Forbidden* (Lois Weber Productions, 1919) was unusual in that it was the wealthy man from the city who teaches his newly wedded wife, a country girl, a moral lesson. Whereas the wealthy man is disgusted with life in New York and desires the tranquility of the country, his country wife craves the excitements of the city and leaves her husband to tour the cabarets and opium dens of Chinatown. She is cured of this craving when she is accosted by a bearded stranger who turns out to be her husband in disguise. Most poor heroines were highly virtuous and their virtue could extend to the moral reformation of the wealthy protagonist. The small-time actress in *Stagestruck* (Triangle, 1917) wins over the wealthy philanthropist mother of a dissolute son by reforming the son. Moral reformation was becoming rare and the virtue of the working-class heroine was more often demonstrated by her sexual reticence. The love of the famous sculptor for the cabaret girl who agrees to pose for him in *The Virtuous Model* (Pathe Exchange, 1919) is reinforced when she refuses to pose for him in the nude. The chorus girl whose high standards of morality gain her a saintly reputation among the other chorus girls in *Spotlight Sadie* (Goldwyn, 1919) is rewarded by marriage to a millionaire.

Poor heroines often demonstrated their moral superiority by their willingness to sacrifice their love in order not to damage the social status or career of the wealthy beloved. The dancer in *A Coney Island Princess* (Famous Players, 1916) lies when she says that she never loved the wealthy sportsman in order that he can marry someone from his own class. In most cases where the heroine is willing to sacrifice her love, the rich hero persists and overcomes her concerns, as in *Sally in Our Alley* (Peerless, 1916) and *Her Social Value* (Katerine MacDonald, 1921). However, in *Wedlock* (Paralta, 1918), not only is Margery, the telephone operator, willing to give up her husband for the sake of his family's social position, but Gregory, the husband, succumbs to his family's pressure to desert Margery. Whereas Margery is rewarded by inheriting a fortune from an old miner, Gregory is punished by being sent to prison for his involvement in business fraud. Margery secures a pardon for Gregory who, now reformed, goes back to his wife who still loves him.[38]

THE CROSS-CLASS ROMANCE AND CONSUMERISM

DeMille's *Saturday Night* (1922) with its failed marriages between wealthy, 'non-ethnic' Americans and working-class Irish Americans could be read as an argument that marriage partners should be from the same class. However, the conservative DeMille was not adverse to successful cross-class romances, particularly if they provided opportunities for the conspicuous consumerism of opulent sets and costumes, as in *Forbidden Fruit* (Paramount, 1921), his remake of a film he directed in 1916, *The Golden Chance* (Jesse L. Lasky Feature Play Co.). In the 1916 version, we are informed by a faded newspaper clipping that Mary, the lower-class protagonist, was the daughter of a judge and that five years earlier she had left home to marry Steve Denby, a man of "questionable reputation." Mary was disowned by her family and now lives with her husband, a wife-abusing drunk and crook, in a squalid tenement slum. Mary finds small jobs as a seamstress, but her breeding explains how she is able to play the role of a rich young socialite when asked to do so by Mrs. Hillary, the wife of a businessman who is trying to convince Roger Manning, a young millionaire, to join him in an investment scheme. The Hillarys' plan is that the charms of Mary will make Roger postpone his intended trip, thereby allowing Mr. Hillary time to persuade Roger to support the investment. Roger falls in love with Mary, and the death of her husband, shot by police after attempting to rob the Hillary home, allows for the possibility of their union in marriage. The film ends with a shot of Roger and Mary standing in her shoddy apartment, each preoccupied with their own thoughts.

Forbidden Fruit retains the basic plot of *The Golden Chance*, but the changes are significant from the point of view of the advance of consumerism. Mary is not given a background as a judge's daughter to account for her ability to pass as a rich socialite. She is a poor seamstress who is able to play the role of a socialite with relative ease because she is transformed by the clothes and jewels provided by the businessman's wife, now called Mrs. Mallory. Whereas in *The Golden Chance*, Mrs. Hillary provides Mary with one of her gowns upon which Mary had been working, in *Forbidden Fruit* Mrs. Mallory assures Mary that she will "be gowned by 'Poiret'—perfumed by 'Coty'—jeweled by 'Tiffany'." Mrs. Mallory orders a maid to phone 'Celeste' to open her shop and send her best selections of gowns, lingerie, slippers, stockings, gloves and furs. *The Golden Chance* only alludes to the Cinderella story when Mary compares a shoe provided by Mrs. Mallory with her own worn out shoe. *Forbidden Fruit* makes the Cinderella element overt: Mrs. Mallory says that she will play the part of fairy-godmother to Mary's Cinderella and Mary day dreams that she is, in fact, Cinderella. Scenes are inserted from the Cinderella fairy tale and these provide even greater spectacle and conspicuous consumption than that of the Mallorys' large mansion and the clothes worn by the contemporary characters. Mary is forgiven by Rogers, the millionaire, for her passing as a socialite when she confesses that she could not resist playing Cinderella because she had been "shabby and lonely and heart-hungry for so long," and, in contrast with the inconclusive ending of *The Golden*

Chance, the Cinderella fantasy is called upon to provide the unambiguous happy ending to *Forbidden Fruit*. An epilogue titled "Life's Springtime" has Mary sitting with Mrs. Mallory in the garden of the mansion; Rogers arrives with a shoe to claim Mary, his Cinderella, and after failing to fit the shoe he kisses her foot[39] (Fig. 5.5).

Fig. 5.5 Frames from *Forbidden Fruit* (Paramount, 1921). Top frames: Mary, the poor seamstress, is transformed by clothes and beauty treatment and meets Rogers, the millionaire. Middle Frames: Mary returns to her husband in their dingy tenement home. Bottom frames: Rogers fails to fit the shoe on Mary and kisses her foot

The combination of consumerism and fantasy in *Forbidden Fruit* is very different from the combination of realism and melodrama in Lois Weber's *The Blot* (Lois Weber Productions, 1921). The cross-class romance in *The Blot* is interpolated within a moral critique of class differences, particularly the differences between professions that cater to the mind and the producers of consumer goods. It is a 'Blot' on society that the college professor and the clergyman should be inadequately compensated and reduced to living in genteel poverty. The Griggs and Olsen families are neighbors, but whereas the family of Griggs, the underpaid college professor, cannot afford even an adequate diet, the family of Olsen, an immigrant shoemaker, eats well, is well-clothed, and has bought a model T Ford car. Professor Griggs, deep in his books, appears oblivious to his family's poverty, and it is Mrs. Griggs who is pained by her family's deprivation and whose grim face shows her feelings as she looks at their worn furniture and carpets. Mr. Olsen feels pity for the Griggs and would like to help them by having his son Peter take private lessons with Professor Griggs, but Mrs. Olsen regards the Griggs as snooty and likes to flaunt her family's prosperity before Mrs. Griggs.

Shoes as a signifier of class and status, central to Weber's earlier film *Shoes*, are prominent in *The Blot*. The worn shoes of the Griggs family, shown in a number of close-ups, are contrasted with the Olsens' new shoes. For the Olsen family, shoes are statements of fashion and conspicuous consumption, as demonstrated when we see that Mrs. Olsen fashionable shoes are too small for her feet and when the youngest of the Olsen family plays with shoes "retailed at $18 a pair." One shot of Amelia, the Griggs' daughter, shows her putting cardboard into her shoes to cover the holes in the soles, and when she exits her workplace, the library, to walk home she looks at her shoes as the rain falls. She is rescued by Phil West, a wealthy student of her father's, who is enamored by Amelia and offers her a lift home in his car, a Packard. Phil's car and the Olsens' Ford 'Tin Lizzie' is part of the contrast between the Olsen family, whose prosperity allows them entrance into the new consumer society, and the 'old' wealth and elite style of Phil and his circle. Weber cross-cuts between a boisterous gathering of the Olsens' teenage daughter's friends at her home with a gathering of the wealthy, young smart set, smoking cigarettes and drinking bootleg alcohol. An intertitle states: "The Country Club party had a smarter setting but the caliber was about the same." The highly demonstrative behavior of both the Olsen teenagers and the college-age smart set are contrasted with the Griggs family spending a quiet evening at home. Phil is part of the smart set but, as a consequence of his growing feelings for the modest Amelia, he shows some dissociation from the raucous behavior of his friends.

Phil's attention to Amelia awakens hope in Mrs. Griggs, but places her in a dilemma: "It is her one big chance and I haven't even decent tea to offer him." Mrs. Griggs scrapes together enough money to buy tea and cakes but when she brings in the tea tray she finds that Phil has already left and finds only the poor clergyman, another suitor of Amelia, with her. Mrs. Griggs is placed in a more desperate situation when Amelia falls ill and she is unable to buy "nourishing food" as prescribed by the doctor. The film takes a melodramatic turn when Amelia sees her mother steal one of Mrs. Olsen's chickens but does not see that her mother puts it back almost immediately. Amelia believers that the cooked chicken that her mother brings to her sick bed is stolen when in fact it is Phil who, after observing Mrs. Griggs' failure to buy a chicken on credit, pays for a large basket of food, including a chicken, to be sent to the Griggs' home.

Phil now feels uncomfortable when he eats the rich foods with his friends at the country club restaurant. He says to Juanita, seated next to him, that he had not previously concerned himself that some people have too much to eat while others have not enough. Although Juanita's hopes for Phil's affection are thwarted by his attraction to Amelia, her jealously gives way to a recognition that he has changed for the good as a consequence of the influence of Amelia who "must be very dear and good and fine." Juanita had earlier made a sarcastic reference to Phil's "working girl," but she now realizes that true worth has nothing to do with wealth and social class. When Juanita gazes upon Amelia as she works in the library, an intertitle reads: "Here was the real thing—a gentlewoman—unbeatable!" Amelia's proud virtue is demonstrated when from her meager librarian's wage she offers money to Mrs. Olsen for the chicken that Amelia believed her mother had stolen. The misunderstanding is cleared up and Phil persuades his father, a trustee of the college, that professors should receive a higher salary. The last scene at the Griggs' home shows that Phil and Amelia are to be a couple and Amelia's two other admirers, the Olsens' son and the Reverend, are saddened as they gaze upon the happy couple. The last shot is of the forlorn clergyman as he walks away from the Griggs' house.

Jennifer Parchevsky writes that *The Blot* was made during a brief period after World War I when the low salaries of middle-class males, such as professors and administrators, were a major subject of public discourse.

When Phil approaches his father on the need for higher salaries of professors and clergymen, he shows him two articles from the *Literary Digest*, a popular middle-class magazine that gave extensive coverage to the plight of the middle class. Parchevsky argues that by centering her film on a professor and a minister, Weber associated the genteel culture of the old middle class with the different problems of dependent white-collar workers. By a contrast between the most impoverished white-collar workers with the most prosperous laborers, defenders of the middle class expressed their anxiety that the line between white collar and blue collar, between 'brain work' and 'hand work', was breaking down. This concern had an ethnic or racially perceived element as the middle class, particularly the old middle class, were predominantly American-born 'Anglo-Saxons', whereas large sectors of blue-collar workers were immigrants. Ethnic or racial suicide was contemplated as brain workers could not afford to have children; the Griggs had only one daughter whereas immigrants like the Olsens, albeit of North European origin, had many children. Weber's film associates blue-collar workers not with production but with vulgar consumerism and assumes that educated men should receive better pay because the nature of their work entitles them to class privilege.

The cross-class romance in *The Blot* allies the Griggs family with Phil's wealthy family after Phil is reformed by his love for Amelia from a life-style of wasteful indulgence to one of reform and virtue[40] (Fig. 5.6).

Fig. 5.6 Lobby card stills from *The Blot* (Lois Weber Productions, 1921). The first shows Phil (Louis Calhern), a wealthy student, pretending to be an avid reader in order to court Amelia (Claire Windsor), a poor librarian, who is at first unresponsive to his attentions. The second shows Amelia, weak from illness and worry, fainting as a now reformed Phil arrives to correct Amelia's misunderstandings and soon after to propose marriage. Images courtesy of Derek Boothroyd

Some critics in 1921 disliked the moralizing or preachy tone of the film, and as the decade advanced, cross-class romances tended to retain the theme of a poor heroine rewarded for her virtue by marriage to a wealthy man, but without the moralizing. In contrast with Weber's critical stance toward consumerism, it was consumerism that became the appropriate context of cross-class romances as well as the reward of the poor protagonist.

THE EMERGENCE OF THE GOLD DIGGER

The appeal of consumerism can also be linked to the appearance of the 'gold digger' in the cross-class romance films of the 1920s. In the last decades of the nineteenth century, prior to the adoption of the term 'gold digger,' an association was made in magazine stories, cartoons, and other media between the gold digger type and burlesque performers and chorus girls. Burlesque posters depicted the girls' male victims as wealthy, elderly, sexually frustrated men, wearing tuxedos and starched shirts, whose fascination with the sexual spectacle made them easy marks.[41] The expression gold digger made its appearance around 1915 and in her investigative book *My Battle With Vice* (1915), Virginia Brooks found that the term was used among the working class to refer to girls who came to a dance hall with the purpose of obtaining material benefits from the young men.[42] Peggy Hopkins Joyce, an ex-chorine who married wealthy men, was written about as the perfect embodiment of the type,[43] and in popular entertainment an association between gold diggers and chorus girls was established in 1919 in Avery Hopwood's play *The Gold Diggers,* which ran for two years on Broadway and then went on tour. Warner Brothers made a film version of Hopwood's play in 1923. As defined by one of the characters, a "gold digger is a woman, generally young, who extracted money and other valuables from the gentlemen of her acquaintance, usually without making any adequate return."[44]

The adoption of the term was part of a broader shift in popular conceptions of women, particularly with respect to those young women who had moved away from their families and lived alone or with other women. Whereas pre-World War I investigators had emphasized the exploitation of unprotected women, sociologists of the 1920s and 1930s found sexually "emancipated" women who knew how to protect themselves and would use their "charm" for "procuring entertainment and perhaps gifts."[45] The gold digger came to replace the vamp as the most prominent type of femme fatale. The heyday of the cinematic vamp was from 1915–1920, and although it was not always possible to make a clear distinction between the cinematic depictions of gold diggers and vamps in the 1920s, it would appear that the number of vamps waned as the number of gold diggers rose. As the term indicates, the motivation of the gold digger is material benefit, whereas the motives of the vamp are often illusive and impenetrable; the vamp may simply take pleasure from the entrapment and destruction of men.[46] Another difference between the vamp and the gold digger is that whereas the class origins of the vamp are unknown, ambiguous, or irrelevant, those of the gold digger are almost always lower or working class.

In a number of films in which the gold digger was not the central character, they were portrayed unsympathetically as women who led men astray from their wives or faithful sweethearts to whom the men invariably returned. However, as the working-girl heroines in cross-class romances, it was revealed that the gold digger tag often had little basis, particularly when applied to chorus girls as in *The Gold Diggers* (Warner, 1923), or when the so-called gold digger has a change of heart and falls genuinely in love. It was suggested by the reviewer for *Variety* that in order to avoid censorship, the play *The Gold Diggers* was altered for the film, of which there is no known surviving print. The play includes chorus girls who are shown to be living off men and these characters appear to have been eliminated from the film. One of the chaste chorus girls, Violet, is genuinely in love with blue-blood Wally, but their marriage is blocked by Wally's Uncle Stephen who believes that all chorus girls are gold diggers and threatens to withhold his nephew's heritage if he marries one. Violet enlists the help of the more experienced chorus girl, Jerry, who is adept at receiving presents from men while remaining chaste. Jerry pretends to Stephen that she is the object of Wally's affection and acts the role of a mercenary gold digger so that Violet will appear like a model of virtue in comparison. Stephen falls in love with Jerry, proposes to her when drunk, and after the deception is revealed he gives his blessing to Wally and Violet and repeats his proposal to Jerry.[47] The film provided opportunities for its female stars to appear in expensive apparel and a number of tie-ups were made with exclusive Fifth Avenue shops. Cartier placed photographs of Hope Hampton, who plays Jerry, wearing $150,000 worth of jewels that she displays in one scene of the film. Other tie-ups were with Mark Cross leather goods shop, Gotham hosiery shop, and prominent shoe shops.[48]

Heroines who were genuine gold diggers began to appear more frequently from the middle of the decade in both dramas and comedies. In the dramas, the gold digger almost invariably underwent a change of heart. In *Women's Wares* (Tiffany, 1927), salesgirl Dolly's gold digging is a consequence of her disillusionment with her boyfriend, who one evening lets his feelings overcome his judgment. Dolly decides that all men are beasts and, encouraged by her sophisticated roommate, she sets forth to take advantage of men without giving them what they want in return. She goes as far as to accept an expensive Park Avenue apartment from a millionaire, but as this results in her losing the respect of another wealthy man she admires, she forsakes gold digging and finds happiness with her original humble boyfriend. In another drama, *Women Love Diamonds* (MGM, 1927), it is indicated that Mavis is the mistress of Harlan, an elderly millionaire she calls "uncle," who supports her in lavish clothes and jewelry. Jerry, a young wealthy man with whom Mavis has fallen in love, takes her to his family's estate where she feels ill at ease with his patrician mother and sisters, and after Harlan explains to Jerry his true relationship with Mavis, Jerry rejects her. In one scene, Mavis and her friend, another gold digger, compare their situation favorably with that of simply dressed working-class women, but Mavis has a change of heart after the death of her chauffeur's sister in childbirth. Mavis has grown fond of Patrick, the chauffeur, and tells him the truth of her relationship with Harlan before leaving to become a nurse in a children's ward. Patrick finds her and the film ends as they kiss. Lea Jacobs notes that the redemption of the gold digger in this film is unusual in that it is a consequence less from love with a working-class man than from identification with the suffering of other women.[49]

Gold diggers in comedies were not required to undergo redemption although, as in *Classified* (Corinne Griffith Productions, 1925), an emphasis is placed upon their chasteness and they finally choose love over money. Babs Comet, the classified ads employee in *Classified* spends much of her time in the office making dinner engagements with any male voice "with a smile." Through gifts from her varied male acquaintances, she is able to array herself as if she belonged to a family of affluence. We are shown, however, that she always guards her virtue. In one comic scene, she has dinner with two men in the rag trade and when one of them tries to kiss her she gives him such a hard slap that he is bowled over on the floor. She succeeds in riding to and from work in a Rolls-Royce or a Renault by the simple method of standing on a street corner and looking anxious but she often has to walk the last few blocks when the driver "gets fresh." When out in the country with a wealthy man whose car "breaks down" conveniently close to an inn, she walks back to the city, riding part of the way on a horse-drawn milk cart. The wealthy man later proposes to her, but Babs prefers to marry a garage mechanic for love. Bab remains chaste but it was presumably her manipulation of men through sexual allure that led the reviewer for *Variety* to describe the film as the "worst kind of trash that can be put upon the screen for young girls and boys."[50]

The reviewer for *Variety* also disliked *Gentlemen Prefer Blondes* (Paramount, 1928), although the criticism here was not the film's (im)morality but rather its "adaption down" in sophistication compared with the highly successful book and the play by Anita Loos upon which the film was based.[51] The reviewer for *The New York Times*, on the other hand, found the film to be an "infectious treat" and noted the assistance of Loos who had made the adaptation and written the intertitiles.[52] A print of the film does not exist but we can gather from contemporary reviews that it included more of the heroine's working-class background than the 1953 musical version. Lorelei Lee, the granddaughter of an unsuccessful goal miner in the Arkansas hills, takes a job as a stenographer and shoots her predatory boss dead when she finds him with another girl. After she is acquitted by a comically depicted jury, the judge stakes her for her fare to California where she becomes a film extra. On a ship to Europe and after their arrival in Europe, Lorelei and her friend Dorothy use their looks and charm to manipulate wealthy men for material ends, particularly diamonds. Among the men conquered by Lorelei is Henry Spoffard, America's richest bachelor, a moral reformer who reads risqué magazines and visits questionable places under the guise of duty. After complications with other wealthy men and with diamonds are resolved, Lorelei and Spoffard marry on their return trip to New York (Fig. 5.7).

A number of exhibitors of *Gentlemen Prefer Blondes* complained that the high price they paid for the film did not justify the business that it brought in and that some patrons had told them that they disliked the film.[53] However, the fan magazine *Photoplay* stated that the film was a "tremendous success."[54] It is possible that for some of the young, working-girl readers of *Photoplay,* the gold digger provided a model for imitation as well as recognition that if they wanted to live beyond their wages of subsistence they had to attract men who would pay for their entertainment, take them out to a restaurant for a decent meal, and from whom they would receive gifts. For some working girls, gold digging appears to have been just another name for their participation in 'treating'. One reader of *Photoplay* wrote to Carolyn Van Wyck, the magazine's columnist

Fig. 5.7 Still from *Gentlemen Prefer Blondes* (Paramount, 1928), a lost film, showing gold diggers Lorelei Lee (Ruth Taylor) and Dorothy Shaw (Alice White). Image courtesy of Elizabeth Evans

who provided "Friendly Advice on Girls' Problems" with the following enquiry: "What do you think of gold-diggers? Do you think a girl should be one? I was brought up in the country and taught no nice girl would take gifts from a man, unless she was engaged to him, much less deliberately work him for presents. Now I am alone, a working girl in a large city. The girls in my office are constantly augmenting their incomes through men's pocketbooks, and getting away with it. They call me an idiot for not doing the same. What do you think?" Van Wyck replied that she had received many letters on whether to be a gold digger and wrote that the gold digger represented women "coming out in the open about their real intensions … it is the business of a girl commercializing her social life as well as her working one." However, Van Wyck did not recommend that girls should follow the example of "hard-boiled Lorelei Lee" in *Gentlemen Prefer Blondes*: "Yet old-fashioned as it may seem, I favor romance … romance and gold-digging are quite impossible together." Van Wyck had reservations about the more practical aspects: "Regarding gold-digging simply as a money making scheme, I don't think its price is worth the spoils. Take the ambitious little girl earning twenty dollars a week and the big butter and egg man who hints at diamonds. Actually few girls get the diamonds." She noted that the unsuccessful side of gold digging is not generally talked about and that it often ends in disaster for the girl.[55] In cross-class romance films, however, gold diggers tended to end up happily after they had fallen genuinely in love.

Ethnicity and the Cross-Class Romance

The great majority of cross-class romances in American films were between native-born, 'non-ethnic' Americans. A few included romantic protagonists from the 'new immigration' from eastern and southern Europe, which numbered 27 million between 1880 and 1924. Among those groups that were clearly distinguished as 'ethnic', the Irish were the most prominent in cross-class romances. The Irish were part of what became known as the 'old immigration'; by 1900, the number of American-born Irish was more than double the number of Irish-born Americans, and in the opening decades of the twentieth century, the Irish accounted for just under 5 % of American immigrants. Irish male immigrants continued to be concentrated in low-paying manual work, but second-generation Irish Americans, especially females, were entering white-collar occupations and were moving into middle-class neighborhoods. In 1910, about half of the marriages of second-generation Irish were with non-Irish; but as Catholics, Irish Americans continued to be set apart from native-born Protestants and had not moved into the elite stratum of the 'Protestant Establishment'.[56]

Many of the cross-class romances involving Irish Americans remained within the ethnic group. These included films in which Irish American girls from nouveau riche families visited Ireland and married into the Irish aristocracy who were either impoverished (*Castles For Two*, Jessie L. Lasky, 1917) or economically sound and able to provide the heroine with an authentic ancestral name and coat-of-arms (*A Yankee Princess*, Vitagraph, 1919). In *Irish Luck* (Famous Players-Lasky, 1925), the working-class, Irish American visiting Ireland is male, a New York traffic cop who has won a trip to Europe in a newspaper contest. He wins the daughter of an Irish aristocratic family after he uncovers a conspiracy to deprive her brother of his inheritance. The status obstacle facing a girl from a nouveau riche, Irish American family marrying into a socially elect American family of apparently aristocratic Irish origins was conveyed in *Marked Cards*

(Triangle, 1918). In this film, the mother of Ted Breslin, Mrs. J. De Barth Breslin, threatens to disinherit her son if he marries Ellen Shannon because her self-made politician father began as a menial laborer. Ellen attends a finishing school hoping to improve herself, but it is only after Ellen risks her reputation to save Ted from the gallows for a crime he did not commit that Mrs. Breslin welcomes her into the family.

The cross-class romances in which only one of the romantically involved couple was of Irish origins included *Spotlight Sadie* (Goldwyn Pictures Cor., 1918), *The Top O' the Morning* (Universal Film, 1922) and *Irene* (First National, 1926). These ended successfully with the marriage of the romantic couple, but in at least two films the Irish American heroines from poor families finally find true happiness within their own class: *Saturday Night*, which as we have seen also includes a failed cross-class marriage between an Irish American male and a wealthy female; and *Amarilly of Clothes-Line Alley* (Mary Pickford Film Corp., 1918) in which the cigarette girl and the wealthy sculptor conclude that their class differences make them unsuitable for each other and Amarilly returns to the Irish bartender.[57] Among the cross-class romance films involving Irish Americans with successful outcomes were those in which the poor protagonist was male, as in *Thirty a Week* (Goldwyn Pictures Corp., 1918) in which the chauffeur marries the daughter of his employer; *Hold Your Horses* (Goldwyn Pictures Corp., 1921) in which a street cleaner marries a society belle; and *Conductor 1492* (Warner, 1924) in which a streetcar conductor marries the daughter of a company president.

In three films, the poor Irish American side of the romantic couple is an orphan who has been brought up, or cared for, by a benevolent Jew. Rosie, an Irish orphan brought up by a Jewish pawnbroker in *Sweet Rosie O'Grady* (Columbia, 1926), rescues Victor McQuade, a youth from a Fifth Avenue family, from some ruffians and after some complications they marry. In the comedy *Old Clothes* (Jackie Coogan Productions, 1925), an elderly Jew and a young Irish boy, Tim Kelly, befriend an impoverished Irish girl, Mary Riley, who falls in love with Nathan Burke, the son of a wealthy Jewish family. Nathan's mother removes her opposition to the marriage after Tim saves the Burke family's fortune. In *The Barricade* (Robertson Cole, 1921), after the death of his Irish partner, the cigar store owner Jacob Solomon adopts the dead man's son, Robert Brennon, and mortgages his home to pay for the boy's education. Robert becomes a physician on the East Side, but the wealthy girl he marries induces him to open a practice on Fifth Avenue. Robert snubs his foster father but when

Jacob is about to be evicted from his store and home, Robert realizes his false pride, rescues Jacob from his financial predicament, and returns to the East Side where he is joined by his wife who also realizes her mistake.

The romance between the poor Irish girl and the wealthy Jewish male in *Old Clothes* was an exception, as most films that focused on the relationships between Irish and Jewish immigrants and included romance among their children were not cross-class romances. The subgenre of Irish Jewish stories with cross ethnic, intra-class romances included *Fools' Highway* (Universal, 1924); *One of the Bravest* (Gotham Productions, 1925); *Sweet Daddies* (First National Pictures, 1926); *Rose of the Tenements* (R-C Pictures Corp., 1926); *The Cohens and the Kellys* (Universal, 1926), which spawned a series of another six films released in the late 1920s and early 1930s; *Clancy's Kosher Wedding* (R-C Pictures Corp., 1927); *Frisco Sally Levy* (MGM, 1927); *Pleasure Before Business* (Columbia, 1927); and *Abie's Irish Rose* (Paramount Famous Lasky Corp., 1928). The Jews with whom the Irish interacted in these films were part of the new immigration that included large numbers of Catholic Poles and Italians, but there were no equivalent Italian Jewish or Polish Jewish subgenres of immigrant families interacting or inter-ethnic romances. One explanation for this was that in the eyes of Hollywood, the earlier arrival of the English-speaking Irish provided the children of Jewish immigrants with a model of assimilation into American society in spite of the fact that they were not part of the dominant Protestant groups.[58]

The Jewish immigrants at that time were closer to the Irish with respect to class than they were to the established native-born Jews of Sephardi descent and to other Ashkenazi Jews, primarily from Germany, who had adapted culturally into the USA. The new Jewish immigration from Eastern Europe, which numbered more than 2 million from 1880–1920, was seen as culturally alien by the established native-born Jews. Although the eastern European Jewish immigrants settled in many parts of the USA, a large proportion concentrated in New York, and films with Jewish characters were mostly set in New York, especially the Lower East Side or Jewish 'ghetto'.[59]

The few cross-class romances with Jewish characters included both intra-ethnic and inter-ethnic romances. In *The Good Provider* (Cosmopolitan Productions, 1927), a Jewish immigrant has moved from poverty to prosperity to bankruptcy and plans to take an overdone of sleeping powder so that his wife and children will receive the insurance on his life. His daughter's marriage into a wealthy Jewish family prevents his suicide and provides a happy end. A cross-class, intra-ethnic romance in *His People* (Universal, 1925) exacerbates the troubled relationship between a traditional immigrant father, Rabbi Cominsky, who has had to become a push-cart peddler in order to make a living, and his upwardly mobile, Americanized son, Morris. Of his two sons, the father prefers Morris who is studying to be a lawyer over Sammy, a prizefighter who is known as "Battling Rooney" and has an Irish sweetheart. The socially ambitious Morris becomes engaged to Ruth Stein, the daughter of a wealthy former judge with his own law firm, and to impress the judge and avoid the embarrassment of his ghetto parents Morris presents himself as an orphan who has advanced without any help from a family. Rabbi Cominsky endangers his life in the winter weather when he pawns his overcoat in order to buy Morris a dress suit, but Morris refuses to recognize him when he arrives at the Judge's home to confront his son. The old man apologizes before the Judge and his guests and leaves. It is Sammy, the loyal son despite his father's preference for Morris, who drags Morris home where, realizing his ungratefulness and disloyalty, Morris begs and receives forgiveness from his father. The grateful father gives his blessing to Sammy's union with his Irish sweetheart. In this film, the cross-class, intra-ethnic romance of one brother threatens the Jewish family whereas the intra-class, cross-ethnic romance of the other brother signals its union.[60]

Romances between Jews and non-Jews, whether intra-class, as in many of the Irish Jewish films, or cross-class, focus on the opposition of one or both families to religious intermarriage. In *Should a Baby Die?* (Hanover Film Company, 1916), the relationship of Lydia, the daughter of Jacob, a Jewish pawn broker, and Burton, the son of a wealthy Gentile family is opposed first by Jacob who suspects Burton's motives and then by Burton's parents. The religious and social obstacles are removed when Jacob proclaims that Lydia is not his daughter and it is discovered that Lydia's natural parents, who died when she was a baby, were Gentile millionaires.[61]

Two cross-class romances with Jewish heroines, one intra-ethnic and the other inter-ethnic, were based on stories written by Anzia Yezierska who had come as a young girl to America with her family and had moved from work in a sweatshop to becoming an author and celebrity. In *Hungry Hearts* (Goldwyn Pictures, 1922), the attempts by Rosenblatt, a prosperous, greedy owner of tenements, to prevent the marriage of his nephew David Kaplan, a newly accredited lawyer, to the daughter of a poor Jewish immigrant family living in one of his East Side tenements are defeated.

The film concludes with shots of David with his wife and her family living in a comfortable suburban home.[62] The happy ending of the film that conformed to Hollywood's cross-class romance formula is entirely at odds with Yezierska's short story, *When Lovers Dream,* on which the cross-class romance section of *Hungry Hearts* is based. In the story, the uncle of the medical student, David Novak, disapproves of his nephew's intention to marry Sara, the daughter of an impoverished "greenhorn" family. The uncle persuades David to leave Sara, who later marries a man whom she does not love. Yezierska was appalled at the happy ending that the studio appended to her story.[63]

Yezierska wrote what she perceived as a happy ending to her novel *Salome of the Tenements,* but her happy ending was not in accord with Hollywood's endings for cross-class romances and it was changed accordingly in the film. The cross-class, inter-ethnic romance in *Salome of the Tenements* (Famous Players-Lasky, 1925) begins when Sonya Mendel, a reporter for a Jewish newspaper, is assigned to interview John Manning, a millionaire who has endowed a settlement house on the East Side and seeks to protect its poor population from loan sharks. Manning is attracted to Sonya who has been named Salome by a co-worker because of Sonya's success as a "head-hunter" of men. Manning invites Sonya to dinner and Sonya persuades a dress designer who has moved up from sweatshop worker to operating a fashionable shop on Fifth Avenue to provide her with an attractive dress for the evening. In order to decorate her flat and thereby impress Manning, Sonya borrows $200 from "Banker Ben," a loan shark, and promises in a note to repay him $1,500 after she has married Manning. Sonya and Manning marry and, knowing nothing of Sonya's dealings with Ben, Manning attempts to secure an indictment against him for usury. Ben refuses to return Sonya's note, tears up her proffered check, and slyly gives her a chance to steal the note from his safe in order to apprehend her and blackmail Manning. Ben proposes to Manning that he will not press charges of theft against Sonya if Manning refrains from prosecuting him. At first Manning is convinced that Sonya married him for his money but Sonya proves her love and is willing to sacrifice herself and go to prison rather than have her husband give up his attempts to help her people living in the East Side. Manning threatens to have the loan shark jailed for blackmail, forces him into accepting payment for the note, and is reconciled with Sonya (Fig. 5.8).

Salome of the Tenements is a lost film but it is clear that its story, which I have reconstructed from reviews of the time,[64] differed radically, particu-

Fig. 5.8   Stills from *Salome of the Tenements* (Famous Players-Lasky, 1925), a lost film. John Manning (Godfrey Tearle), a millionaire WASP, invites Sonya Mendel (Jetta Goudal), a reporter for a Jewish newspaper, to dinner. The second still shows their relationship in crisis after their marriage. Images courtesy of Michel Derrien

larly in its representation of Manning and its ending, from Yezierska's novel. The novel, unlike the film, dwells on the hypocrisy of the 'good works' of the privileged class and presents a radical critique of the settlement projects that aspired to Americanize or 'Anglo-Saxonize' the immigrants—in this case, the Eastern European Jews. Sonya in the novel succeeds in marrying Manning, the WASP, but he is a restrained, aloof man who is unable to respond to Sonya's Jewish emotional nature. Sonya comes to realize that her husband's settlement is like the others that keep the poor down and grateful for the little they receive. Manning is unable to see the hypocrisy behind his liberal reforms, and their marriage breaks down when Sonya reveals her deceit over the loan she took and Manning reacts with anti-Semitic slurs. Sonya leaves Manning and their Fifth Avenue home, returns to the Lower East Side, works for a time as a waitress to save enough to go to a school of design, and becomes a successful designer. Thus, Sonya in the novel achieves socio-economic mobility as a career woman rather than through marriage to a millionaire. The Manning of the novel is described an undermining Sonya's personality, whereas the heroic Manning of the movie is her savior.[65]

All of the cross-class romances that I found with Italian American pro-tagonists are cross-ethnic. A budding romance between Maria Maretti, a manicurist in a large hotel, and James Morgan, a wealthy guest in *The Manicure Girl* (Famous Players-Lasky, 1925), comes to an end when Maria discovers that James is married and she returns to her Italian boyfriend, an electrician. In the other cross-class, cross-ethnic romances between poor Italian girls and wealthy men (*The Criminal*, New York Motion Picture Corporation, 1916, *Who Will Marry Me?* Bluebird Photoplays, 1919, *The Slave Market*, producer uncertain, 1921), the romance ends successfully as does the romance between an Italian American waiter and a society girl in *Society Snobs* (Selznick Pictures Corp, 1921).

There was little possibility that a cross-class romance with African American protagonists would also be a cross-ethnic one in this period. In the first feature-length film produced by a black-owned company, *The Homesteader* (Micheaux Book and Film Company, 1919) an African-American male falls in love with a woman whom he believes is white and they are only able to unite after he discovers that she has an African American heritage.[66] In addition to the very few black-owned film companies, there were also a few white-owned studios that produced films with African American casts for African-American audiences. It was one such company, a Philadelphia studio named the Colored Players that produced a cross-class romance, *The Scar of Shame* (1927).

Like other melodramas produced for African American audiences by both black-owned and white-owned companies, *The Scar of Shame* expressed the values of the black middle-class of the time and was intended to 'uplift' the African American masses. The hero Alvin Hilliard is an ambitious African American composer who lives in a "select boarding house" in a black neighborhood in Philadelphia. An intertitle introduces him as "a young man of refined tastes, a love of music and the finer things in life." Clear contrasts are made in the opening scenes between Alvin and the drunken, brutal Spike, the step-father of the beautiful mulatto, Louise, who is seen washing clothes and dreaming of a comfortable life with a maid and a wealthy beau who brings her flowers. Alvin rescues Louise from Spike when he attempts to strike her, and takes her into the boarding house where the good-hearted landlady agrees that Louise can work and live there. Alvin opines: "This is another instance of the injustices some of the women of our race are constantly subjected to, mainly through lack of knowledge of the higher aims in life."

After Alvin rescues Louise from further attempted assaults, one by Eddie, a cigar-smoking, loudly-dressed gambler, and another by Spike, Alvin proposes marriage to Louise, telling her that Spike would not molest her once she becomes his wife. After their marriage, Eddie and Spike conspire to kidnap Louise and put her to work to attract customers in a speakeasy that Eddie intends to establish. Eddie sends Alvin a false telegram that his mother is ill, and it is at this point that the class differences between Alvin and Louise sets them apart. Alvin cannot take Louise with him to his mother because he has not told his mother of his marriage and when Louise protests Alvin explains: "Caste is one of the things mother is very determined about—and you—don't belong to our set." The use of the world caste in this and other intertitles of the film denotes a more rigid system than the more appropriate term class and was used later by some scholars to refer to the racial stratification of whites and blacks in America. Louise is hurt and annoyed and when she picks up her brown doll that Alvin trod on unintentionally when he was leaving, she exclaims: "Poor little thing! You too had to be a victim of caste!"

Louise discovers a letter to Alvin from his mother recommending a girl who would make him a good wife because she is a "lady and socially one of our set." Louise tears up the letter as well as their marriage certificate, packs her clothes, and leaves her wedding ring. The plot takes a heightened melodramatic turn when Alvin discovers he has been tricked and returns; he confronts Eddie, Louise is shot in the affray leaving a "scar of shame" on her neck, Louise gives a false testimony against Alvin who is jailed. Alvin escapes from jail, takes up a new life under an assumed name as a piano teacher and falls in mutual love with Alice, the daughter of a lawyer. By coincidence, Eddie has set up his club in the same town as Alvin has settled and Alice's father who appears to be having an affair with Louise, and unaware of her relationship to Alvin, introduces them to each other in Eddie's club where she works. Louise tries to win Alvin back and when she fails she takes poison and leaves a letter for Alice's father in which she explains that she had been the wife of Alvin but that their "stations in life were different" and that Alvin had married her without loving her to protect her from a cruel step-father. Alvin is vindicated and Alice's father pronounces on Louise: "A child of environment!—If she had been taught the finer things in life, the higher aims, the higher hopes, she would not be lying cold in death—Oh! Our people have much to learn." The film ends with Alvin and Alice embracing.

Whites are entirely absent from *The Scar of Shame* and it is the "environment" that is blamed for producing criminals like Eddie, drunks like Spike and fallen women like Louise. The film suggests that, whereas lower-class African Americans are harmed by the environment, middle-class African Americans had freed themselves from it and, in these circumstances, a marriage between a middle-class and lower-class African American was bound to fail.[67] Films of romance across the classes among 'non-ethnic' Americans or between WASPs and ethnic whites were more likely to have happy endings.

NOTES

1. After 1920 far fewer films depicted women as victims of rape or attempted rape. The number of such films listed in the American Film Institute Catalog dropped from 24 in 1920 to 4 in 1921, and this low number continued throughout the 1920s.
2. Lea Jacobs, *The Decline of Sentiment: American Film in the 1920s* (Berkeley: University of California Press, 2008), 184–187.
3. *Exhibitors Trade Review*, June 9, 1923, 73.
4. *Variety*, June 23, 1922, 34. On the distaste of film critics in the 1920s for melodrama see Jacobs, *The Decline of Sentiment*.
5. Scott Simmon, *Program Notes to DVD More Treasures From American Film Archives 1894–1931* (San Francisco: National Film Preservation Foundation, 2004), 151–155; Kevin Brownlow, *Behind the Mask of Innocence: Films of Social Conscience in the Silent Era* (New York: Alfred A. Knopf, 1990), 151–156.
6. Stephen Sharot, "The 'New Woman', Star Personas, and Cross-Class Romance Films in 1920s America," *Journal of Gender Studies* 19.1 (2010): 73–86.
7. Susan Porter Benson, *Counter Cultures: Saleswomen, Managers, and Consumers in American Department Stores, 1890–1940* (Urbana: University of Illinois Press, 1986), 134–138, 181–187.
8. Benson, *Counter Cultures*, 5, 131, 230.
9. Daniel Horowitz, *The Morality of Spending; Attitudes toward the Consumer Society in America, 1875–1940* (Baltimore: Johns Hopkins University Press, 1985), xxvii; Chip Rhodes, *Structures of the Jazz Age: Mass Culture, Progressive Education, and Racial Disclosures in American Modernism* (London: Verso, 1998), 84; William Leach, *Land of Desire: Merchants, Power, and the Rise of a New American Culture* (New York: Vintage Books, 1993), 272.
10. Stuart Ewen, *Captains of Consciousness: Advertising and the Social Roots of the Consumer Culture*, (New York: Basic Books, 2008 [1974]), 57–58.
11. Susan Porter Benson, *Household Accounts: Working-Class Family Economies in the Interwar United States* (Ithaca, NY: Cornell University Press, 2007); Lizabeth Cohen, *Making a New Deal: Industrial Workers in Chicago, 1919–1939* (Cambridge: Cambridge University Press, 1990), 109–112, 157, 325–327, 356–357.

12. David M. Gordon, Richard Edwards, Michael Reich, *Segmented Work, Divided Workers: The Historical Transformation of Labor in the United States* (Cambridge: Cambridge University Press, 1982), 151.
13. William H. Chafe, *The Paradox of Change: American Women in the 20th Century* (New York: Oxford University Press, 1991), 65–71.
14. Rita Felski, *The Gender of Modernity* (Cambridge, MA: Harvard University Press, 1995).
15. Nancy F. Cott, *The Grounding of Modern Feminism* (New Haven, CT: Yale University Press, 1987), 172–174.
16. Joshua Zeitz, *Flapper: A Madcap Story of Sex, Style, Celebrity, and the Women Who Made America Modern* (New York: Three Rivers Press, 2006), 203–5; Angela J. Latham, *Posing a Threat: Flappers, Chorus Girls, and Other Brazen Performers of the American 1920s* (Hanover: Wesleyan University Press, 2000).
17. Christina Simmons, "Modern Sexuality and the Myth of Victorian Repression," in Kathy Peiss and Christina Simmons, eds., *Passion and Power: Sexuality in History* (Philadelphia, PA: Temple University Press, 1989), 157–177.
18. Joanne J. Meyerowitz, *Women Adrift: Independent Wage Earners in Chicago, 1880–1930* (Chicago: University of Chicago Press, 1988), xxii–xxiii, 117–125.
19. Ewen, *Captains of Consciousness*, 177–179.
20. Cott, *The Grounding of Modern Feminism*, 147–9, 156–60, 189–91; Lois Scharf, *To Work and To Wed: Female Employment, Feminism, and the Great Depression* (Westport, Conn.: Greenwood Publishing Group, 1980), 41.
21. Eva Illouz, *Consuming the Romantic Utopia: Love and the Cultural Contradictions of Capitalism* (Berkeley: University of California Press, 1997).
22. Unless otherwise stated the major source for the details of the narratives of the films discussed in this chapter is the American Film Institute online catalog.
23. Motion Picture News (hereafter MPN), April 19, 1919, 2526.
24. *Young Romance* can be seen on DVD (Image Entertainment).
25. Motion Picture World (hereafter MPW), February 13, 1915, 1046.
26. MPW, April 7, 1917, 153.
27. MPW, February 22, 1919, 1110.
28. MPN, June 14, 1919, 4025.
29. MPW, October 20, 1917, 446, 440.
30. MPW, June 14, 1919, 1110.
31. MPW, February 12, 1916, 973.
32. MPW, October 26, 1918, 545.

33. *Exhibitors Herald*, March 25, 1922, 55; *Exhibitors Trade Review*, June 17, 1922, 167.
34. Quote in Steven J. Ross, *Working-Class Hollywood: Silent Film and the Shaping of Class in America* (Princeton, NJ: Princeton University Press, 1998), 207.
35. Ross, *Working-Class Hollywood*, 203, 207. *Saturday Night* can be seen on DVD (Alpha Home Entertainment).
36. Keren M. Chandler, "Agency and *Stella Dallas*: Audience, Melodramatic Directives, and Social Determinism in 1920s America," *Arizona Quarterly* 51.4 (1995): 27–44. *Stella Dallas* can be seen on DVD (Sunrise Silents).
37. *Fine Manners* is on DVD (Grapevine Video).
38. MPW, July 27, 1918, 586.
39. *The Golden Chance* can be seen on DVD and *Forbidden Fruit* can be seen on YouTube. See also, Sumiko Higashi, *Cecil B. DeMille and American Culture: The Silent Era* (Berkeley: University of California Press, 1994), 93–100.
40. Jennifer Parchesky, "Lois Weber's *The Blot*: Rewriting Melodrama, Reproducing the Middle Class," *Cinema Journal* 39.1 (1999): 23–53. Additional useful discussions are Shelly Stamp's commentary on the DVD and E. Ann Kaplan, *Motherhood and Representation: The Mother in Popular Culture and Melodrama* (London: Routledge, 1996), 135–138.
41. Robert C. Allen, *Horrible Prettiness: Burlesque and American Culture* (Chapel Hill: University of North Carolina Press, 1991), 201–212.
42. Virginia Brooks, *My Battle With Vice* (New York: Macauley, 1915), 114.
43. Constance Rosenblum, *Gold Digger: The Outrageous Life and Times of Peggy Hopkins Joyce* (New York: Metropolitan Books, 2000), 84–85.
44. Jacobs, *Decline of Sentiment*, 200–201.
45. W.I. Thomas quoted in Meyerowitz, *Women Adrift*, 137.
46. Janet Straiger, *Bad Women: Regulating Sexuality in Early American Cinema* (Minneapolis: University of Minnesota Press, 1995), 151–55; Janet Straiger, "*Les Belles Dames sans Merci*, Femmes Fatales, Vampires, Vamps, and Gold Diggers: The Transformation and Narrative Value of Aggressive Fallen Women," in Vicki Callahan, ed., *Reclaiming the Archive: Feminism and Film History* (Detroit: Wayne State University Press, 2010), 41.
47. *Variety*, September 13, 1923, 28; Jacobs, *Decline of Sentiment*, 200–201.
48. MPN, October 20, 1923, 1891.
49. Jacobs, *The Decline of Sentiment*, 209–215.
50. *Variety*, November 11 1925, 39; Jacobs, *Decline of Sentiment*, 203–204; *New York Times*, November 2, 1925.
51. *Variety*, January 8, 1928, 13.
52. *New York Times*, January 16, 1928, 26.

53. *Exhibitors Herald and Moving Picture World*, March 17, 1928, 56, March 24 1928, 48–49; MPN, January 28, 1928, 276, February 18, 1928, 571, February 25, 651, March 3, 1928, 747.
54. *Photoplay*, February, 1927, 82.
55. *Photoplay*, February, 1927, 82.
56. Jay P. Dolan, *The Irish Americans: A History* (New York: Bloomsbury Press, 2008), 92–94; Kevin Kenny, *The American Irish: A History* (Abingdon, Oxon: Routledge, 2014), 181, 184–185; Timothy J. Meagher, *The Columbia Guide to Irish American History* (New York: Columbia University Press, 2005), 95, 103–107.
57. *Amarilly of Clothes-line Alley* is available on DVD (Milestone Collection).
58. Patricia Erens, *The Jew in American Cinema* (Bloomington: Indiana University Press, 1984), 81–82; M. B. B. Biskupski, *Hollywood's War with Poland, 1939–1945* (Lexington: University Press of Kentucky, 2010).
59. By 1910 Jews accounted for about one-quarter of New York's population, and in 1927 forty-four percent of American Jews lived in New York. Hasia R. Diner, *The Jews of the United States, 1654 to 2000* (Berkeley: University of California Press, 2004), 106, 194.
60. *His People* is available on DVD (Grapevine). A detailed account of the film, including its critical and commercial success, is provided by Kevin Brownlow, *Behind the Mask of Innocence: Films of Social Conscience in the Silent Era* (New York: Alfred A. Knofp, 1990), 392–406.
61. *Motography*, February 12, 1916, 375–376.
62. *Hungry Hearts* is on DVD (Yiddish Film Collection) and there is a detailed account in Brownlow, *Behind the Mask of Innocence*, 392–406.
63. Louis Levitas Herriksen, *Anzia Yezierska: A Writer's Life* (New Brunswick, NJ: Rutgers University Press, 1988), 167. See also, Lisa Botshon, "Anzia Yezierska and the Marketing of the Jewish Immigrants in 1920s Hollywood," *Journal of Narrative Theory* 30.3 (2000): 287–312.
64. *Film Daily*, March 8, 1925, 10; *New York Times*, February 24, 1925; *Variety*, February 25, 1925, 31.
65. Anzia Yezierska, *Salome of the Tenements* (University of Illinois Press, 1995 [1923]). On the novel see the introduction to this edition by Guy Wilentz. See also, Catherine Rottenberg, *Performing Americanness: Race, Class and Gender in Modern African-American and Jewish-American Literature* (Lebanon: University Press of New England, 2008), 53–69, and Douglas J. Goldstein, "The Political Dimensions of Desire in Anzia Yezierska's 'The Lost Beautifulness' and Salome of the Tenements," *Studies in American Fiction* 35.1 (2007): 43–66.
66. Jacqueline Najuma Stewart, *Migrating to the Movies: Cinema and Black Urban Modernity* (Berkeley: University of California Press, 2005), 220–221.

67. *The Scar of Shame* can be seen on YouTube. For analyses see Thomas Cripps, "Race Movies as Voices of the Black Bourgeoisie: The Scar of Shame (1927)," in John E. O'Connor and Martin A. Jackson, eds., *American History/American Film: Interpreting the Hollywood Image* (New York: Ungar Publishing Company, 1988), 39–55; Jane Gaines, "The Scar of Shame: Skin Color and Caste in Black Silent Melodrama," *Cinema Journal* 26.4 (1987): 3–21.

BIBLIOGRAPHY

Allen, Robert C. *Horrible Prettiness: Burlesque and American Culture.* Chapel Hill: University of North Carolina Press, 1991.

Benson, Susan Porter. *Counter Cultures: Saleswomen, Managers, and Consumers in American Department Stores, 1890–1940.* Urbana: University of Illinois Press, 1986.

———. *Household Accounts: Working-Class Family Economies in the Interwar United States.* Ithaca, NY: Cornell University Press, 2007.

Biskupski, M. B. B. *Hollywood's War with Poland, 1939–1945.* Lexington: University Press of Kentucky, 2010.

Brooks, Virginia. *My Battle With Vice.* New York: Macauley, 1915.

Botshon, Lisa. "Anzia Yezierska and the Marketing of the Jewish Immigrants in 1920s Hollywood," *Journal of Narrative Theory* 30.3 (2000): 287–312.

Brownlow, Kevin. *Behind the Mask of Innocence: Films of Social Conscience in the Silent Era.* New York: Alfred A. Knopf, 1990.

Chafe, William H. *The Paradox of Change: American Women in the 20th Century.* New York: Oxford University Press, 1991.

Chandler, Keren M. "Agency and *Stella Dallas*: Audience, Melodramatic Directives, and Social Determinism in 1920s America," *Arizona Quarterly* 51.4 (1995): 27–44.

Cohen, Lizabeth. *Making a New Deal: Industrial Workers in Chicago, 1919–1939.* Cambridge: Cambridge University Press, 1990.

Cott, Nancy R. *The Grounding of Modern Feminism.* New Haven, CT: Yale University Press, 1987.

Cripps, Thomas. "Race Movies as Voices of the Black Bourgeoisie: The Scar of Shame (1927)," in John E. O'Connor and Martin A. Jackson, eds. *American History/American Film: Interpreting the Hollywood Image.* New York: Ungar Publishing Company, 1988, 39–55.

Diner, Hasia R. *The Jews of the United States, 1654 to 2000.* Berkeley: University of California Press, 2004.

Dolan, Jay P. *The Irish Americans: A History.* New York: Bloomsbury Press, 2008.

Erens, Patricia. *The Jew in American Cinema.* Bloomington: Indiana University Press, 1984.

Ewen, Stuart. *Captains of Consciousness: Advertising and the Social Roots of the Consumer Culture*. New York: Basic Books, 2008 [1974].

Felski, Rita. *The Gender of Modernity*. Cambridge, MA: Harvard University Press, 1995.

Gaines, Jane. "The Scar of Shame: Skin Color and Caste in Black Silent Melodrama," *Cinema Journal* 26.4 (1987): 3–21.

Gordon, David M., Richard Edwards, Michael Reich. *Segmented Work, Divided Workers: The Historical Transformation of Labor in the United States*. Cambridge: Cambridge University Press, 1982.

Herriksen, Louis Levitas. *Anzia Yezierska: A Writer's Life*. New Brunswick, NJ: Rutgers University Press, 1988.

Higashi, Sumiko. *Cecil B. DeMille and American Culture: The Silent Era*. Berkeley: University of California Press, 1994.

Horowitz, David. *The Morality of Spending; Attitudes toward the Consumer Society in America, 1875–1940*. Baltimore: Johns Hopkins University Press, 1985.

Illouz, Eva. *Consuming the Romantic Utopia: Love and the Cultural Contradictions of Capitalism*. Berkeley: University of California Press, 1997.

Jacobs, Lea. *The Decline of Sentiment: American Film in the 1920s*. Berkeley: University of California Press, 2008.

Kaplan, E. Ann. *Motherhood and Representation: The Mother in Popular Culture and Melodrama*. London: Routledge, 1996.

Kenny, Kevin. *The American Irish: A History*. Abingdon, Oxon: Routledge, 2014.

Latham, Angela J. *Posing a Threat: Flappers, Chorus Girls, and Other Brazen Performers of the American 1920s*. Hanover: Wesleyan University Press, 2000.

Leach, William. *Land of Desire: Merchants, Power, and the Rise of a New American Culture*. New York: Vintage Books, 1993.

Meagher, Timothy J. *The Columbia Guide to Irish American History*. New York: Columbia University Press, 2005.

Meyerowitz, Joanne J. *Women Adrift: Independent Wage Earners in Chicago, 1880–1930*. Chicago: University of Chicago Press, 1988.

Parchesky, Jennifer. "Lois Weber's *The Blot*: Rewriting Melodrama, Reproducing the Middle Class," *Cinema Journal* 39.1 (1999): 23–53.

Rhodes, Chip. *Structures of the Jazz Age: Mass Culture, Progressive Education, and Racial Disclosures in American Modernism*. London: Verso, 1998.

Rosenblum, Constance. *Gold Digger: The Outrageous Life and Times of Peggy Hopkins Joyce*. New York: Metropolitan Books, 2000.

Ross, Steven J. *Working-Class Hollywood: Silent Film and the Shaping of Class in America*. Princeton: Princeton University Press, 1998.

Rottenberg, Catherine. *Performing Americanness: Race, Class and Gender in Modern African-American and Jewish-American Literature*. Lebanon: University Press of New England, 2008.

Scharf, Lois. *To Work and to Wed: Female Employment, Feminism, and the Great Depression.* Westport, CT: Greenwood Publishing Group, 1980.

Sharot, Stephen. "The 'New Woman', Star Personas, and Cross-Class Romance Films in 1920s America," *Journal of Gender Studies* 19.1 (2010): 73–86.

Simmon, Scott. *Program Notes to DVD More Treasures From American Film Archives 1894–1931.* San Francisco: National Film Preservation Foundation, 2004.

Simmons, Christina. "Modern Sexuality and the Myth of Victorian Repression," in Kathy Peiss and Christina Simmons, eds. *Passion and Power: Sexuality in History.* Philadelphia, PA: Temple University Press, 1989, 157–177.

Staiger, Janet. *Bad Women: Regulating Sexuality in Early American Cinema.* Minneapolis: University of Minnesota Press, 1995.

———. "*Les Belles Dames sans Merci*, Femmes Fatales, Vampires, Vamps, and Gold Diggers: The Transformation and Narrative Value of Aggressive Fallen Women." in Vicki Callahan, ed. *Reclaiming the Archive: Feminism and Film History.* Detroit: Wayne State University Press, 2010, 32–57.

Stewart, Jacqueline Najuma. *Migrating to the Movies: Cinema and Black Urban Modernity.* Berkeley: University of California Press, 2005.

Yezierska, Anzia. *Salome of the Tenements.* Champaign, IL: University of Illinois Press, 1995 [1923].

Zeitz, Joshua. *Flapper: A Madcap Story of Sex, Style, Celebrity, and the Women Who Made America Modern.* New York: Three Rivers Press, 2006.

CHAPTER 6

The Cross-Class Romance in the Depression

The Great Depression of the 1930s proved to be as congenial a context for the cross-class romance film as did the unequal prosperity and surge of consumerism of the 1920s. The most basic elements of the formula remained the same: in 74 films of my list of 111 cross-class romance films released between 1929 and 1942, the male protagonist is rich and the female protagonist is poor; most of the romances are successful insofar as 84 of the films end with marriage or the promise of marriage. Three of the films had two cross-class romances, one between a poor girl and rich man and another between a rich girl and poor man, and in all three films the poor protagonists forsake their wealthy would-be lovers and end up together. The proportion of cross-class romances in which the wealthy protagonist is female (30 %) was considerably higher in the 1930s than in the 1910s and 1920s, but in some of these films the relationship of the rich female is not with a working-class man but with a middle-class man, often a reporter, and in these, mainly screwball comedies, the romance is almost inevitably successful. Where the male is wealthy, the female is almost invariably working or lower class in occupation, such as maid, sales-girl, stenographer or chorus girl.

Only two of the cross-class romances of this period were directed by a woman (Dorothy Arzner) and, whereas females were involved in the writing of 61 of the 111 cross-class romances, only 9 of the films were written exclusively by women. Of the total number of script-writing credits for the cross-class romances, 91 were female and 156 were male.

© The Author(s) 2017
S. Sharot, *Love and Marriage Across Social Classes in American Cinema*,
DOI 10.1007/978-3-319-41799-8_6

Many of the motifs of the cross-class romance films of the 1920s continued into the 1930s, but although in some films there is little if any acknowledgement of the Depression, in other films the Depression is shown to weigh heavily on the dilemmas faced by the working-class heroines. There is greater reflexivity with respect to issues of class in the 1930s films, there are more frequent negative portrayals of upper-class characters, and gold digging heroines are more numerous. Even when there were no explicit references to the Depression, its effects were hard to ignore even in the often fairy tale-like narrative of the cross-class romance. The effects of the Depression may explain the increased ratio of cross-class romance dramas to comedies in the early 1930s. The predominance of comedies in the second half of the 1920s was reversed in the early 1930s, with a peak in 1931 of thirteen dramas, two comedies and one comedy-drama. In the second half of the decade, comedies again predominated over dramas by a ratio of about two to one.

DEPRESSION AND DOWNWARD MOBILITY

The New York Stock Exchange crash in October 1929 was not immediately perceived as the beginning of an extraordinary recession, and it was not until the collapse of hundreds of banks as depositors withdrew their savings in late 1930 that the extent of the crisis became apparent. Americans realized that they were living in a great crisis as numerous banks and businesses failed, factories closed, thousands lost their life savings, and hundreds of thousands lost their homes. The winter of 1932–1933 was the most desperate of the Depression; unemployment rose from 1.5 million, or 3 % of the labor force in October 1929, to 12–14 million or a quarter of the workforce in 1933, and an estimated one-third of those who remained in work held their jobs by working part-time and for lower wages. National income declined from $81 billion in 1929 to $41 billion in 1932, and, taking into account price decreases, per capita income fell from $681 in 1929 to $495 in 1933. Roosevelt's presidential campaign, his promises of vigorous action, and his administrative reforms, following his inauguration in March 1933, reduced feelings of fear and despair among large sections of the population, but the economy remained stagnant and the first signs of economic recovery appeared only in 1935. The improvement was short-lived as the cutting back of government spending in 1937 precipitated a recession almost as severe as 1932–1933. Increased government spending in 1938 saw some recovery but the Depression only came to an end when America entered World War II. Unemployment never dropped much below 8 million during the 1930s, and nearly 10 million—over 17 % of the labor force—remained out of work in 1939.[1]

Most cross-class romances involved the upward mobility of the poor protagonist, in most cases a female, but the experience of many workers, male and female, during the Great Depression was of downward mobility.[2] Downward mobility is to be expected during economic recession, and there was little structural change in the economy and occupational structure that would have provided opportunities for upward mobility. One obvious form of downward mobility for many was the loss of jobs and failure to secure alternative work. Many were made homeless and perhaps as many as 2 million took to the road as 'tramps'.[3] The youths who succeeded to enter the labor force often did so by lowering their expectations, and many workers remained in work by accepting reductions in wages or by downward occupational mobility.

For a sizeable sector of the population, having almost nothing was nothing new, but the continuing advance of consumerism encouraged feelings of economic deprivation. An ostentatious display of wealth no longer seemed appropriate and there were some signs of downscaling, such as the decline in sales of luxury cars, but there were clear indications of the advance of consumerism, such as the increase in the number of new commercial products and the doubling of loans for household durables between 1933 and 1939.[4] The low and irregular incomes of a large sector of the working class meant that they remained marginal to consumerism,[5] but the continuation of the consumerist trend in the 1930s encouraged material aspirations even among the poor. For those who had formerly succeeded to move into the middle class and had higher aspirations, the Depression caused anger and consternation over unrealized expectations of mobility and material well-being. Belief in the American Dream was shaken, but it was not destroyed.[6]

Discontent was widespread but amorphous during 1930–1932, the last years of the Hoover administration. Organized looting of food and anti-eviction struggles ('rent riots') were common and the unemployed marched in protest in a number of cities. The victory of Roosevelt injected some optimism among Americans, but despite some successes, it soon became clear that there was no radical improvement. Many of the letters sent by thousands of Americans to President Roosevelt and Mrs. Roosevelt included requests for material support and expressed shame and humiliation over the outward signs of the writers' deprivation. The young were extremely sensitive to the symbols of class difference and were angry that they were unable to afford the clothes worn by their more fortunate class-mates. Some letters expressed resentment at the extremes of inequality, and although they supported the work ethic and acquisitive individualism, there was also a vague anti-capitalist sentiment. A significant minority of the letter writers wrote of the injustice of a society where a few enjoyed luxuries and the many had not even the bare necessities.[7]

Economic necessity forced many married women into the work force, but despite the increase in married women workers, they remained a minority, and even at the lowest family income levels only about a quarter of married women worked.[8] Opposition to the employment of married women increased as men lost their jobs, and it was legislated against by government at all levels.[9] The argument against married women working was that they took jobs from men, but the gender segregation of occu-pations made this unlikely; 36 % of married women were employed in domestic and personal services, and another 30 % worked in apparel and canning factories. A large proportion of women's jobs were part-time and seasonal, and although minimum wage legislation improved their situa-tion, most women at the end of the decade barely earned a living wage. Opportunities in the higher occupational ranks were limited by profes-sional college quotas on women,[10] and by widespread discrimination against women in the appointment of professionals and managers. Many women in managerial positions were replaced by men and were only able to remain in employment by accepting demotion. Many young women dropped their academic or vocational pursuits, lowered their career goals, and sought security in marriage.[11]

Downward mobility was common among many categories of workers during the Depression, but downward mobility as a strategy for remaining in the labor force appears to have been more common among women. Although the sex segregation of occupations initially provided some pro-tection for women workers, white-collar jobs, sales, and services were not unaffected, and many women remained employed by taking less desirable jobs. When they lost their positions, women clerics took jobs as waitresses, waitresses moved into laundries, and laundry workers became domestic workers. At the bottom of the employment hierarchy, black women and older white women were forced out of employment.[12] The dominant images of the Depression were those of males seeking work and relief at employment and welfare offices and queuing at soup kitchens and in bread lines.[13] The suffering of women received less exposure, but many young girls joined boys on the road as hobos, and some turned to prostitution as an alternative to hunger.[14]

Mobility through marriage was considered an important trajectory of mobility for women, but the Depression cast a shadow on this possibility as the marriage rate declined. Many unemployed men defended the norm of the male breadwinner role and forbade their wives to go out to work. Families reduced their expenditures and drew upon their savings in order to avoid the wife working. However, many families were left with no choice and it has been estimated that in the worst Depression years a third of all women workers were the sole support of their families, while over half augmented the income earned by other family members. Men insisted that their wives' employment was a temporary expedient until they regained employment, but this became difficult to maintain as the Depression continued.[15] In some families, the loss of the male breadwinner role resulted in a partial or complete emancipation of the wife from her husband's authority, and some men felt a sense of deep humiliation as a consequence of their economic dependence on their wives and daughters.[16] Thus, the Depression accentuated fundamental social anxieties of both women and men regarding class and gender divisions.

MOBILITY FOR WOMEN

Mobility for women through marriage rather than work was legitimized by what a social critic, Ruth McKenney, called in 1940 the "immense body of propaganda for the dream world of romantic love."[17] Most films, like most popular literature, promoted this "dream world," but a bestseller that was critical of a woman's sacrifice for love, *Back Street* by Fannie Hurst, was soon followed up by a film version. The heroine, Ray Schmidt, played in the 1932 film by Irene Dunne, leaves her job as a clothing store clerk-buyer to become a kept woman by a married banker, and her life becomes a tragic one with dire psychological and, finally, economic consequences. Laura Hapke analyzes the book as one of a few but significant number of 1930s novels that "dramatized the soul- and potentially life-destroying effects of feminine love slavery."[18] Hapke admits, however, that none of the book's readers at the time understood that *Back Street* contained a "coded warning to women workers in the Depression on the wages of love." Contemporary reviewers "misread the cautionary message at the novel's core as embracing the social ostracism leveled at the 'other woman'."[19] Although Fannie Hurst supported women wage earners and was critical of those women able to work who let men support them, the film, like the novel, was not read as a call for women to work rather than marry. An alternative reading was that a woman should not become dependent on a man without the benefit of wedlock.

When women succeeded in business or the professions in spite of limited opportunities, they were unlikely to find approval. Business magazines of the 1930s were wary of ambitious women and were critical of those who were more interested in a career than in marriage.[20] Working women appeared in films of the 1930s more frequently than in later decades, but the message conveyed by the films was that even if a woman was successful in her profession or in business, she would only be happy and find meaning in her life if she gives up working for love, marriage, or her husband's esteem.[21]

It was rare in cross-class romance films for a woman's commitment to a career to influence her decision to decline a rich man's offer of marriage, but this could occur if the career was in entertainment. An example is *Dancing Lady* (MGM, 1933) in which Janie (Joan Crawford) is first seen by Todd (Franchot Tone), a rich playboy, doing a partial striptease in a cheap burlesque where Todd is slumming. He introduces her to the MGM world of gorgeous gowns and art-deco interiors, and when Todd proposes marriage, his family, a sister and a grandmother, have no objections. The major obstacle to their marriage is Janie's preference for a dancing career, and she succeeds by starring in an expensive musical in a large theater. Broadway attracts her more than the idle life of Park Avenue, and the more masculine Patch (Clark Gable), her producer, replaces Todd as the man in her life. The notion that a career in entertainment should not be abandoned for marriage was reinforced by fan magazine discourse that on occasion presented female stars, particularly after their divorces, as career women who did not forsake their careers for men.[22]

THEMES OF CROSS-CLASS ROMANCE FILMS

A number of common motifs in cross-class romance films of the 1930s relate to the representation of class and gender and their relationships: firstly, the fluidity of the class structure as demonstrated by the victory of disinterested love over class and by class passing; secondly, the negative representations of the lifestyle of the upper class and—somewhat less common—of the lower class; thirdly, the redemption of the wealthy character by the working-class character who has internalized middle-class values; and fourthly, the reinforcement of the gender distinction. Some of these motifs did not fundamentally differ from those in the cross-class romance films of the previous two decades, but two motifs—the negative portrayal of the upper class and the redemption of the wealthy character by the working-class character—are more prominent and appear more frequently in the films of the 1930s. Although the portrayal of the wealthy as idle and insensitive to the plight of others was not new (the films of D. W. Griffith provide a number of examples), the Depression encouraged filmmakers to take a jaded view of the 'leisure class' whose extravagance and irresponsibility were seen by many as a cause of the economic woes.[23] Economic plight sharpened perceptions among many working-class and impoverished middle-class Americans of the disparities of wealth and social status in their society, and audiences were no doubt receptive to the critical and satiric portrayals of wealthy characters and the sympathetic portrayals of poor characters who demonstrated their moral superiority and their ability to reform the wealthy. However, the triumph of poor characters was accompanied by providing the audience with a vicarious experience of wealth, and criticism of wealthy characters did not extend to a critique of the class structure per se.

FLUIDITY OF CLASS STRUCTURE

It was rare for characters in cross-class romance films or in any other Hollywood films to discuss classes in an abstract or explicit manner. When they did approach the subject, the discussion was not on the class structure as such, but rather on the location of individuals within that structure. One such discussion takes place in the opening scene of *The Bride Wore Red* (MGM, 1937) between the elderly Count Amalia (George Zucco) and his young friend Rudi Pal (Robert Young). Although the exact nationality of the characters is left unclear, they are Europeans conducting their discussion in a casino in Trieste, and this non-American milieu might have been regarded by American filmmakers as an appropriate one for a discussion of class.

The Count proclaims that the location of individuals in the class structure is a matter of chance: "Life is a great roulette wheel." Rudi disagrees with the Count's assertion that all men are created equal and that there is nothing to distinguish Rudi from the waiter who is serving them apart from their clothes and societal locations; one waits at tables while the other is waited upon. In reply to the Count, who notes that the manners of waiters are often better than those of the people they serve, Rudi asserts that "breeding" separates him from the waiter and breeding is more than clothes and manners. 'Breeding' is a somewhat ambiguous term; it could have a biological connotation, but supposedly it is meant to refer here to Rudi's notion of the superior culture and patterns of behavior into which he and other members of the upper class were socialized.

The Count believes that class is a matter of appearances, and when they go slumming in the "lowest dive in Trieste" he tells Rudi that if he could take one of the poor girls working in the dive and have her properly washed, dressed and coiffured, Rudi would not be able to tell her apart from his fiancée. After Rudi leaves, the Count decides to act on his proposition and picking Anni (Joan Crawford), who sings in the dive, he enables her to buy expensive clothes and pose as a rich socialite at an exclusive hotel in the Austrian Alps where Rudi and his fiancée are staying. The Count's initiative suggests a Pygmalion theme, but he does not teach, rehearse or accompany Anni. He only provides the financial means for Anni's transformation from low-dive singer, with its suggestion of prostitution, to a wealthy lady, and, as befits Crawford's star persona, it is Anni who is responsible for her own transformation. It is established by the Count's comments that Anni speaks well and has "charming manners," which Anni admits she learnt from watching the ladies of the Count's world in the movies.[24] Anni only requires the appropriate clothes and the appearance of money to convince the upper-class guests of the hotel that she is from their class. The first time she dines at the hotel she does not have the knowledge of the appropriate table etiquette, but this is not noticed by other guests as she is dining alone. A waiter, who we have to infer is more perceptive of class signs than the upper-class guests, tells her what to order and what cutlery to use. The cross-class romance proceeds until Rudi proposes marriage to Anni, but it is evident that Rudi would not have proposed had he known her status and, after a telegram from the Count exposes her masquerade, Rudi reunites with his fiancée and Anni unites with the local postman in a true love match.[25]

Class consciousness proves to be an obstacle to cross-class romance in *The Bride Wore Red*, but the successful class passing in the film suggests that class consciousness is not based on essential class differences. The unsuccessful outcome of the cross-class romance in the film may be attributed, in part, to the assumption that class consciousness was stronger in Europe than in America. Most Hollywood cross-class romances occur in America and their most central theme is that class boundaries can be crossed and class obstacles can be overcome by disinterested love even in the depths of an economic depression.

There were a few unsuccessful cross-class romances but these were often not romances in the strict sense because the characters from poor backgrounds decide to leave—sometimes after marriage—their rich partners who in most cases they do not really love, for 'true' love with a non-wealthy, generally more worthy, partner. This is what happens in *Bought* (Warner, 1931), *Bed of Roses* (RKO, 1933) and *The Gilded Lady* (Paramount, 1935). In *Sinners in the Sun* (Paramount, 1932) and *Hands Across the Table* (Paramount, 1935), there are two poor protagonists who succeed in capturing rich partners, but they decide that love is more important than money and they end up with each other. A reversal of the pattern of a heroine giving up a rich man for a poor man is found in *Ten Cents a Dance* (Columbia, 1931). The dance hall girl refuses a rich businessman, who at first offers her arrangements that do not include marriage, for a poor, unemployed college graduate. The poor man turns out to be a womanizer, liar and thief, and the girl leaves him to return to the rich man who proposes that they marry after her divorce.

Two of the frequent obstacles that are generally overcome in cross-class romance films are that, firstly, one of the lovers (usually the poor character) has reservations as to the appropriateness of their relationship because of their class differences, and secondly, family members, usually of the rich character, oppose the relationship. The hesitation or reservations of the poor characters concerning the possibilities of crossing the class boundary are countered by the encouragement and arguments of the rich character. In *Gambling Lady* (Warner, 1934), when the wealthy Gary (Joel McCrea) proposes marriage to Lady Lee (Barbara Stanwyck), a professional gambler, she objects that she is from the 'other side of the tracks'. When he replies that she can move over the tracks, she says that his folks would not let her. When she repeats this concern as they arrive at the mansion of Gary's father, Gary responds that it is Lee who has to like "us," that is, his family and circle of friends, and he is confident that his widowed father will not object. In fact, when alone with Lee, Gary's father tests her by offering her a large sum of money, which, of course, she refuses.

In *Private Number* (Twentieth-Century Fox, 1936), Richard, the wealthy son (Robert Taylor) tries to overcome the reservations of his love object, Ellen, the parlor maid (Loretta Young) by stating the random placement of individuals within the class structure. When Ellen tells him she cannot go swimming with him in the mansion's lake because there is an hour reserved for the servants to go swimming, he replies that she has old-fashioned ideas: "In this day and age we believe in social equality."

She responds: "I'll believe in it to when I'm able to have servants." He then tries to overcome her objection by noting that class location is a matter of chance: "it's just an accident that I'm not working for your family. If it had gone the other way I would have been your chauffeur. Who knows!" As in many cross-class romances, the poor heroine is quickly convinced that the class obstacle can be overcome, but the opposition of the wealthy parents has to be faced. Near the end of the film, Richard proclaims that he understands completely his parents attempt to break up his marriage to a maid ("it was only natural"), but he says that they were wrong. His parents objected to the union because of the social inequality between him and Ellen, but he asserts that the only inequality was that he was not worthy to be Ellen's husband.

Films portrayed the opposition of wealthy parents, particularly mothers, to the cross-class marriage of their offspring as a consequence of their snobbishness, their fears of status loss, or their failure to appreciate the overwhelming power of love. The response of the wealthy family in *Brief Moment* (Columbia, 1933) to the son's intention to marry a nightclub singer is fairly typical. Prior to meeting Abbey (Carole Lombard), the family express concern about how the marriage will affect their status, and after meeting, her the mother states that the girl has "no breeding, no poise, nothing." Spectators are not given any indication by Abbey's behavior that this is in fact the case.

If the rich partner's family succeeds in preventing the cross-class marriage of their offspring, this success is usually temporary. The wealthy mother in *The Jazz Cinderella* (Chesterfield, 1930) persuades her son to give up the model working in their department store in favor of a wealthy socialite, but the son finally revolts in favor of the model. The wealthy society woman in *Shopworn* (Columbia, 1932) has her son's love object, a waitress, convicted on a trumped up charge of prostitution, and after the girl has served time in a reformatory and become a successful showgirl, the mother almost convinces her to give up her son before having a change in heart. The wealthy family in *The Most Precious Thing in Life* (Columbia, 1934) succeed in separating an impoverished waitress from their college-educated son and from the child the waitress bears him, but years later, working as a cleaning woman, she encounters her now-grown child and, without revealing her identity, advises him to stand up to his father and marry his impoverished girlfriend.

Other examples of parents opposing and then relenting or being put in their place by the spunky heroine are *The Social Register* (Columbia, 1934),

Stolen Sweets (Chesterfield, 1934) and *Splendor* (Samuel Goldwyn, 1935). In all these cases of family opposition, the man is rich and the girl is poor. Where the girl is rich and the man is poor, the girl's father was more likely to support and smooth the path for the couple, as in *It Happened One Night* (Columbia, 1934), *Happiness Ahead* (First National, 1934) and *Hard to Get* (Warner, 1938).

Many a poor heroine proved her disinterested love by her willingness to sacrifice her love when she is convinced, often by one of the hero's parents, that her marriage would impede the son's career or status. In *Love among the Millionaires* (Paramount, 1930), the railroad magnate father says he wants nothing else to do with his son if he intends to go through with his intended marriage to a waitress. When Pepper (Clara Bow), the waitress, realizes how much the son's work in the development of the railway network means to him, she decides to break up their relationships by acting in an obnoxious manner at a party given by the father. She pretends to be drunk and makes fun of the upper class guests, complete with a phony English accent. It is this performance that convinces the father that Pepper really loves his son and she would be the perfect wife for him.

In *Ladies of Leisure* (Columbia, 1930), the wealthy mother tells Kay Arnold (Barbara Stanwyck), a former "party girl," that she believes Kay loves her son Jerry, and that it is because Kay loves him that she should give him up. In this film, the mother is not represented as a snob but as a sincere person who is truly concerned about the effects such a marriage would have on her son's life. The mother explains that Kay would be a handicap to her son and that although she, the mother, would understand, others, her son's "people, his world," would not. In an attempt to alienate Jerry's affections, Kay sets off for Havana with his friend, but in despair she tries to commit suicide by jumping off the ship. She is saved, and Jerry comes to her bedside to tell her that everything will be all right. The film's sentimental end does not solve the tension between disinterested love and the social acceptance of a girl with a disreputable background. Like most cross-class romance films, the life of the couple is not shown beyond the promise of marriage.

The sacrifice made by the "dime a dance" girl, Madeleine McGonegal (Nancy Carroll) in *Child of Manhattan* (Columbia, 1933), occurs after her marriage to Paul Vanderkill (John Boles), a middle-aged widower and one of the richest men in New York. Madeleine had agreed to become Paul's mistress because of Paul's concerns about the impression that a marriage to a dance hall girl would have on his daughter, who does not appear in the film. We are given to understand that it is the mistress' task to prevent pregnancy, because when Madeleine becomes pregnant she apologizes profusely to Paul and is surprised when Paul proposes marriage. They marry secretly, and when the baby dies shortly after birth, Madeleine's sacrifice is to leave for Mexico in order to obtain a quick divorce. Madeleine's belief that Paul only married her out of a feeling of obligation is reinforced by John Boles' undemonstrative performance, but after some misunderstanding, Paul arrives in Mexico and after overhearing Madeleine's true love for him, the couple is reunited.

Even without the pressures of rich parents or other family considerations, heroines from poor backgrounds were willing to give up their love for the sake of the man's career. The character played by Joan Crawford in *Possessed* (1931, MGM) persuades the lawyer whom she loves that she plans to wed another in order not to handicap his chances of being nominated for Governor. In *Gambling Lady,* the heroine, Lady Lee, pretends that she is leaving the wealthy Gary for alimony when, in fact, this is the only way for her rival to agree to give Gary an alibi when he is falsely accused of murder. Gary's father accuses her of being a fortune hunter, but after he discovers the truth he is instrumental in reconciling the couple.

Proof of the disinterested love of the poor character is provided when the poor character falls in love with the rich character before she discovers that he is rich. The frequent class disguise or class passing in cross-class romance films represents the class hierarchy as a fluid system in which it takes little more than a change in clothing for a person from one class to be accepted in another. The ambitious young career woman in *A Man of Sentiment* (Chesterfield, 1933) jilts a wealthy man for a poor man only to find that he is the errant son of a wealthy family who eventually accept him back with his bride. The heiress in *The Luckiest Girl in the World* (Universal, 1936) falls in love with a resident of the cheap boarding house in which she lives because of a bet with her father that she can make it alone in New York without his assistance. The unemployed girl in *If You Could Only Cook* (Columbia, 1936) assumes that the man sitting on a park bench with her is as desperate as she is. He is, in fact, wealthy, but he does not disclose his identity when the girl talks him into passing as her husband in order to secure work as a cook and butler. In *Hard to Get* (Warner, 1938), the rich girl changes places with the maid as part of her elaborate plan to seek revenge against an attendant at a gas station who had made her clean the rooms of the station's adjoining motel when she had no cash on her to pay for the petrol he put in her car. Of course, she falls in love with him, and he is the one who has to be persuaded to marry her.

There is the double disguise theme in *The Gay Deception* (Fox, 1935) in which the prince obtains work as a bellhop in order to learn about American hotels, and the small-town stenographer, after winning $5,000 in a lottery, stays at the exclusive Walsdorf-Plaza in New York and is mistaken for a rich girl. The double disguise could serve as an intra-class romance: in *The Maid's Night Out* (RKO, 1938), a milk magnate's son works as a milkman as part of a bet with his father, and he mistakes a socialite for a housemaid. They keep their identities secret for fear that class differences will disturb their relationship, but they are both happy when they discover the truth.

The wealthy son in *The Maid's Night Out* does not appear to notice that the girl he believes to be a maid is wearing well-tailored, obviously expensive, clothes. In cross-class romance films, it is more often the poor characters that are slow to identify indications of cultural class differences. Madeleine (Nancy Carroll), the dance hall girl in *Child of Manhattan*, believes at first that Paul (John Boles), who is remarkably well-dressed, is unemployed and hard up. The difference in their clothes is soon overcome when Paul buys Madeleine an entire wardrobe and the major class cultural difference between them is represented as accent and speech. A lot is made of Madeleine's lower-class Brooklyn accent (she says 'appertment' instead of appointment) and that she does not understand Paul's sophisticated way of talking. These differences are understood as part of the appeal the characters have for each other, but in some other films the absence of cultural capital proves a hindrance to the acceptance of the poor characters. The dress shop model in *Hard to Get* (First National, 1929) finds that she has to put on phony airs for the wealthy man and she realizes that she will be happier with the garage mechanic. The brashness of the Jean Harlow character in *Red Headed Woman* (MGM, 1932) does not endear her to her rich husband's friends. The loud clothes and vulgar behavior of *Stella Dallas* (Samuel Goldwyn, 1937) makes her an inappropriate wife and mother in the cultured upper- middle class into which she married.

In most cross-class romance films, however, cultural differences were overcome by true love. The boarding house servant in *Compromised* (Warner, 1931) who marries into the Boston aristocracy is shamed by her lack of cultural knowledge, and her husband has to rescue her after she leaves to live in a poor apartment. The would-be society belle *Alice Adams* (RKO, 1935) is embarrassed by the behavior of her parents when she invites the wealthy man to their house for dinner, but love wins out in a tacked-on happy end. The navy man in *Let's Talk It Over* (Universal, 1934) chews gum and wears loud clothes and, at first, the heiress is only interested in him because of a wager she made with her blue-blooded friends that she could make him acceptable socially, but she finds at the end that she really loves him. Thus, with few exceptions, of which *Stella Dallas* is perhaps the best known, lack of the appropriate cultural capital does not prove an insurmountable obstacle to a cross-class union. Unlike *Stella Dallas*, most cross-class romance films do not continue beyond marriage or the promise of marriage, and thus the differences in cultural capital are not shown to be tested within marriage.

REPRESENTATION OF THE CLASSES

The upper class or wealthy stratum is negatively represented in many cross-class romance films. The women in particularly are shown to be flighty, spoilt, thoughtless about those who do not have their privileges, and sometimes vindictive. The upper-class lifestyle is represented as unproductive; it is either hedonist and frivolous, especially if the focus is on the young, or stuffy and boring, especially if the focus is on the middle-aged. An example of the former type is *Dynamite* (MGM, 1929), which contrasts the wildness of the wealthy young of the 'roaring twenties' before the Depression set in with the solidness of the working class. The improbable plot introduces Hagon Derk (Charles Bickford), a coalminer sentenced to death for a murder he did not commit, and Cynthia Crothers (Kay Johnson), a wealthy girl who must marry a man within a month before her 23rd birthday if she is to fulfill the terms of her grandfather's will and inherit millions. Cynthia is in love with a married man, Roger Towne (Conrad Nagel), whose wife will only divorce him if Cynthia agrees to pay her a large sum. As a way out of her dilemma, Cynthia marries the condemned man in exchange for $10,000 to be used for the care of Hagon's beloved kid sister. After Hagon is discovered to be innocent and released, he arrives at Cynthia's luxurious art-deco apartment just before Roger arrives with many of his and Cynthia's wealthy friends who proceed to have a boisterous party in which they get drunk and behave in a dissipated fashion. Hagon is repelled by the opulence of Cynthia's apartment and by the antics of her friends and, after he reveals himself as Cynthia's husband, he forces her friends to leave. Hagon's tough masculinity contrasts with the femininity of some of Cynthia's male friends, and he continues to demonstrate his roughness when he breaks down the door of Cynthia's bedroom after she locks herself in and he uses force to kiss her. He then shows his contempt for her by throwing her money back at her and stating that he has no wish to be married to her; unlike the women from where he comes, she is not a "real woman."

The film moves from the milieu of the rich, who spend their time on sports and drunken parties, to the coalmining town where Hagon works. As Cynthia's grandfather's will includes the provision that she must be living with her husband on her twenty-third birthday, she arrives in her expensive car to ask Hagon to come to stay with her temporarily. Hagon only agrees to such an arrangement if Cynthia comes to stay with him, and now it is Cynthia's turn to find herself out of place as she tries to live the life of a miner's wife. Cynthia's attempts to cook are disastrous and she is saved by Hagon's young sister who prepares his evening meal. After Cynthia shows her honesty by admitting to Hagon that his sister cooked his meal, he tells her: "There would be some hope for you if you didn't travel with such a rotten bunch." Cynthia shows her mettle and endears herself to the local women when she drives speedily to bring a doctor from the city to save a small boy injured in an accident. Further plot developments place Hagon, Cynthia and Roger trapped together in the mine, and after Cynthia admits her love for Hagon, Roger performs an act of self-sacrifice by igniting a dynamite explosion that kills him and enables Hagon and Cynthia to escape. Thus, at least two members of the decadent rich demonstrate heroism when extraordinary circumstances place them in a working-class environment[26] (Fig. 6.1).

One motivation for a character from a wealthy family to take on a class disguise was to escape the monotonous lifestyle of the upper-class family and to join the fun-loving life of the working class. In *Happiness Ahead* (First National, 1934), a bored heiress, Josephine Hutchinson (Joan Bradford) leaves the stuffy New Year's Eve party of her parents and goes out by herself to enjoy the lively festivities of the working class. Josephine enters a nightclub with a Chinese floorshow where the joyful singing of Auld Lang Syne is intercut with the sober, somewhat mournful, singing at her parent's party. At a nightclub she meets Bob Lane (Dick Powell), who works in an office as a dispatcher for a window cleaning business but, when the plot requires it, joins the window cleaning of a high-rise building. Josephine pretends to be a working-class girl without a job and the girls among Bob's friends encourage her to seek work in the places where they work. The Depression is not mentioned and the working class is represented as secure and content; they have enough money and they have fun in places like skating rinks, where Bob takes Josephine. As in many other cross-class romance films, the obstacle is a misunderstanding

Fig. 6.1 Still and poster of *Dynamite* (MGM, 1929). The still shows Hagon (Charles Bickford), a tough coalminer, confronting his socialite wife (Kay Johnson) in her luxurious, art-deco apartment. The poster shows the coalminer, his wife, and her lover (Conrad Nagel) from her wealthy social circle trapped together in a collapsing mine. Images courtesy of Jerry Murbach, http://www.doctormacro.com/

arising from the class difference rather than the class difference itself, but the obstacle is easily overcome when the truth comes out. When Bob discovers Josephine's deception he is not fazed by her wealth and her father overcomes the expected objections of her mother by telling her that he is going into the window-cleaning business with his son-in-law. As in a number of rich girl–poor boy films, it is the girl's father who understands that love is more important than money or status and encourages the match against the objections of the snobbish mother.

The problems of the upper or upper-middle class in the Depression films are shown to be particularly acute where there is no father, as in *Three-Cornered Moon* (Paramount, 1933). When upper-class parents are portrayed, it is more often the mother who is represented in a negative fashion, as either scatterbrained or snobbish. When the lower-class parents are portrayed, it is more often the father who receives the most negative representation,[27] as in *The Easiest Way* (MGM, 1931) and *Blind Date* (Columbia, 1934). Although in most cross-class romance films, upper-class families are given more screen time than the families of poor characters, the early scenes of some films include negative representations of the working- or lower-class family in order to show the milieu from which the ambitious daughter of the family wishes to escape. In *Personal Maid* (Paramount, 1931), the films begins with a moving shot as a "dumb waiter" travels up a tenement building, floor by floor, until it arrives at the apartment of the Ryan family who are arguing among themselves. Nora Ryan (Nancy Carroll) complains that during the day she has the noise of the machinery in the mill where she works and when she arrives home it is worse with "bickering, yelling, and screaming." She tells her family that she is leaving for a place where "men are polite and handsome and women going to bed luxuriously." However, she finds that when she goes to work as a personal maid for a wealthy family, both the father and son make sexual advances, the apathetic mother complains of having to go to the opera through which she sleeps, and the daughter returns so drunk that Nora has to help to put her to bed. Both the lower class and the upper class are portrayed negatively in *Personal Maid*, but Nora defines herself as middle class and it is her middle-class values that enable her to reform Dick Gary (Gene Raymond), the dissolute wealthy son.

Middle-class values and pride are the subject of *The Idle Rich* (MGM, 1929), an adaption of a 1925 play titled *White Collar*, but here the subject receives a satiric treatment. When wealthy William (known as Bill) van Luyn (Conrad Nagel) proposes marriage to his secretary, Joan Thayer (Leila Hyams), she accepts but expresses her concern that problems will arise from the differences in their respective classes. In contrast to the predicament of the poor female in many cross-class romances, Joan is not worried that Bill's family, whom we never see, will not accept her but that her proud lower-middle class will not accept him. Joan agrees to marry Bill on the condition that he moves in with her family, and much of the comedy derives from Bill's attempt to cope in the hot apartment with its lack of space and privacy and Joan's family, including Henry, an unemployed cousin who delivers tirades on the hardships of white-collar workers. Joan's kid sister, Helen (Bessie Love) is engaged to marry a truck driver and is ready to enjoy the advantages of a wealthy brother-in-law, but the parents refuse Bill's offer of a home on Riverside Drive and a house in the country. Bill says that Joan's family have a class consciousness, thereby implying that he has none; he only has money. Bill overcomes the family's middle-class pride when his announcement that he intends to give away his fortune to build a hospital for the benefit of the "great middle class" causes them consternation. Joan and her parents have a quick change in heart and they joyfully accept that they will be able to enjoy the life of the wealthy.

The changes made in *Rich Man, Poor Girl* (MGM, 1938), the remake of *The Idle Rich*, made it conform to the more common class issues in cross-class romances. This time Joan is reluctant to accept Bill's proposal of marriage because she is concerned that he will come to think that he has married beneath him. Her reservation is reinforced when she invites Bill to dinner at her home and the behavior of her family, who spruce themselves up for their guest, and the noise of neighbors causes her embarrassment. Bill hurts Joan's pride when he makes the mistake of telling her that he wants to "take her away from all of this," and when he proposes to her family that they accept his material support, including a new home, their pride does not allow them to accept "charity." However, there is less emphasis in the remake on middle-class consciousness; it is confined to cousin Henry who lectures Bill on the "great middle class" which, he says, comprises 80 % of the population. Bill sets out to prove to Joan that her family's class is not important to him by moving in with them, which annoys Joan and delights her mother. As in *The Idle Class*, it is Bill's pretense that he intends to give away all his money that persuades Joan and her family to welcome the benefits of wealth.

REDEMPTION OF THE WEALTHY BY THE POOR

The reform of Dick Gary by Nora Ryan in *Personal Maid* includes the adoption of the work ethic and appropriate sexual behavior. In an early scene when Dick attempts to kiss Nora and she repulses him, he remonstrates, "Don't act like this Nora, it's so darn middle class." Although she is from a poor tenement family and works as a maid, Nora replies that she is middle class and that Dick should act like the gentleman he is supposed to be. Nora's response earns her Dick's respect and he sets out to reform himself by getting a job and supporting himself without his family's wealth. Dick, like many other wealthy males in cross-class romances, drinks too much until he is redeemed by the working girl. The heavy drinking of the millionaire in *Night World* (Universal, 1932) can be excused by the fact that his unloving mother shot his unfaithful father, but he sobers up sufficiently to propose to the nightclub dancer who is clearly going to be his salvation. The wealthy lawyer in *The Girl from 10th Avenue* (First National, 1935) is drinking himself to destruction after a high-society woman has rejected him for an even wealthier man, and it is a shop girl who saves him both from drink and from the society woman who tries to reclaim him.

The rich male is not always inclined to prove to the working-class or middle-class girl that the work ethic is superior to his hedonistic way of life, but he has no choice if he is to redeem himself in the eyes of his loved one. The problem of Rodney Deane (Gene Raymond) in *Brief Moment* is that, in the words of a contemporary reviewer, his "4000 a month allowance has prevented him from experiencing the joys of toiling for his daily bread."[28] Unlike most cross-class romances, this film begins with marriage. Rodney marries Abbey (Carole Lombard) who quickly becomes dissatisfied with her husband's lifestyle of night clubs and drinking. She wants a proper marriage in which the couple spends some of their evenings at home and is not forever surrounded by others in a constant merry-go-round. She tells Rodney that he "cannot spend [his] life having a good time," and that he needs to work in order to attain self-respect and for her to be proud of him. Rodney goes to work for his father but he quickly tires of the boring, routine work that he is given, and, while pretending to Abbey that he goes to the office every day, he spends his time at the races. When Abbey discovers his deceit she berates him: "Where would you be if you didn't have your father's money. You could not make a living if you tried ... How little you amount to." Abbey prefers to work and support herself, and after she leaves him Rodney is propelled to search for work. His lack of experience results in refusals until his emotional appeal to an employer finally gets him a job. The film does not show the work he does but it shows his happiness after he receives his first pay check and shows it to Abbey. She exclaims in delight: "You did this for me!" He replies: "I did it for myself." Proud of her working husband, Abbey is now content to leave her work and become a housewife (Fig. 6.2).

Some working-class heroines induced their wealthy men to adopt the work ethic, but a workaholic wealthy husband could be just as unsatisfactory as a non-working wealthy husband if his behavior results in the inability of the woman to perform her appropriate roles as wife and mother. In *She Married Her Boss* (Columbia, 1935), when Julia Scott (Claudette Colbert), an executive secretary, marries her boss, Richard Barclay (Melvyn Douglas), an upper-middle class owner of a department store, the major issue is that the hard-working boss wants his wife to continue to help at work whereas she protests that marriage is "a woman's real career." Richard expresses his feelings when, instead of helping him in his business, he finds his wife singing nursery rhymes with his daughter from a previous marriage: "I've always known you as a competent, sensible woman whose career means something to her. All of a sudden you are pouncing

Fig. 6.2 Still from *Brief Moment* (Columbia, 1933). Abbey (Carole Lombard), a former night club singer, looks disapprovingly at her wealthy, gambling husband (Gene Raymond) whose hedonistic lifestyle she disavows. Image from Photofest

about in soft things, wearing negligees, being coy and things like that." Julia submits to no longer acting like her idea of a woman and returns to work where a female assistant tells her that Julia is her role model because "she is important in the business world and a career is important." When the assistant tells Julia that her career comes before her beau, Julia replies that instead of working she should go and be with her beau and "do something which is really important." Only after Richard gets drunk with his butler is he able to loosen up and finally take time off from work and go on a cruise with Julia (Fig. 6.3).

The need to rescue wealthy partners from devotion to their work was far rarer, however, than the need to reform them from a lifestyle of wasteful pleasure, a particularly vinous sin during the Depression. The irresponsible and unproductive siblings—a sister and brother—of a wealthy family

Fig. 6.3 Still from *She Married Her Boss* (Columbia, 1935). The secretary marries her workaholic boss, but he wants her to continue helping him in his business whereas the only 'career' she wants is to be a wife and mother to his child. Image courtesy of Derek Borthroyd

are seen at the end of *Fast and Loose* (Paramount, 1930) to be on the way to redemption as a consequence of their relationships with working-class characters. The sister, Marion Lenox (Miriam Hopkins), rejects the pompous English lord to whom she is engaged after she falls for the motor mechanic and chauffeur, Henry Morgan (Charles Starrett). The redemption of Marion's brother, Bertie (Henry Wandsworth), who drinks heavily, is in the hands of a chorus girl, Alice O'Neil (Carole Lombard), whose sober and responsible character is contrasted with her friend, also a chorus girl, who is a wild gold digger. The reform of Marion and Bertie and the middle-class values of their prospective partners are made evident in the last scene of the film, which takes place in a court room after the sister and brother have been arrested in a raid on a nightclub. Marion and Bertie behave badly in front of the judge and their father, but they apologize after they are told to do so by Henry and Alice. The father is impressed and tells the judge that rather than spend a night in jail his children should get married to "fine upright people" who will make his children like themselves. When the siblings' snobbish mother arrives Alice tells her that she wants to marry Bertie in spite of the fact that he is a "drunken little fool." Alice turns the table on the mother who protests and appeals to the status of her family by telling her that her own mother "would never get over the disgrace if I married a man like Bertie." Henry says that his "old man" would feel the same way about Marion and explains that his home town has "pretty high standards." When Marion's father asks him if he believes that his daughter is not good enough for him, Henry explains that she would be good enough if she had "to wrestle with something tough." Both Henry and Alice tell the wealthy parents that the only hope for their children is if they forgo their family's money. Alice explains that her influence over Bertie would only last if he does not have the family money and he has "something to work for." For Henry, it is a matter of gender authority: "I like money all right but when I marry I want to be the guy that has it. How can Marion be a good wife unless she respects me and how is she going to respect me if she has more than me."

The attempts of a working-class man to reform a wealthy girl and convince her to adopt his standard of living and style of life were not always successful, especially if there is another girl from his own social class who loves him. In *Chance at Heaven* (RKO, 1933), Blacky Gorman (Joel McCrea), the owner of a gas station in a small New England town, marries wealthy Glory Franklin (Marian Nixen), whose family has a villa in the town for summer vocations. Glory's snobbish mother, who opposed the match, tries to convince Blacky to settle in New York, but Blacky asserts his independence and the couple establish their home in Blacky's modest bungalow. The spoilt Glory attempts to become a good middle-class housewife and she depends on Marje Harris (Ginger Rogers), Blacky's former sweetheart, to decorate the house and make Blacky's favorite chicken pie. When she becomes pregnant, the frightened Glory agrees to her mother's proposal to return alone to New York where she will be well looked after. After some months, Glory decides not to return to Blacky and tells him that she is unable to leave the style-of-life to which she is accustomed. She is no longer pregnant and although Blacky immediately accepts the explanation that Glory had been wrongly diagnosed by the small town doctor, the implication is that she has had an abortion. Blacky returns to Marje who is happy to be making his chicken pie.

GENDER DISTINCTION

There are far more rich male–poor female romances than there are rich female–poor male romances, but in both variations the representations of class and class values are regulated by gender and the authority of the male is maintained. Of course, the maintenance of male domination rarely poses problems where the male is wealthy and the female is poor. The love of the wealthy male for the poor female is generally accepted as sufficient reason to explain his choice despite the frequent opposition of status-conscious parents, but in a rare admission in *Working Girls* (Paramount, 1931), the wealthy male explains to his buddy the benefits of a union with a poor girl to the male's ego. He tells his friend that "little working girls have something that society girls have not got." He would give up his wealthy fiancée for the poor girl because the wealthy girl has had everything she has wanted and would not get exited whatever a man did for her, whereas the poor girl (the "little kid") looks up to him.[29]

Where the male was poor in the cross-class romance, he was likely to either reject the money of the girl's family (e.g. *Fast and Loose*) or accept the money in order to develop his own business and thereby retain his independence (e.g. *Happiness Ahead*). The steelworker who marries the daughter of the factory boss objects to becoming one of the *Kept Husbands* (RKO, 1931), and he eventually convinces her to live on his salary without the help of her wealthy father. The wealthy heiress who marries a working-class man in *Saleslady* (Monogram, 1938) accepts his refusal of her father's offer to help them out. The riveter in *The Hot Heiress* (First National, 1931) tells the wealthy girl that they will live on his wages and insists that she will not work.

The poor males are often macho and compare favorably with the sometimes feminized upper-class fiancés of the wealthy heroines. The fiancé of Marion, the socialite in *Fast and Loose*, is an aristocratic, foppish Englishman, a familiar stock character who provides a radical contrast to Henry, the car mechanic. Marion meets Henry when her car gets stuck in the sand on the seashore where Henry is swimming. It is Henry's physical strength and practical know-how that enable her to drive the car out. Henry explains to her why men are stronger than women: "Because they [women] never were intended to be their equal. Don't forget that. Women were intended ... to charm men in their lighter moments, to sooth them when they're tired." Henry's sentiments appear to be part of the reason that Marion is attracted to him.

The attraction of the virile, underclass male to the wealthy or upper-class female takes on added meaning when that male is a gangster, as in the film *A Free Soul* (MGM, 1931). The gangster's combination of machismo and illegality excites the wealthy woman's sexual desire and she is prepared to flout sexual convention to be with him. She is not, however, necessarily interested in marriage, and the ending of what Esther Sonnet calls "the gangster-infected social melodrama" usually finds the gangster dead or otherwise absent and the upper-class female reunited with a class-appropriate partner.[30] Within the category of cross-class romance films, the flagrant active sexuality of the upper-class females in relationship with gangsters is unusual. Among the poor females in cross-class romances, heightened sexuality is generally restricted to gold diggers.

STAR PERSONAS AND THE CROSS-CLASS ROMANCE FORMULA

One consequence of the large number of cross-class romance films was that almost all of the prominent female stars of the 1930s appeared in at least one cross-class romance. However, certain stars appeared far more frequently in cross-class romances than others. Three stars, Joan Crawford, Barbara Stanwyck and Carole Lombard, were particularly ubiquitous in cross-class romances. In total, 12 of Crawford's 30 feature films released between 1929 and 1941 were cross-class romances; apart from the wealthy girl role in her first two sound films, from *Our Blushing Brides* in 1930 to *The Women* in 1939, she consistently played the poor side of the romantic couple. Of Stanwyck's 39 films from 1929 to 1941, 11 were cross-class romances. From her first success, *Ladies of Leisure,* in 1930 to *Ball of Fire* in 1941 she played the poor role or, as in *Ball of Fire,* the culturally lower-class girl. Of Carole Lombard's 41 films during the period, 11 were cross-class romances, and she is exceptional insofar as she played the wealthy side of the romantically paired couple (six films) more frequently than the poor side (five films).

An examination of popular fan magazines finds a number of correspondences between the personas of the stars and the roles they played in their cross-class romance films. Both Crawford and Stanwyck were reported as having fought their way out of a background of poverty and broken or dysfunctional families through their ambition, labor and drive. Before their breaks in films they worked in low-paid jobs—Crawford as hat-check girl and Stanwyck as telephone operator—and as chorus girls. They were described as Cinderellas and as feminine counter-parts of the socially mobile heroes in the stories of Horatio Alger. The fan magazines' accounts of Crawford's and Stanwyck's lower-class background and the effects of this background upon them (Crawford's driving ambition, Stanwyck's toughness) corresponded to their on-screen personas, particularly in their cross-class romance films. In her cross-class romance films as the poor girl, Crawford begins as a department store girl (*Our Blushing Brides*), a paper-box factory girl (*Possessed*, 1931), a housemaid (*Sadie McKee*, 1934), a secretary (*Chained*, 1934), a low-dive cabaret singer (*The Bride Wore Red*, 1937), and a button-factory girl (*Mannequin*, 1937). In contrast with Crawford, not many of Stanwyck's characters could be described as respectable working girls. She was a 'party girl' in *Ladies of Leisure* (1930), a 'taxi dancer' in *Ten Cents a Dance* (1931), a girl prostituted by her father in *Baby Face* (1933), a gambler in *Gambling Lady* (1934), a shoplifter in *Remember the Night* (1940), a card sharp in *The Lady Eve* (1941), and a criminal's showgirl mistress in *Ball of Fire*. She was more respectable in two other cross-class romances, as a small-town librarian in *Forbidden* (1932), although in this film she becomes a kept woman, and a waitress in *Shopworn* (1932). Stanwyck's image as a tough, wisecracking, hard-boiled dame with a soft core was reinforced in some of her other (without a cross-class romance) working-girl films, such as her nurse in *Night Nurse* (Warner, 1931) and her gangster moll in *Ladies They Talked About* (Warner, 1933), and in her interviews for fan magazines, Stanwyck projected an off-screen persona that was as tough and independent as her on-screen one.

Fan magazines focused on stars' off-screen love lives and marriages and Crawford's two marriages during the 1930s—to Douglas Fairbanks Jr. in 1929 and Franchot Tone in 1935—followed in many respects the narratives of her cross-class romance films. Both of Crawford's marriages were viewed as steps in Crawford's mobility as she was transformed by her husbands and by herself into a cultured lady. Fairbanks Jr. was the son of Douglas Fairbanks Sr. and the stepson of Mary Fairbanks, who held court in their home, Pickfair, nicknamed 'The Buckingham Palace of Hollywood.' In accord with a common motif in cross-class romances, the 'royal' parents were reported to oppose their son's union with a girl whom they regarded as common and immoral. To become a lady fit for the prince, Crawford took French lessons, read books labeled classics, dressed more sedately and softened her hairstyle. Her marriage to Tone was another step up because, unlike Fairbanks Jr. who was from Hollywood's nouveau riche, Tone was from an East Coast patrician family, the well-educated son of a socially prominent industrialist. *Picture Play* reported in 1938 that Crawford's marriage to Tone had "raised eyebrows," but she now "reads all the new books, sees as many of the new plays as she can, attends practically every Philharmonic concert, goes to all good art exhibitions."[31] (Fig. 6.4)

Unlike Crawford, Stanwyck in the 1930s did not follow the cross-class romance narrative of mobility through marriage and gentrification. Fan magazines did transmute one theme from the films in their coverage of Stanwyck, however, which was the dilemma faced by the heroine in choosing between self-interest and the interests of the man who has enabled her advancement and with whom she is now in love. At the end of the films, the heroine is willing to sacrifice her own advancement in order to save the man's standing in society. Stanwyck played out this scenario in her marriage with Frank Fay, a leading vaudeville performer of the 1920s and the star of a number of successful musical films in 1929–1930. Fay married Stanwyck in 1928 when she was relatively unknown but after his film career dimmed and Stanwyck's rose, Stanwyck demonstrated her willingness to sacrifice her film career for her husband by joining him working in vaudeville. After Stanwyck divorced Fay in 1935, fan magazines replaced

Fig. 6.4 Lobby cards for *Sadie Mckee* (MGM, 1934). One of many films in which Joan Crawford plays a working-class girl who marries a wealthy man. The first card shows her as a maid serving the mother and son (Franchot Tone) of the wealthy household. The second card shows her together with the playboy alcoholic (Edward Arnold) whom she marries and divorces, and the wealthy son (Tone) with whom she unites at the end. Crawford married Tone in 1935, the year after this film's release. Images courtesy of Jerry Murbach, http://www.doctormacro.com/

the image of a devoted, self-sacrificing wife with that of an independent career woman immersed in her work. Stanwyck's autonomous image was reinforced by the fact that, unlike most stars, she had chosen not to sign a seven-year contract with a studio. She worked for five studios during the 1930s, and fan magazines as well as studio publicity pointed to this free-lancing as evidence of courage and independence.

Although Carole Lombard starred in as many cross-class romance films as Crawford and Stanwyck, the association of the formula with her per-sona was relatively weak. She starred in a number of cross-class romances before her distinctive persona as a 'screwball' emerged, and she alternated between playing the poor female to the rich male (for example, in *Sinners in the Sun*, 1932, and *Brief Moment*, 1933) and the rich female to the poor male (for example, in *No More Orchids*, 1932, and *We're Not Dressing*, 1934). Lombard had an upper middle-class, WASP background and early fan magazine coverage tended to emphasize her high-class glamour, rein-forced by her marriage in 1931 to the suave, man-about-town William Powell. A few months after Lombard divorced Powell in 1933, the fan magazines found a star happy in her unmarried state, and this image became part of her wider image as the foremost screwball female star. Onscreen, the screwball image became well established with her wacky socialite role in *My Man Godfrey* (1936). Off-screen, Lombard led a free-spirited life-style, organized crazy parties and was widely known as 'America's madcap Playgirl Number One'. This screwball image was tempered by Lombard's romance with and, in 1939, marriage to Clark Gable, and by their move to live on a ranch where Lombard was reported to share Gable's interest in 'masculine' activities such as hunting and fishing. Lombard had finally conformed to a variation of the cross-class romance formula, in which the upper-class female sacrifices her own lifestyle and independence to become part of the lifestyle of the proletarian male—even if that proletarian male was the acknowledged 'King of Hollywood'.

Tension between the cross-class romance formula and star personas was caused when the achieved class of the star, as emphasized especially in the rags-to-riches stories of Crawford and Stanwyck, was in conflict with the formula's narrative of class achievement through marriage with a wealthy man. This was intensified when the female star married an actor whose stardom was inferior to her own, as occurred with Crawford and Stanwyck, which paralleled the situation of many women who had become the breadwinners during the Depression. When the formula has a poor male and wealthy female, the potential conflict with gender norms is rectified by the male's insistence that the female be dependent on him, but the top female stars did not appear to conform to these gender norms. The tension between formula and persona was resolved in favor of the formula by the domestication of the star when she married, and in favor of the persona when she divorced. Fan magazines reported the newly married star's willingness to sacrifice her career for the good of the marriage (Stanwyck) or her adoption of the lifestyle of her husband (Crawford's gentrification and Lombard's proletarianization). Stars never actually sacrificed their careers for their marriages with lesser stars and these marriages in any case did not last long. When the star divorced, fan magazines emphasized the star's independence and the importance of her career above all else. A number of cross-class romance films included narratives of the heroine's success in show business, but this was generally subordinate to the narrative of romance, which for Hollywood films, if not always for fan magazines, was the major trajectory for a woman's social mobility.[32]

NOTES

1. Robert S. McElvaine, *The Great Depression, America, 1929–1941* (New York: Times Books, 1984), 134–137; Gerald D. Nash, *The Great Depression and World War II: Organizing America, 1933–1945* (New York: St. Martin's Press, 1979), 6–7; David E. Kyvig, *Daily Life in the United States 1920–1940* (Chicago: Ivan R. Dee, 2004), 209, 221–222; Michael E. Parrish, *Anxious Decades: America in Prosperity and Depression, 1920–1941* (New York: W. W. Norton, 1994), 376–378, 386; Gary S. Cross, *An All-Consuming Century: Why Consumerism Won in Modern America* (New York: Columbia University Press, 2000), 68; Paul Ryscavage, *Income Inequality in America* (New York: M. E. Sharpe, 1999), 139.

2. We do not have a national study of mobility rates for this period, but Thernstrom calculates that in Boston during the 1930s only 11 percent of workers were upwardly mobility while 16 percent were downwardly mobile. Stephan Thernstrom, *The Other Bostonians: Poverty and Progress in the American Metropolis* (Cambridge, MA: Harvard University Press, 1973), 56.

3. Nash, *The Great Depression and World War* II, 36.

4. Gary Cross, *An All-Consuming Society*, 68–75.

5. Susan Porter Benson, *Household Accounts: Working-Class Family Economies in the Interwar United States* (Ithaca, NY: Cornell University Press, 2007).

6. Beth S. Wenger, *New York Jews and the Great Depression: Uncertain Promise* (New York: Syracuse University Press, 1999), 16–20, 29, 55, 71, 201.
7. Robert S. McElvaine (ed.), *Down & Out in the Great Depression: Letters from the "Forgotten Man"* (Chapel Hill: University of North Carolina Press, 1983); Robert Cohen, *Dear Mrs. Roosevelt: Letters from Children of the Great Depression* (Chapel Hill: University of North Carolina Press, 2002), 37–41, 57–71.
8. Susan Ware, *Holding Their Own: American Women in the 1930s* (Boston: Twayne Publishers, 1982), 29.
9. William H. Chafe, *The Paradox of Change: American Women in the 20th Century* (New York: Oxford University Press, 1991), 116; S.J. Kleinberg, *Women in the United States, 1930–1945* (London: Macmillan Press, 1999), 219.
10. Chafe, *The Paradox of Change*, 69–71, 97, 116–117.
11. Lois Scharf, *To Work and To Wed: Female Employment, Feminism, and the Great Depression* (Westport, CT: Greenwood Press, 1980), 92, 95, 108.
12. Lois Rita Helmbold, "Downward Occupational Mobility During the Great Depression: Urban Black and White Working Class Women," *Labor History* 29.2 (1988), 137–138, 152, 187.
13. Scharf, *To Work and To Wed*, 110–111.
14. Ware, *Holding Their Own*, 33–34.
15. Scharf, *To Work and To Wed*, 140–141; Kleinberg, *Women in the United States*, 246.
16. Mira Komarovsky, *The Unemployed Man and His Family: The Effects of Unemployment Upon the Status of the Man in Fifty-Nine Families* (New York: Octagon Books, 1971 [1940]), 29.
17. Laura Hapke, *Daughters of the Great Depression: Women, Work, and Fiction in the American 1930s* (Athens: University of Georgia Press, 1995), 126.
18. Hapke, *Daughters of the Great Depression*, 141.
19. Hapke, *Daughters of the Great Depression*, 118.
20. Hapke, *Daughters of the Great Depression*, 183.
21. [Susan] Elizabeth Dalton, "Women at Work: Warners in the 1930s," in Karyn Kay and Gerald Peary, eds., *Women and the Cinema: A Critical Anthology* (New York: E.P. Dutton, 1977), 267–281; Carolyn L. Galerstein, *Working Women on the Hollywood Screen* (New York: Garland Publishing, 1989).
22. Emily Susan Carman, "Independent Stardom: Female Film Stars and the Studio System in the 1930s," *Women's Studies* 37 (2008): 583–615.
23. One of Lary May's graphs shows that the percentage of films with plots in which the central protagonist perceives that the rich endanger society rose sharply from 1932 to 1936 and remained high until 1940. Larry May,

The Big Tomorrow: Hollywood and the Politics of the American Way (Chicago: University of Chicago Press, 2000), 273.

24. McDonald notes this instance of self-reflexivity in the film; Crawford was labeled "The Most Copied Girl in the World." Tamar Jeffers McDonald, *Hollywood Catwalk: Exploring Costume and Transformation in American Film* (New York: I.B.Tauris & Co., 2010), 118.

25. For analyses of this film that link the film's meanings to the clothes that Anni (Crawford) wears see Sarah Berry, *Screen Style: Fashion and Femininity in 1930s Hollywood* (Minneapolis: University of Minnesota Press, 2000), 34–39 and McDonald, *Hollywood Catwalk*, 35, 126.

26. The radical scriptwriter John Howard Lawson, who joined the Communist Party in 1934, was involved in writing the dialogue for *Dynamite*, but the story was written by Jeanie Macpherson, Cecil B. DeMille's regular scriptwriter.

27. Exceptions are those films where the mother is dead or absent and the daughter works with her father as in *Love among the Millionaires* and *Blind Date*.

28. *New York Times*, September 30, 1933.

29. The overt expression of this sentiment may be related to the fact that the director was Dorothy Arzner, one of the very few female directors of the period.

30. Esther Sonnet, "Ladies Love Brutes: Reclaiming Female Pleasures in the Lost History of Hollywood Gangster Cycles, 1929–1931," in Lee Grieveson, Esther Sonnet, and Peter Stanfield, eds., *Mob Culture: Hidden Histories of the American Gangster Films* (New Brunswick, NJ: Rutgers University Press, 2005), 98.

31. *Picture Play*, February 1938, 34–35, 73.

32. I provide a more detailed and comprehensive analysis of the relationship between star personas and the cross-class romance formula in Stephen Sharot, "Social Class in Female Star Personas and the Cross-Class Romantic Formula in Depression-era America," *Screen* 56.2 (2015): 172–194.

BIBLIOGRAPHY

Benson, Susan Porter. *Household Accounts: Working-Class Family Economies in the Interwar United States*. Ithaca, NY: Cornell University Press, 2007.

Berry, Sarah. *Screen Style: Fashion and Femininity in 1930s Hollywood*. Minneapolis: University of Minnesota Press, 2000.

Carman, Emily Susan. "Independent Stardom: Female Film Stars and the Studio System in the 1930s," *Women's Studies* 37 (2008): 583–615.

Chafe, William H. *The Paradox of Change: American Women in the 20th Century*. New York: Oxford University Press, 1991.

Cohen, Robert. *Dear Mrs. Roosevelt: Letters from Children of the Great Depression.* Chapel Hill: University of North Carolina Press, 2002.

Cross, Gary S. *An All-Consuming Century: Why Consumerism Won in Modern America.* New York: Columbia University Press, 2000.

Dalton, [Susan] Elizabeth. "Women at Work: Warners in the 1930s," in Karyn Kay and Gerald Peary, eds., *Women and the Cinema: A Critical Anthology.* New York: E.P. Dutton, 1977, 267–281.

Galerstein, Carolyn L. *Working Women on the Hollywood Screen.* New York: Garland Publishing, 1989.

Hapke, Laura. *Daughters of the Great Depression: Women, Work, and Fiction in the American 1930s.* Athens: University of Georgia Press, 1995.

Helmbold, Lois Rita. "Downward Occupational Mobility During the Great Depression: Urban Black and White Working Class Women," *Labor History* 29.2 (1988), 135–172.

Kleinberg, S.J. *Women in the United States, 1930–1945.* London: Macmillan Press, 1999.

Komarovsky, Mira. *The Unemployed Man and His Family: The Effects of Unemployment Upon the Status of the Man in Fifty-Nine Families.* New York: Octagon Books, 1971 [1940].

Kyvig, David E. *Daily Life in the United States 1920–1940.* Chicago: Ivan R. Dee, 2004.

May, Lary. *The Big Tomorrow: Hollywood and the Politics of the American Way.* Chicago, University of Chicago Press, 2000.

McDonald, Tamar Jeffers. *Hollywood Catwalk: Exploring Costume and Transformation in American Film.* New York: I.B.Tauris & Co., 2010.

McElvaine, Robert S. *The Great Depression, America, 1929–1941.* New York: Times Books, 1984.

———— (ed.) *Down & Out in the Great Depression: Letters from the "Forgotten Man".* Chapel Hill: University of North Carolina Press, 1983.

Nash, Gerald D. *The Great Depression and World War II: Organizing America, 1933–1945.* New York: St. Martin's Press, 1979.

Parrish, Michael E. *Anxious Decades: America in Prosperity and Depression, 1920–1941.* New York: W. W. Norton, 1994.

Ryscavage, Paul. *Income Inequality in America.* New York: M. E. Sharpe, 1999.

Scharf, Lois. *To Work and To Wed: Female Employment, Feminism, and the Great Depression.* Westport, Conn.: Greenwood Publishing Group, 1980.

Sharot, Stephen. "Social Class in Female Star Personas and the Cross-Class Romantic Formula in Depression-era America," *Screen* 56.2 (2015): 172–194.

Sonnet, Esther. "Ladies Love Brutes: Reclaiming Female Pleasures in the Lost History of Hollywood Gangster Cycles, 1929–1931," in Lee Grieveson, Esther Sonnet, and Peter Stanfield, eds. *Mob Culture: Hidden Histories of the American Gangster Films.* New Brunswick, NJ: Rutgers University Press, 2005, 93–119.

Thernstrom, Stephan. *The Other Bostonians: Poverty and Progress in the American Metropolis.* Cambridge, MA: Harvard University Press, 1973.

Ware, Susan. *Holding Their Own: American Women in the 1930s.* Boston: Twayne Publishers, 1982.

Wenger, Beth S. *New York Jews and the Great Depression: Uncertain Promise.* New York: Syracuse University Press, 1999.

CHAPTER 7

Male Seducers and Female Gold-Diggers

WORKING GIRLS AND MALE SEDUCERS

Sexual harassment and exploitation was frequently shown in films made between 1914 and 1919 and became rare in the films of the 1920s. In accord with the optimism of the 1920s, the working girl in cross-class romance films was able to marry a wealthy man, often her boss, without compromising her virtue. In fact, a girl's defense of her virtue was a condition of her mobility through marriage, a principle that was reinforced by the occasional negative example of the heroine's friend who threw her chances away by succumbing to her seduction. A film that retained this principle, with a greater emphasis than the films of the 1920s on the economic deprivations of working girls, was *Our Blushing Brides* (MGM, 1930).[1]

Our Blushing Brides was made before the worst years of the Depression and there is no direct reference to the economic crisis, but the acute economic dissatisfaction of working girls and their hopes of overcoming it through their relationships with men are stated clearly in the film's early scenes. The focus is on three young women who work in a department store: Jerry (Joan Crawford), a model; Connie, a perfume salesgirl; and Franky, who works in linen sales. The regimentation of the workers is shown in the first scene as the three girls are part of a long line of workers, mostly women, clocking into work and, after a bell rings, quickly moving to their sales tables where they are addressed as numbers by the floorwalkers. As the girls put their hats and coats into their lockers, Franky says that she would be ashamed to be caught dead in her coat but she does not

© The Author(s) 2017
S. Sharot, *Love and Marriage Across Social Classes in American Cinema*,
DOI 10.1007/978-3-319-41799-8_7

know when she will be able to afford another one. The girls' complaints about their economic state continue later in the apartment that they share. Connie protests how little they get in life "living on a measly 22.50 a week" without decent clothes and unable to go places. Franky exclaims, "What have we got to look forward to! To stay behind a counter until we drop dead or marrying some sap from the store … and spend the rest of your life in the Bronx washing dirty dishes."

Connie and Franky agree that they will not achieve anything if they continue to be "dumb and virtuous" and refer to the example of a worker in the store who receives a couple of thousand dollars from a man every month for clothes. When Jerry says that, "you should get a load of the guy who pays the bills," Franky replies, "Well, what does that matter." It matters a lot to Jerry who turns down opportunities to profit from relationships with wealthy men. In an earlier scene in which she models lingerie, a well-dressed male customer asks if the lingerie she is modeling is very expensive. Jerry replies that he will have to ask the saleslady and when he says that he would hate to bother the saleslady, Jerry responds, "We are quite used to being [pausing for emphasis] bothered." Franky sarcastically accuses Jerry of seeking "some beautiful, pure romance" whereas Franky wants money and is going to get it before it's too late: "This town picks them young." Jerry adds, "And finishes with them young too." Jerry admits that she is also miserable about their life but she believes that with regard to men she is practical rather than romantic and advises her friends to be cautious because it is difficult to find a man who is not a fake. When she says that men "always act the same in a taxi cab" her friends remind her that she has talked about Tony, the elder son of the store owner, as being different. Jerry qualifies, "I said he seemed different" and that she has not been with him yet in a taxi cab.

The girls' feelings of deprivation are sharpened by scenes in the store where wealthy women buy the expensive perfume sold by Connie and order the extremely expensive clothes modeled by Jerry. The scene in the girls' tenement apartment is followed soon afterwards by a scene in the enormous mansion of the store's owner where Jerry and the other mannequins of the store model the clothes of a Parisian designer. After the fashion show, Tony takes Jerry to his luxurious tree house where, with its sunken couch and disappearing staircase, Jerry discovers that Tony is no different from other men. He forcefully kisses her and when she resists he says, "Don't tell me you didn't know why I bought you here alone." Jerry replies that she had hoped that for once in her life she would be wrong and asks if he cannot believe that a girl might have a sense of virtue. He replies, "When it comes to the subject under discussion, I wouldn't believe any modern girl." Jerry resists Tony's advances once more in a later scene when Jerry is alone in her underwear in the models' dressing room of the store. Tony enters the room without knocking and when he says he was waiting to be invited Jerry says, "Why stand on ceremony. Surely your position gives you this [indicating her undressed state] privilege." Jerry accuses Tony of being immature and he leaves.

Unhappily, Jerry's flat mates do not take her advice or follow her example of upholding virtue. Franky marries a man who impresses her with his wads of hundred dollar bills. He turns out to be a criminal, the head of a gang who have been stealing from the store, and after his arrest she returns to her farming parents' home in Ohio. Connie allows herself to become a kept woman in a luxurious apartment provided by the younger son of the store owner, and when he marries a girl of his own class she commits suicide by drinking poison. Tony forces his brother to leave his wedding to go to Connie's bedside where the brother's declaration of love makes Connie happy as she dies. This tragedy is followed by a happy ending, in which Jerry and Tony, now a loving couple, have returned to the tree house. A male worker at the store who at the beginning of the film offered to take Jerry to a "million dollar movie" phones up to repeat the offer, but Jerry is now engaged to marry a million dollar husband. Once again, virtue is rewarded.

Another film that set out in stark terms the options available to working-class girls and then provides, in its last minutes, a happy solution was *Under 18* (Warner, 1932). The film begins with a happy event in a contented working-class family prior to the Depression. Margie (Marion Marsh), the younger daughter of the family, expresses her beliefs in the value of love and marriage as her older sister Sophie marries Alf and moves out of the their parents' home. A few still shots rapidly deflate the upbeat beginning: the father's gravestone, a 'room for rent' sign, and a pawnbroker's store sign. The year is now 1931 and Margie is living with her mother in a poor apartment in a crowded tenement neighborhood. Margie's hard-working boyfriend Jimmie drives a truck delivering goods and is optimistic that a break is just around the corner, but the situation only gets worse as Sophie, Alf and their baby move in with Margie and her mother after it transpires Alf has gambled away rent money by participating in billiard tournaments. Sophie now has only contempt for the work-shy Alf and Margie's former belief in marriage is undermined by the bickering and shouting between Sophie and Alf. An alternative life-style presents itself in the fashionable gown shop where Margie works as a seamstress and listens to the shop's models as they discuss the benefits that they receive from rich admirers. By chance, Margie is given the opportunity to model a beautiful fur coat before a customer who is accompanied by wealthy Raymond Harding (Warren William) who eyes Margie admiringly, particularly when, believing that she is unobserved, Margie reveals herself in her lingerie beneath the fur coat. Harding's gesture of sending orchids to Margie's mother sparks a crisis between Sophie and Alf as Alf grabs the orchids with the intention of selling them and using the money on a pool game. Sophie chases after Alf, he strikes her, and Margie decides that she has seen all she wants of marriage. She tells her mother and sister, "Anytime I hand myself to a man for life its cash on delivery."

Sophie discovers that she is pregnant with a second child and asks Margie to help her obtain a divorce. A lawyer tells the sisters that it will cost $200 to obtain a divorce and Margie tries unsuccessfully to obtain a loan from the models at work, from her boss, and from Jimmie. Margie decides to ask Harding and goes to his sumptuous apartment where he is hosting a large party and frolicking with a woman in his pool. Harding says to Margie, "Why not take off your clothes and stay awhile," and asks a servant to show her to a room where she is provided with a swimsuit and kimono. Harding soon enters in his kimono and begins to apply his seduction technique on Margie, plying her with champagne. When Margie asks him for a loan of $200 and promises to pay it back in installments from her weekly salary, Harding asks her if she will take it as a gift. Margie indicates by her expression that she understands the implication and says, "Yes, if necessary … I suppose that's the only way you lend money to girls like me." Harding answers, "Yes, that seems to be the customary arrangement." Margie says she understands and shows her willingness to accept the type of relationship that Harding is suggesting by declaring that "Marriage is bunk, at least for poor people." When Harding says that he does not think she would like the high life, Margie replies, "I'll learn to like it." Margie's honesty impresses Harding ("I find you very refreshing"), and it becomes apparent that he will give her the money without requiring a sexual exchange. At this point, Jimmie arrives to rescue his girl and, after some complications that arise from Jimmie punching Harding, the film ends happily. Margie agrees to marry Jimmie; Harding and Margie's boss each send her $200; and the money is no longer needed for Sophie's divorce because Alf has won a big billiards game and is taking his pregnant wife, child, and mother-in-law for a vacation in Atlantic City. The film's portrayal of extreme inequality, sexual exploitation and an irresponsible, work-shy husband who abuses his wife are forgotten as a stream of happy tidings give an impression of almost deliberate absurdity (Fig. 7.1).

As the Depression deepened, sexual harassment and exploitation were portrayed vividly in a number of films. Although an infrequent occurrence in the films of the 1920s, sexual harassment had no doubt remained widespread in society, but it is possible that the Depression made sexual harassment an even greater threat to working women.[2] There is little documentation to support claims for the widespread nature and trend in sexual harassment, simply because sexual advances and requests for sexual favors were considered an expression of masculinity and were expected as part of a working woman's life. There was no generally accepted name for this behavior (the term 'sexual harassment' was adopted in the 1970s) and, as there were no legal remedies, neither men nor women were likely to view it as a crime. A book on business etiquette for women published in 1935 instructed them on what they could expect in the workplace: "When it appears that the man has 'intentions', honorable or otherwise, the standard technique is to pretend not to see them, or else to continue to act as if they were not serious." The author acknowledged that this strategy did not always work, but women were warned against complaining to

Fig. 7.1 Still and frame from *Under 18* (Warner, 1932). Still shows Margie (Marion Marsh) at the beginning of the film in an optimistic mood with her sister who is getting married. Frame shows Margie suddenly aware of the presence of Raymond Harding (Warren William) who has been gazing at her in her lingerie beneath the fur coat that she has modelled. Still courtesy of Derek Boothroyd

management: "The front office does not want to be put in a position of having to take sides, to sit in judgment, and, possibly, to risk losing a valuable man or a good customer." If the harassment persisted, the only solution was to leave: "occasionally a girl does have to give up a perfectly good job in order to extricate herself from a situation for which she is entirely blameless."[3] However, in the depths of the Depression, most working women were unlikely to leave a job when the chances of obtaining another were slight and the only other option available to many women was prostitution. Social workers reported a dramatic increase in the number of women who resorted to casual prostitution and increasingly cited economic need rather than immorality as the primary reason for engaging in prostitution.[4]

The unpleasant consequences of the loss of a job for working women were indicated by Trixie, one of the showgirl gold diggers in the musical *Gold Diggers of 1933* (Warner, 1933). The success of the show requires that Brad, a blueblood who is trying to conceal his true identity, take a leading part, and in order to convince him to take the part, Trixie explains the consequences for the female performers if the show does not go on: "It means that all those girls, all those poor kids who gave up jobs, and who'll never get other jobs in these times ... [are] depending on you! ... God knows what will happen to those girls—They'll have to do things I wouldn't want on my conscience."[5] The film suggests that chorus girls would turn to prostitution if they did not have a job, but actual chorus girls often found that to obtain and retain their jobs, they had to submit to sexual advances. Chorus girls, like other working women, were unlikely to make an issue of sexual harassment, but documentation has surfaced from the Shubert brothers' production of *Hooray for What!* in 1937. The chorus girls were subjected to sexual demands from management and, through them, the production's investors. Casting was a sexual transaction and in addition to their onstage work, the chorus girls were expected to attend parties where they had to make themselves available to the Shubert's investors and business associates who would 'party' with them in hotel rooms paid for by the management. Those women who refused to perform sexually at the management's command were fired.[6]

Big Business Girl (Vitaphone, 1931) shows that even a woman with a college degree had to be lucky to find work during the Depression and that she was also likely to be considered a sexual object in the workplace. Claire McIntyre (Loretta Young) has borrowed money to attend college and at her graduation she tells her boyfriend that she wants to postpone their marriage as she intends to succeed in business. A short montage sequence shows the hurdles for a woman graduate in finding any kind of a job and when, by chance, she is hired by a large advertising firm, she quickly understands that her sex appeal is more important in her advancement than her intelligence and capability. The boss likes Claire's copy and gives her a promotion, but Claire's face changes from an expression of pride to one of humiliation when she inadvertently overhears the boss tell his partner that even if her copy was an accident she is worth her salary "as an office decoration." Claire concludes that her sexual appeal is more likely to advance her than her work abilities, and when the boss comes into her office she provides a good display of her legs. The boss instructs her to dress well in order to soften up their clients.[7]

If, for many working women, sexual negotiations with bosses, investors and customers accompanied what they regarded as their major work tasks, for some women, known as 'customer girls' or 'client girls', it was their major occupation. The cross-class romance heroines in *The Devil's Holiday* (Paramount, 1930) and *Girls About Town* (Paramount, 1931) are customer girls employed by businessmen to attract and soften up their buyers. *She Had to Say Yes* (First National, 1933) focuses on the (mis) adventures of a stenographer-turned-customer girl who seeks to remain virtuous. One advert for the film described it as the "story of a beautiful stenographer who *played* overtime to keep the customers from saying no!"[8] In this film, Sol Glass, the head of a large clothing company, announces to his managers that business is bad and that clients are no longer being properly enticed by the "worn-out, gold-digging, customer girls." Glass adopts the suggestion of Tommy Nelson, a salesman of the company, that they should use their stenographers to entertain their buyers. When Glass introduces the idea to the stenographers, he clarifies the benefits that they should accept from their relationships with buyers: "Theatre tickets, silk hose, or a box of candy is okay. But you will not accept expensive presents or money. Remember, you are receiving a bonus from the firm." At first Tommy refuses to let his fiancée, Florence Denny (Loretta Young), to participate in the scheme and tells her that if she is going to be manhandled, he will be the guy to do it. However, Tommy is also attracted to one of the most popular of the new customer girls, Birdie Reynolds, and he arranges to take her out by telling Florence that Birdie is sick, and by persuading Florence that she should take Birdie's place and entertain an important buyer. The buyer, Danny Drew, takes Florence to a nightclub and then asks her to accompany him to his hotel to take some dictation. At the hotel, Florence struggles against Danny's advances and when she tells him that she hates being pawed he replies that, "maybe you've never been pawed properly. It's really nice." After Danny apologizes and explains that he thought her play of innocence was "part of the racket," it is Florence's turn to apologize: "I guess it was *my* fault. I suppose you do feel cheated. I'm just not a good sport, that's all."

Florence learns of Tommy's affair with Birdie, breaks off their engagement, and continues as a customer girl. Tommy accuses her of "going the limit" with customers and one night he arrives drunk at her apartment, thrusts money on her, and tells her to close her eyes and pretend he is a buyer. When she yells to him to stop, he accuses her of knowing "all the professional tricks." Florence decides to quit being a customer girl and the consequence is that she is fired from her job as stenographer. Danny has fallen in love with Florence, but after he asks her to help him complete a merger and she obtains the necessary signature, it is his turn to question her innocence. Like Tommy, once Danny has persuaded himself that Florence is not innocent she becomes fair game. He tricks her into coming with him to a friend's house, which is unoccupied, tells her that he was a sap to fall for her line of being "untouched," and proceeds to sexually attack her. He chases Florence into a bedroom where she faints onto a chaise lounge. Danny is pleased that she has "decided not to fight it," but before he advances further Florence says softly, "Is this all I mean to you, Danny?" This appears to have an effect on Danny's conscience and he exclaims, "I give up. I guess I just don't understand you." When Danny realizes that Florence is really innocent he remorsefully asks her to forgive him and to marry him. Florence agrees as "a matter of choosing the lesser evil."

Sexual harassment could be played for laughs in comedies as in *Love, Honor and Oh, Baby* (Universal, 1933) and have tragic consequences in dramas as in *$20 a Week* (Alexander Brothers Studio, 1935) in which a manager's sexual harassment leads to the suicide of one of his victims. The advertising campaign for *Employees' Entrance* (Warner, 1933) firmly established the connection for young working women between finding and retaining a job and sexual exploitation and harassment. One advertisement asked: "Has the depression brought BARGAINS IN LOVE? Is there a panic in morals … when millions of heartsick girls will pay <u>any price</u> for a job."[9] Another advertisement claimed that it was the first film "to reveal the 'inside' of department store life—what happens when girl need jobs— 'Love Bargains' shoppers never see!" "Why don't you leave me alone? All I want is my job" was the text that accompanied an image of the heroine as she struggles in her boss' overpowering clinch.[10] Kurt Anderson (Warren William), the unscrupulous managing director of the department store, finds Madeline (Loretta Young), out-of-work and hungry in the store after it has closed for the day. Madeline intends to spend the night in the store's model house. Anderson takes her for a sumptuous meal, hires her, and takes her to his apartment where he blocks her from leaving with a kiss and makes it clear that she is expected to show her gratitude by allowing herself to be seduced. Madeline begins work at the store and starts to date a store manager, Martin, whose ideas for improving sales make an impression on Anderson who makes him his assistant and warns him that the job is not for a married man. Martin and Madeline marry secretly but their relationship suffers as Anderson monopolizes Martin's time. After Madeline quarrels with Martin, they both get drunk at the employees' dance and the inebriated Madeline accepts Anderson's invitation to take a key to a room that he has reserved and lie down for a while. Madeline finds the room, flops down on the bed and passes out. Anderson soon follows and is shown walking down the hallway and entering the room. What happens after Anderson closes the door is left to our imagination and we may suppose that Madeline was in no state to offer resistance. Anderson is furious at work when he discovers that Madeline and Martin are married and he lets Martin overhear a conversation he has with Madeline in which their intimacy is revealed. Overcome with shame, Madeline takes poison but survives and, at her bedside, Martin tells her that they will start anew together. Anderson remains the same unscrupulous, rapacious man at the end of the film as he was at the beginning, and apart from taking a shot in the arm he is not punished for his nefarious deeds. He is about to be fired by the store's board of directors but is saved by some last minute proxy votes.

Warren William played a suave male seducer or would-be seducer in a number of other films including *Skyscraper Souls* (MGM, 1932) in which his unscrupulous businessman is shot by his secretary-mistress when he is about to take another female employee with him to Europe. In comparison, female bosses who seduce their male employees were comparatively uncommon but one was portrayed in *Female* (Warner, 1933). Alison Drake (Ruth Chatterton) successfully manages an automobile factory that she inherited from her father and she uses her position to seduce young men who work in the office, rewarding them with a pay bonus after their night with her. One new employee she invites to her home suggests that the factory workers chant each morning to work up their enthusiasm.

Alison grabs a pillow off the couch, throws it onto the rug and says, "Are you … naturally enthusiastic." She is only interested in one-night stands and if a man becomes too serious she banishes him to the company's branch in Montreal.

The gender reversal portrayed in the first part of the film is upset by the arrival of Jim, a senior engineer who rejects the boss' advances: "I was engaged as an engineer, not a gigolo." On the advice of a secretary, Alison adopts the "gentle and feminine" role and Jim succumbs to her charms. After she scorns his proposal of marriage as old-fashioned, he castigates her for believing that she is "superior for marriage, love and children, the things women were born for" and for thinking that she could make her own rules. Jim leaves town, Alison realizes that she is truly in love, and when she catches up with him she tells him that she will marry him and that he will run the factory while she has nine children. This reestablishment of gender roles in the last few minutes of the film was not sufficient compensation for James Wingate, chief censor of the Studio Relations Committee, who objected strongly to Alison's "satisfying a too definitely indicated sex hunger, by frequently inviting any young man who may appeal to her to her home and there bringing about a seduction."[11] Alison, however, was an exception among the seductresses of the 1930s. More common were those women who had a reputation for seducing men but who did not challenge the rules of gender: the gold diggers.

GOLD-DIGGERS OF THE DEPRESSION

The popular press took little interest in the everyday complaints of working women who fought off the sexual overtures of their bosses and clients. It took far greater interest in the accounts of designing women who exploited wealthy men and escaped punishment when they successfully "blackmailed" them. Investigators reported that waitresses and sales-girls realized the need for them to exploit their sex appeal, and with the increase of women into the lower ranks of white-collar work, the press carried sensational stories of secretaries and typists who purposely set out to seduce and blackmail their bosses. Sociologists, legislators and legal scholars joined in depicting sexually emancipated women as a threat to men; lawyers and politicians labeled men who had become embroiled in breach of promise and alienation of affection suits as "blackmail victims." Beginning in 1935, many states passed anti-heart balm statutes that disallowed taking legal action for breach of promise. The new legislation was intended to end "sexual racketeering" by legal actions that were held to place innocent men at the mercy of ruthless women. The statutes often included abolishing related common law actions including seduction, which was no longer perceived as the conquest by an active male over a passive female. The more liberated sexual activity induced one commentator in 1934 to proclaim that seductions had become "largely mutual," but men were seen to require more protection as a consequence of the greater willingness of women to make their cases in public. It was assumed that men should not be held responsible for giving way to their natural urges in response to women's wiles.[12]

In contrast to sociologists and judges, popular novels and magazine stories portrayed sexually emancipated women, and even some gold diggers, sympathetically. Unlike the earlier heroines of popular literature, who faced threats to their virtue or whose illicit sex led to death or ruined lives, the sexual activism of the new heroines did not necessarily prevent them ending up happily married to the men they loved. When the manipulative gold diggers in some magazine stories were redeemed by love, they were no longer expected to pay for their sins, and they would often succeed in their goal of marrying wealthy men.[13]

Films joined with judicial critics in presenting alimony as a form of female extortion, but the gold digger, particularly if unmarried, was often portrayed, as in magazine stories and popular songs, as ultimately good-hearted. Angus McLaren writes that, whereas courtroom judges decried the activities of gold diggers, movie audiences cheered them on. In answer to the question of whether women were ever justified in exploiting sex, McLaren claims that the courtroom and the movies provided two conflicting responses.[14]

The American Film Institute lists only one film with a gold-digger theme in 1929 (*Gold Diggers of Broadway*), but as the Depression deepened, the number increased: six in 1930, nine in 1931, ten in 1932 and 14 in 1933. A decline in the number of gold-digger films after 1933 may have been the consequence of the more optimistic mood following the election of Roosevelt and the imposition of stricter censorship from 1934. The AFI lists six in 1934, three in 1935, six in 1936, five in 1937, four in 1938, five in 1939 and two in 1940.[15] The list is not comprehensive but it indicates the trend during the Depression years. There were both continuities with, and differences from, the films of the 1920s in the representations of gold diggers in the films of the Depression years. Musicals such as *Gold Diggers of 1933* continued the association of gold diggers with chorus girls, but gold diggers appeared in a range of occupations and milieu. The addition of sound provided more opportunities for the gold-digging protagonists to demonstrate, often through wisecracks, their cynical view of the relationships between the sexes.

The prominence of the gold digger in films of the early 1930s was also evident in popular music. Although a case can be made that the gold digger was already a common type in popular culture in the latter half of the 1920s, Timothy Scheurer, in his article on popular music of the 1930s, writes that the gold digger was the one really original new woman of the 1930s and that probably only the Depression could have created her. Songs about gold diggers, like those about prostitutes and dance hall hostesses, focused on the theme of survival, an issue that had been of little or no concern in the music of the previous decades. The gold digger struggles to survive: "she is a woman who knows what a woman can achieve in the world and is hardened by that knowledge, and is intent upon having the world on her terms."[16]

The representations of gold diggers in films related to fundamental social anxieties of both women and men, which had been accentuated by the Depression. The films with gold diggers transformed these anxieties in ways that conformed to gender norms and allowed for imaginary solutions. These transformations and solutions assumed that the gold digger was a female. The gigolo, credited as the male counterpart of the gold digger, made far fewer appearances than the gold digger and was generally a secondary character.

Male anxieties about obtaining or retaining employment and supporting their families were linked to divisions of gender. The sexual division of occupations within the labor market provided men with some measure of protection from the competition of women, but this division was not complete and many men believed that women were taking jobs that rightfully belonged to men. The occupations in which women were concentrated, particularly clerical and services, contracted less during the first years of the Depression, and the unemployment rate was higher for men than for women. Public disapproval of working married women, which many women shared with men, was sharpened by the Depression, and when a Gallup poll in 1936 asked whether wives should work if husbands were employed, 82 % answered no.[17]

The portrayals of gold diggers in films displaced male anxieties from the economic and occupational realms to a moral realm. The motivations and actions of gold diggers were based on the assumption that women were dependent economically on men. Men were portrayed as the source of capital and status, and although the gold digger would use her sexuality to exploit male weaknesses, she was not in competition with them. The gold digger represented a moral predicament, but this could be diffused by narrative solutions, particularly romantic ones.

THE FILM INDUSTRY IN DEPRESSION AND THE PRE-CODE PERIOD

The greatest number of gold digger films were made from 1930–1933, the years of economic crisis in the film industry and of the so-called 'pre-Code' films. By the end of 1929, the major studios were committed to making only talking pictures and as the novelty of 'talkies' attracted large audiences, there were those in the film industry who believed that it was Depression proof. This illusion was shattered in 1931 when admissions fell and continued to fall in 1932 and 1933. Admission prices were cut and many theaters closed down. The crisis led to further consolidation of the oligopoly as smaller production companies and many independent film theaters went out of business. Of central importance to the effects of the Depression on the major film companies was the ownership of chains of cinema by the 'Big Five': Paramount, Loew's/MGM, Warner Brothers, Fox (after 1935 Twentieth Century Fox) and RKO, which were vertically integrated corporations of production, distribution and exhibition.[18] The cinema chains owned by the Big Five constituted about 20 % of the country's film theaters; however, they included 80 % of the first-run houses, which in the large cities took in over 50 % of the total box-office revenue and in some cities as much as 80 %.

Almost all the major film corporations showed losses in 1931, and those that had invested most heavily in real estate for exhibition—RKO, Paramount and Fox—went into bankruptcy or receivership. With a relatively small chain of theaters, MGM was the least affected by the Depression; its costs of sound conversion were not so heavy, and it had fewer mortgage payments. The major studios survived the crisis as they were refinanced by banking interests that moved to secure the capital they had invested in the industry. Recovery was assisted by Roosevelt's National Industrial Recovery Act (NIRA), which went into effect June 1933. The Act enabled the promotion of certain monopoly practices and the eight major film corporations exploited the opportunity to consolidate what had been a loose affiliation into a solid oligopoly. The NIRA was declared unconstitutional by the Supreme Court in 1935, but by then the majors had achieved an effective market control. Economic recovery of the industry began in 1934, and with the exception of the economic set-back in 1938, the industry's economic situation continued to improve throughout the decade.[19]

The years of economic crisis and recovery of the major film corporations correspond roughly to the division made by many historians of film between the 'pre-Code' period from 1930 to July 1934 and the 'post-Code' period from July 1934. A Code intended to govern the morality of films was published in 1927 by the public relations organization of the industry, the Motion Pictures Producers and Distributors of American (MPPDA), but it is common to date the beginning of the pre-Code period to 1930 when a revised code, largely formulated by two Catholic reformers, was adopted by the major companies who pledged to abide by it. The Code was administered by the Studio Relations Committee (SRC), which came to be known as the Hays Office after Will H. Hays, the president of MPPDA. Studios often ignored the Code as they saw the SRC as largely advisory and it was possible to appeal to a committee of producers who could overrule the SRC directives.

Pressure from various groups mounted on the industry to tighten its censorship. By the end of 1932, nearly 40 religious and educational organizations passed resolutions calling for regulation by the federal government. A sensationalized digest of the findings of research on the deleterious effects of movies on youth was widely circulated, and the Catholic Legion of Decency, established in 1933, launched a crusade against Hollywood immorality. The economic problems of the industry made it appear vulnerable and, early in 1933, Hays advised that a stronger enforcement of the Code would attract public sympathy and take the pressure off for federal intervention. In June 1934, the SRC was renamed the Production Code Administration (PCA) with Joseph I. Breen as its director. The members of the MPPDA agreed to release a film only if it received a certificate from the PCA, and violation of this was subject to a penalty of $25,000. The PCA became involved in the regulation of films from their script stage, and Breen submitted detailed suggestions for changes when he believed that a film was likely to deviate from the Code. In order to outmaneuver those still demanding federal regulation, the MPPDA launched a public relations campaign to persuade its critics and the public that Hollywood had turned over a new leaf; it advertised Hollywood's commitment to moral films and emphasized that the establishment of the PCA signaled a clear dividing line in the regulation of film content. By the end of 1934, the upsurge in box office revenues encouraged the industry to believe that the toughened censorship was good for business.[20]

Thomas Doherty characterizes the pre-Code period as one of lax censorship, during which films portrayed illicit sexual liaisons, marriage was ridiculed, economic injustice was exposed, political corruption was rampant, vice was unpunished, and virtue was unrewarded.[21] Although most films, including the newsreels, ignored the Depression, there were films of the early 1930s that expressed "the anguish of the dispossessed and fearful," with "a fevered, pursued, despairing quality."[22] Hollywood changed as the morale of the nation changed, from the despair under Hoover to the optimism and the restoration of cultural equilibrium under Roosevelt.[23] It took little time for the newly established PCA to erase "the genres, tones, and textures of pre-Code Hollywood."[24] Hollywood underwent a process of desexualization and depoliticizing. It was not just a matter of women no longer appearing in scanty clothing; little was now seen of the dire economic conditions in which a third of the nation remained, or of the protests against those conditions.[25]

The terms 'pre-Code' and 'post-Code' have been adopted almost unanimously in discussions of the films of the 1930s, but some historians, particularly Richard Maltby, have expressed reservations with respect to making a clear division between these periods. Maltby argues that it is misleading to claim that censorship was not seriously administered in the early 1930s, and he notes that the stricter imposition of the Code from 1934 resulted in films of greater ambiguity, especially in representations of sexuality. A related controversy concerns the groups and motivations behind the stricter censorship. One view is that censorship was imposed by pressure groups from outside the industry, particularly the Catholic Legion of Decency on an industry afraid of boycotts and on a passive and easily manipulated movie going public. An alternative view is that the industry cooperated with the Catholic moral campaign in order to protect its oligopoly and business methods against broader attacks from Protestant interest groups and moral reformers and from the threat of federal regulation. Maltby contends that it was not the hostile criticism of the content of films that was the major concern of the industry, but rather the complaint directed against the studios' oligopoly and business practices that left little room for competition and penalized independent exhibitors. The industry welcomed the involvement of the Catholic Church because the Church helped the industry to displace the public debate from economic issues to the morality of films, and by acquiescing to the call for more censorship, the industry succeeded in protecting its economic interests.

Maltby contends that far from the pre-Code cinema reflecting a breakdown of morals as a consequence of the Depression, a revival of moral conservatism was already evident in the early 1930s. Ralph Brauer points to 1934 as a year of "conservative counterrevolution,"[26] and Nick Smedley writes that a significant cultural change in America from 1932 provided the milieu for Hollywood's comfortable support for the "high moral tone" of the New Deal.[27] The collapse of the economy and the accompanying strain on the patriarchal family as a consequence of male unemployment was seen by some, especially small town Protestants, as a result of the permissiveness of the Jazz Age. Maltby admits that in the early 1930s the movie industry failed to keep pace with the growing demand for a "return to decency" and that there was some variation from Hollywood's established norms, but he insists that this variation occurred within strict limits and that the change between the films of the early and late 1930s was gradual.[28] An examination of the portrayal of gold diggers in cross-class romance films provides support for Maltby's arguments.

GOLD DIGGERS IN CROSS-CLASS ROMANCE FILMS

In considering the film narrative trajectories of gold diggers and the public response to them, it is important to distinguish between comedies and dramas. The humor that accompanied Mae West's blatant sexuality in her pre-Code films, together perhaps with the films' non-contemporary settings, allowed her portrayals of successful unchaste women to be widely accepted.[29] The comedy in the Jean Harlow film *Red Headed Woman* (MGM, 1932) made palatable the theme of an unredeemed gold digger who did not pay for her sins.[30] Although Harlow's character does not achieve her goal of acceptance into upper society, she is last seen with a bearded old sugar daddy in a car driven by her chauffeur lover. It became evident with the stricter imposition of the Code that not all Americans, and least of all Joseph Breen, the head of the Production Code Administration from June 1934, shared the view that comedy diffused the offense of a successful, unrepentant gold digger. In dramas, even in the pre-Code period, women who exploited their sexuality to gain wealth and social status were almost invariably punished in some way; they were returned to their working-class origins, or, even worse, they suffered the loss of a child or other loved one.

It was not unusual for a gold digger to undergo a change and forego her predatory ambitions for disinterested love. The sentimental ending tacked on to *Baby Face* (Warner, 1933) in response to censorship pressures is perhaps the best known example. Barbara Stanwyck's character in this film redeems herself in the last minutes of the film by sacrificing her jewelry for love, but the censors insisted on an absurd ending in which we hear that she has returned to a working-class life, albeit with the man—the disgraced former bank president—she loves.[31]

The gold digger films transposed economic anxieties to a moral realm, and whereas the studios were not likely to suggest structural economic and social solutions to the economic crisis, they were able to provide narrative solutions to a moral problem or dilemma. The typical narrative trajectories of the gold digger dramas were punishment and redemption. These were combined in various ways, and most cases of redemption were through the gold digger's conversion to disinterested love, which in some cases took the form of the heroine leaving their rich partners, who in most cases they do not really love, for 'true' love with a non-wealthy partner. This is what happened in *Bought* (Warner, 1931), *Bed of Roses* (RKO, 1933), *The Gilded Lily* (Paramount, 1935) and *The Bride Wore Red* (MGM, 1937).[32] In *Sinners in the Sun* (Paramount, 1932), both the poor heroine and her poor boyfriend succeed in capturing rich partners before they decide that love is more important than money and end up with each other. However, it is the woman who, at the beginning, decides that she does not want to live in poverty. Rare cases of a central male protagonist presenting himself as no less a gold digger than the heroine with whom he falls in love appear in the comedies *Hands Across the Table* (Paramount, 1935) and *Three Blind Mice* (Twentieth-Century Fox, 1938). Whereas the heroines in these two films are working class with marital ambitions, the males are impoverished but originate from the upper class.

In the majority of gold digger films, the gold digger's conversion to true love did not require that she end up with a penniless man. The gold digger's conversion to disinterested love is rewarded in most cases by both love and wealth. However, not all gold diggers underwent redemption and the unredeemed in dramas were punished by disappointment or worse. Death was the punishment of a particularly immoral gold digger in the 1930 film *Party Girl*, a sexploitation film of poverty-row Tiffany Productions. Leeda (Judith Barrie) dupes Jay Rountree (Douglas Fairbanks Jr.), the son of a wealthy manufacturer, into marrying her. She is punished by falling from a fire escape when attempting to escape the police, and this enables Jay to return to his true love, his father's secretary, who is a reformed party girl. In contrast with the appearance of party girls in the films of the major studios, this film leaves the audience with little doubt that the party girls are upscale prostitutes who are employed to attend specially organized parties whereby in wining, dining and providing sexual services, they ensure that business deals will be completed. As with some of the gangster films of the period, *Party Girl* begins with a written statement that its intentions are moral and reformist: "the 'Party Girl' racket threatens to corrupt the morals of thousands of young girls who seek to earn their living decently. It is our earnest hope that this film will arouse you and other public-spirited citizens to forcibly eliminate the vicious 'Party Girl' system." However, the arousal intended is more accurately reflected in one of the film's advertisements, which the New York Times refused to print: "Girls for hire for the out-of-town buyer. See the road to din, sin and gin."[33]

In the films of the major studios, even in the so-called pre-Code era, gold diggers tended to be chaste, or at least their sexual activities were never made explicit. The early 1930s films of Mae West and the well-known films *Baby Face* and *Red-Headed Woman* were among the exceptions in this respect. The sexual favors provided by a sympathetic gold digger in her relationship with a wealthy man who she does not love were understood but rarely shown. Blondie McClune (Marion Davies) in *Blondie of the Follies* (MGM, 1932) is set up in a luxurious apartment by an elderly oil tycoon, but the film does not show them together in the apartment or having any physical contact that could be construed as sexual. The ellipses reinforce the favorable portrayal of Blondie who ends up with a wealthy man whom she really loves.

The chastity of the gold digger was required in most cases if she was to undergo redemption through disinterested love, and this was the case even when she was employed in occupations that were associated with prostitution, such as party girls and escort services. The services provided by a party girl were left almost solely to the imagination in *Ladies of Leisure* (Columbia, 1930). Jerry Strong (Ralph Graves), the artist son of a railroad titan, meets a party girl in the person of Kay Arnold (Barbara Stanwyck) after he leaves a riotous party with drunken women and stops his car by a lake. Kay has escaped from a noisy yacht party by leaving in a canoe and rowing herself ashore. We are not told why she left the party, but she tells Jerry that she was there as a party girl ("that's my racket"), and, although she makes a point of having to explain what a party girl does, her description is hardly informative: a party girl acts as a "filler-in" when girls are needed for parties. The avoidance of a suggestion of prostitution may have been one reason why the title of the film was changed from the play upon which the film was based, *Ladies of the Evening*. Although Kay begins by pocketing Jerry's wallet it soon becomes clear that she is more than ready to reform for a man who does not want her solely for sex.

A gold digger's chastity, despite what one might expect from her profession, is established in an early scene in *Girls About Town*. Wanda (Kay Francis) and Marie (Lilyan Tashman) are paid well by Jerry as 'escorts' to entertain and soften up his business associates. The girls are shown using a trick, which indicates to the audience that they do not go as far as prostitution. When the men they have been entertaining accompany them back to their flat, the girls tell them that their mother is waiting up for them and point to a silhouette of a woman sitting by their window. In fact, this is their Afro American maid. However, the difference between the two girls in their tolerance of providing sexual favors is also established early on in the film when Wanda tells Marie how she is fed up with having to hire herself out for the evening and asks Marie if it doesn't make her sick "to be pawed by a bunch of middle-class Babbits." Marie replies that she is always revived by the checks they receive, and although Wada acknowledges that someone's got to pay for her dress, her candidacy for redemption through disinterested love is set in place. This duly occurs when Wanda proceeds to fall in love with Jim (Joel McCrea), one of Jerry's wealthy clients, and demonstrates her disinterested love by tearing up the check she receives for entertaining him (Fig. 7.2).

In the comic and more light-hearted gold digger films, the gold digger's conversion to disinterested love was often accomplished with little soul-searching and without punishment. In a drama or melodrama, plot contrivances could lead the gold digger to have overwhelming feelings of guilt and her redemption could take on a quasi-religious character. This occurs for Hallie (Nancy Carroll) in *The Devil's Holiday* who is introduced as a manicurist who supplements her income by 'loosening up' the clients of businessmen in order to ensure their deals are completed. She shows Charley, who gives her a commission for helping him to sell farm equipment, her extensive wardrobe, which is made possible by her 'commissions'. She declares that she will never fall in love because she knows too much about men and that her only interest in them is the 'old bankroll'. When David Stone, one of the sons of a wealthy, strait-laced farmer comes to New York to buy equipment he quickly falls in love with Hallie who

Fig. 7.2 Still from *Girls About Town* (Paramount, 1931). Jerry (Alan Dinehart) employs Marie (Lilyan Tashman) and Wanda (Kay Francis) as 'escorts' to soften up his business associates. Image from Photofest

manipulates him by acting as an innocent girl. Marc Stone, the older brother, arrives to rescue David and he tells Hallie to "take her dirty hands off the cleanest boy who stepped out of the wheat." Marc reports to their father that "Her trade's written on her face." Indignant at Marc's suggestion that she is a prostitute, Hallie marries David intending to demand $50,000 from his family to divorce him. Her scheme goes according to plan but David is injured when, in an argument with his brother, he falls down stairs. Hallie returns to New York where, despite her spending, she is unhappy and starts to drink. She returns to the house of the Stones, but when she has to admit to David, who still believes in her innocence, that she took money to leave him, he looses consciousness. Hallie then tells the father that, although she fought against it, she truly loves David, and she asks if there is a chance for someone like her, no matter what they have done. Hallie's declaration of her love for David, who is portrayed as weak, gullible and entirely innocent, has been given little support by their rather passionless scenes together, and her return to him appears motivated by her guilty conscience and shame. The father forgives and embraces her and

Fig. 7.3 Still from *The Devil's Holiday* (Paramount, 1930). Hallie (Nancy Carroll) shows indifference toward the pleas of David, whom she has married, and his father. Charley who has employed her as a 'customer girl' looks on. Still courtesy of Derek Boothroyd

prays to God ("bless them both"). The film ends with Hallie embracing David, who has returned to consciousness (Fig. 7.3).

Most conversions of gold diggers to disinterested love received a lighter treatment than the formula received in *The Devil's Holiday*. One way for a gold digger to demonstrate her conversion was to refuse the proposal of marriage from the wealthy man she now truly loves. This scenario was played out in a most explicit form in *Lady By Choice* (Columbia, 1934). The gold digger in this film is Alabam Lee (Carole Lombard) who, having become convinced that her talents as an entertainer are limited to her fan dance, decides to pursue a wealthy attorney, Johnny Mills. Unbeknownst to Alabam, Johnny is the son of a man who had been loved by Patsy, the mother that Alabam adopted as a publicity stunt. When Patsy tries to dissuade Alabam from her plan, Alabam exclaims, "Why is he different from any other sucker! Why shouldn't I be the one to take him." Inevitably, Alabam falls in love with Johnny, and when he asks her to marry him the following conversation (slightly abridged) in which Johnny pretends that he will be disinherited ensues:

Alabam:	"I can't marry you."
Johnny:	"Why can't you?"
Alabam:	"Because I love you ... I'm a phony Johnny and a half-baked one at that ... I went after you because you had money, that's what I was interested in from the start."
Johnny:	"OK. Will you marry me?"
Alabam:	"Darling, you don't understand!"
Johnny:	"Look, why do women become interested in men anyway? Because they're rich or strong or attractive or smart. All right, in my case it was money."
Alabam:	"Doesn't that bother you?"
Johnny:	"It would except for one thing. Why do you tell me about it now."
Alabam:	"I meant to take you for a ride, but somehow ... [uncompleted sentence]"
Johnny [cuts in]:	"You went after a rich young man, but that man who is proposing to you now is practically broke ... All the money in my family belongs to my mother and she objects very strenuously to you ... She finally told me that if I marry you she will cut me off without a cent, and I do insist on marrying you. That is, if you are willing to marry a man who has to work for his living, and, at present, has a very modest income."
Alabam:	"Johnny. If you only promise me to stay poor for the rest of your life."
Johnny:	"We're practically paupers ..." They kiss.

The redemption of gold diggers in dramas sometimes required them to endure periods of hardship and poorly paid work before they could receive the rewards of their conversion to disinterested love. This occurs in *Tarnished Lady* (Paramount, 1931) to Nancy Courtney (Tallulah Bankhead), an impoverished socialite, who marries for money, becomes destitute after she leaves her unhappy marriage, and finally returns to her husband after realizing that she is truly in love with him. A reformed gold digger may undergo hardship even if her reward is to be a poor man rather than a rich one. *Bed of Roses* (RKO, 1933) begins with Lorry (Constance Bennett) and Minnie (Pert Kelton) released after a stretch in a reformatory with no signs of their having been reformed. Minnie immediately suggests the promise of sex to a driver for a lift into town. Lorry tricks a wealthy publisher who, although he comes to understand her manipulations, takes her as a mistress and sets her up in a luxury apartment. Lorry's redemption through love occurs when she falls for Dan (Joel McCrea), a barge owner, and leaves the publisher. However, because she feels unworthy of her true love, instead of going to him, she moves into a small one-room apartment and finds work in a department store. It is Minnie, the ongoing gold digger, who brings Lorry and Dan back together again.

As in a number of other films with more than one gold digger, the redemption through disinterested love of the heroine in *Bed of Roses* is offset, to some extent, by the continuing gold digging spirit of her friend. The last shot shows Minnie observing the couple and then admiring the bracelet on her wrist which Lorry had refused to take from the rich publisher. Minnie has the last line in the film: "I like to see true love triumphant." This can be read both as an expression of the material benefits that Minnie has gained from taking Lorry's place after she had rejected the rich man and as a somewhat cynical admission of the film makers that they have followed the conventional formula.

In the early 1930s, the heroine's friend could continue her gold-digging ways without disapproval as long as she helped the heroine to find happiness in disinterested love. When there were three or more gold diggers, alongside the gold digger who reforms, a further differentiation could be made between unreformed but good-hearted gold diggers and the unreformed, cold-hearted gold diggers. The true love found by one of the three gold diggers in *The Greeks Had a Word for Them* (Goldwyn/ United Artists 1932, re-released as *Three Broadway Girls*) constituted a change from the original stage production, which had all three girls continuing their gold digging activities at the end. The film emphasizes the differences among the girls: the one for whom it makes no difference if the man she loves will not inherit the wealth of his father, the manipulative one who double-crosses her friends in order to obtain wealthy men, and the one who, although she is quite willing to be supported by a sugar daddy, is good-hearted and supports her friend to obtain her true love.

Gold Diggers of 1933 contains a range of cross-class romances and gold-digging chorus girls. The purest disinterested love is that which Polly has for Brad, whom she thinks is a penniless songwriter but is, in fact, a Boston blueblood. Two of her friends are genuine gold diggers, but whereas one of them, Trixie, is clearly only after the material benefits that can be provided by an elderly lawyer, Peabody; the other, Carol, finds romance as well as money with Brad's older brother whom, at first, she was only interested in fleecing. Another chorus girl, Fay Fortune, is excluded from the rewards of matrimony because she offers sex too overtly as a bargaining commodity. The film divides the gold diggers into the good-hearted, whose circumstances account for their behavior and who are rewarded, and the cold-hearted, who resort to unacceptable methods. It is, however, a fine line dividing the predatory tactics of the more sympathetically portrayed Trixie and the unsympathetically portrayed Fay in their pursuit of Peabody.[34]

A number of changes, including the political climate and stricter censorship, brought an end to the representations of successful gold diggers. As Lea Jacobs has shown, the rapid rise in class and relatively easy class crossing, as represented by material accoutrements such as clothes and jewels, of the heroines of the early 1930s films became less common after 1934. Jacob's major example of the change is the remake of *Stella Dallas* (Goldwyn/United Artists, 1937) which, like the first silent version, transforms the class rise motif into one of maternal sacrifice.[35] This was a theme that did not encounter problems of censorship, and, in general, the dwindling number of cross-class romance films of the late 1930s provided few problems for the censors. Fewer films were produced with genuine gold diggers, and when they made an appearance, as in *Three Blind Mice*, there was no doubt as to their chastity and innocence. At the end of the decade, the heroine could only be suspected or accused of gold digging (*Josette, The Rage of Paris*, both 1938). The heroine in *Fifth Avenue Girl* (RKO, 1939) only poses as a gold digger at the bequest of a wealthy older man who is neglected by his family. The girl has an impact on the members of the family, including the son who starts taking an interest in the family business as well as in the girl.

THE GIGOLO

Whereas gold diggers were all-American girls and most were portrayed sympathetically, gigolos had accents and were either clownish characters in comedies or unpleasant villains in dramas. An example of the comic version of the gigolo is Carlo (Mischa Auer) in *My Man Godfrey* (Universal,

1936); he is a playmate of the daffy mother of the family and amuses her by doing a monkey imitation. The villainous type is found in *Secrets of a Secretary* (Paramount, 1931) in which it becomes evident that the man with whom socialite Helen Blake (Claudette Colbert) marries on a whim, Frank D'Agnoll, is an unscrupulous gigolo. When Helen's father dies and she discovers that she is penniless as a consequence of the stock market crash, D'Agnoll leaves her in a petulant rage. Frank uses his gigolo talents to steal jewelry from wealthy, older women, and he is killed when he tries to double-cross his criminal boss.

The gigolo in *Ladies' Man* (Paramount, 1931), James Darricott (William Powell), was the central character and beneath his smooth charm there are indications of a man who knows that he is living on borrowed time. Like many a gold digger in films, this gigolo falls genuinely in love, but unlike most gold diggers his end is not a happy one. In a fight with the husband and father of the wife and daughter who fall in love with him, James falls to his death from the balcony of his hotel residence. In addition to the dark ending, the representation of the gigolo in this film differs from most gold diggers. His story is not one of social mobility; his socio-economic family background is not shown or indicated, there is no reference to the Depression or to the problems of making a living, and from the beginning of the film we see James living a lifestyle of an upper-class playboy, paid for by the gifts he receives from the older married women for whom, we have to assume, he provides sexual services.

Whereas gold diggers are generally represented as highly active agents in their paths to wealth, James' account of how he became a gigolo is that of an almost passive object in the hands of women. He explains to Norma Page (Kay Francis), with whom he has fallen in love, that ever since he could remember, from the cradle on, he was picked up by women and that he came to understand that he could make money by it. He became at some point a bonds' salesman but he found that the "skittish dowagers" to whom he tried to sell bonds were more interested in him. He reasons that women spend the money that men make, and when the women make their husbands work themselves almost to death and then complain that the husbands neglect them they spend their husbands' money on him, which he admits to Norma is "low and unspeakable." When Norma asks him why he adopted his way of life, he answers, "I suppose because I couldn't help myself. I was wrong." However, before he can reform and marry the woman he loves, he is killed. William Powell told the fan magazine *Screenland* that he had hated playing the part of the gigolo because the character was weak, passive and pitiable.[36] Even though in *Ladies' Man* the gigolo has a sympathetic side, unlike the gold digger, he was not a character with whom spectators were invited to identity.

GOLD DIGGERS, CENSORSHIP AND THE NEW DEAL

Unlike the morally scrupulous working girl, whose love for the wealthy man is disinterested from the beginning, the manipulative, sexually designing gold digger is interested in the material benefits of her relationship with the male. In a society where the options for women to advance in the work force were severely limited, female spectators in particular could appreciate the rationale of the gold digger and possibly identify with her success. As the barriers to the occupational opportunities and mobility of women are reinforced, the gold digger demonstrates with particular clarity that the solution for women is to find the right man. However, although the assumption that female sexuality has commodity value is made apparent in many films, it is also assumed that a chaste, virginal woman has a higher value in the marriage market than the sexually experienced woman. Thus, although the conception of a gold digger is of a woman who used her sexuality for material gain, a number of films go out of their way to establish that she is nevertheless chaste. The sexuality of the gold digger is displayed, but, if there is to be a happy ending in a love-based marriage, it has to be simultaneously repressed, and only in a few films is it made evident that the gold digger engages in actual physical sexual activities as a means of socio-economic mobility. In most cross-class romances with gold diggers, the redemption of the gold digger is not from her sexual behavior, which is basically chaste, but from her materialistic motivation in her pursuit of the male.

The portrayal of gold diggers in cross-class romance films is of relevance to the controversy over whether the stricter imposition of censorship from June 1934 represented a clear division between the cinema of the early 1930s and the remainder of the decade. The revisionist questioning of a pre-Code period, made most forcefully by Maltby, has been based on a close consideration of censorship processes and documents.[37] An examination of the narratives of the cross-class romances in general and of the gold digger romances in particular provide some support for the revisionist view. With regard to the number of cross-class romance films, the dividing year is not 1934 but 1941, after which far fewer films of this type were made. The high moral tone of some of the cross-class romance films of the early 1930s suggests that the notion of a morally daring pre-Code cinema is dependent on a selective choice of films. One change that was evident from 1934 is a decline in the number of gold diggers; films with cynical narratives of class rise through sexual allurement were no longer produced. A stricter censorship may have played a part here, but probably more important was that the differences between men and women in unemployment and downward mobility became less obvious after 1934, and male anxiety concerning competition with women in the labor market may have declined. Again, this change should not be overstated. Even in the early 1930s, most gold diggers were redeemed by disinterested love, which in many cross-class romance films continued to be rewarded by class rise.

Among the major studios, gold diggers were particularly numerous in the films of Warner Brothers, and a case can be made that a change in the content and tone of films from 1934 was most obvious in that studio. However, the changes in the films of Warner Brothers were related as much to its executives' support of Roosevelt's administration and the New Deal as it was to the stricter censorship. With its enthusiastic support of Roosevelt and the New Deal, the bleakness to be found in some Warner Brothers films of the first years of the decade gave way to optimism and confidence of pulling through, as exemplified by its musicals of 1933.[38] Not just Warner Brothers but Hollywood in general is seen by some historians as adopting the optimism that Roosevelt's administration conveyed. Ralph Brauer wrote that Hollywood movies constituted a "popular New Deal" and that the years 1934 and 1935 were a crucial watershed, "a counterrevolution in consciousness" whereby the previous years' films of violence, sexual freedom, and social consciousness were replaced by the films of Shirley Temple Frank Capra, and screwball comedies.[39] Similarly, Nick Smedley wrote that Hollywood supported and articulated the values and ideal of the New Deal, its "high moral tone," and the "radical reorientation in 1930s America towards a more communal, less competitive social ideology."[40] Just as the New Deal was interventionist and regulatory, so was the "preachy, regulatory and interventionist" PCA whose Code received virtually universal support because it "accurately reflected the prevailing moral atmosphere."[41] Cross-class romances could accommodate to the Code, but cross-class romances with cynical gold diggers were problematic.

NOTES

1. Mary Beth Haralovich, "The Proletarian Woman's Film of the 1930s; Contending with Censorship and Entertainment," *Screen* 31 (1990): 177–181.

2. The number of films in the 1930s listed by the American Film Institute Catalog as including rape or attempted rape increased considerably in comparison with the 1920s; from one a year in 1927, 1928 and 1929 the number increased to 13 in 1932 and 18 in 1933, The number dropped in 1934 together with the stricter censorship code.

3. Frances Maule, *She Strives to Conquer: Business Behavior, Opportunities and Job Requirements for Women* (New York: Funk & Wagnalls, 1934), 155–158. Quoted in Margaret A. Crouch, *Thinking About Sexual Harassment: A Guide for the Perplexed* (New York: Oxford University Press, 2000), 28–29.

4. Elizabeth Alice Clement, *Love for Sale: Courting, Treating and Prostitution in New York City, 1900–1945* (Chapel Hill: University of North Carolina Press, 2006), 197, 206–208.

5. On references to prostitution and the showgirls mock prostitution in *Gold Diggers of 1933* see Philip Hanson, *This Side of Despair: How the Movies and American Life Interrelated during the Great Depression* (Cranbury, NJ: Associated University Press, 2008), 36–39; Bruce Babington and Peter Willim Evans, *Blue Skies and Silver Linings: Aspects of the Hollywood Musical* (Manchester: Manchester University Press, 1985), 61, 71–72; Pamela Robertson, *Guilty Pleasures: Feminist Camp from Mae West to Madonna* (Durham, NC: Duke University Press, 1996), 79–83; Patricia Mellencamp, *A Fine Romance: Five Ages of Film Feminism* (Philadelphia: Temple University Press, 1995), 60–61.

6. Jennifer Cavenaugh, "Hooray for What!: A Glimpse into the Golden Age of Sexual Harassment," *Journal of American Drama and Theater* 20.3 (2008): 5–28.

7. Berry emphasizes the importance of a scene, extended beyond its narrative significance, in which Claire chooses her clothes and dresses prior to meeting clients. The focus on clothes shows that Claire is unable to separate her professional from her sexual identity. Sarah Berry, *Screen Style: Fashion and Femininity in 1930s Hollywood* (Minneapolis: University of Minnesota Press, 2000), 171–172.

8. Advertisement reproduced in the internet site *Immortal Ephemera*.

9. Haralovich, "The Proletarian Woman's Film of the 1930s," 181–182

10. Ad reproduced in *Immortal Ephemera* site

11. Quoted in Mark A. Vieira, *Sin in Soft Focus: Pre-Code Hollywood* (New York: Harry N. Abrams, 1999), 118.

12. Angus McLaren, *Sexual Blackmail: A Modern History* (Cambridge, MA: Harvard University Press, 2002), 169–74.

13. Joanne J. Meyerowitz, *Women Adrift: Independent Wage Earners in Chicago, 1880–1930* (Chicago: University of Chicago Press, 1988), 126–41.

14. McLaren, *Sexual Blackmail.* 175–81

15. *AFI Catalog.*

16. Timothy E. Scheurer, "Goddesses and Golddiggers: Images of Women in Popular Music of the 1930s," *Journal of Popular Culture* 24 (1990): 34

17. Susan Ware, *Holding Their Own: American Woman in the 1930s* (Boston: Twayne Publishers, 1982), 13–17; William H. Chafe, *The Paradox of Change: American Woman in the 20th Century* (New York: Oxford University Press, 1991), 115–16.

18. In her book on economic control of the motion picture industry, published in 1944, Mae Huettig wrote that two-thirds of the total capital of the five integrated majors was invested in cinemas and most of the corporations' income was derived from their theaters. Mae E. Huettig, "The Motion Picture Industry Today," in Tino Balio, ed., *The American Film Industry* (Madison: University of Wisconsin Press, 1976), 241 [From *Economic Control of the Motion Picture Industry* (Philadelphia: University of Pennsylvania Press, 1944)].

19. Janet Wasko, *Movies and Money: Financing the American Film Industry* (Norwood, NJ: Ablex Publishing Corporation, 1982), 49–52; Lewis Jacobs, *The Rise of the American Film: A Critical History* (New York: Teacher College Press 1968 [1939]), 422–25; Tino Balio, *Grand Design: Hollywood as a Modern Business Enterprise, 1930–1939* (Berkeley: University of California Press, 1995), 13–15, 30–32; Thomas Schatz, *The Genius of the System: Hollywood Filmmaking in the Studio Era* (New York: Pantheon Books, 1988), 98, 160.

20. Richard Maltby, "Censorship and Self-Regulation," in Geoffrey Nowell-Smith, ed., *The Oxford History of World Cinema* (Oxford: Oxford University Press, 1996) 235–248; Thomas Doherty, *Pre-Code Hollywood: Sex, Immorality, and Insurrection in American Cinema 1930–1934* (New York: Columbia University Press, 1999), 321–31; Thomas Doherty, *Hollywood's Censor: Joseph I. Breen and the Production Code Administration* (New York: Columbia University Press 2007), 57–70, 77–85.

21. Doherty, *Pre-Code Hollywood*, 2, 45; Doherty, *Hollywood's Censor*, 53.

22. Doherty, *Pre-Code Hollywood*, 44, 53, 85–9, 213–4.

23. Doherty, *Pre-Code Hollywood*, 85–9, 320.

24. Doherty, *Pre-Code Hollywood*, 331.

25. Doherty, *Pre-Code Hollywood*, 337.

26. Ralph A. Brauer, "When the Lights Went Out-Hollywood, the Depression, and the Thirties," in Michale T. Marsden, Johen G. Nachbar, Sam L. Grogg, Jr. (eds.), *Movies as Artifacts: Cultural Criticism of Popular Film* (Chicago: Nelson-Hall, 1982), 29.

27. Nick Smedley, *A Divided World: Hollywood Cinema and Émigré Directors in the Era of Roosevelt and Hitler, 1933–1948* (Bristol, UK: Intellect, 2011), 47.

28. Richard Maltby, "The Production Code and the Hays Office," in Balio, *Grand Design*, 37–72; Richard Maltby, "The Genesis of the Production Code," in Thomas Schatz, ed., *Hollywood: Social Dimensions: Technology, Regulation and the Audience* (New York: Routledge, 2004), 85–119; Richard Maltby, "More Sinned Against than Sinning: The Fabrications of 'Pre-Code Cinema'," *Senses of Cinema* 29 (2003) online journal.

29. Ramona Curry, *Too Much of a Good Thing: Mae West as Cultural Icon* (Minneapolis: University of Minnesota Press, 1996), 78–79.

30. Lea Jacobs, *The Wages of Sin: Censorship and the Fallen Woman Film, 1928–1942* (Berkeley: University of California Press, 1997), 82–83.

31. We only hear about her return to the industrial town. We do not see it because Stanwyck was unavailable to film additional scenes. Richard Maltby, "Baby Face or How Joe Breen Made Barbara Stanwyck Atone for Causing the Wall Street Crash," *Screen* 27.2 (1986): 22–45. Jacobs states that, in most of the gold digger films in which the gold digger is triumphant, the ending is at odds with the more typical romantic or sentimental classical happy end, but her own analysis of the films shows that happy endings with gold diggers who have retained their cynicism were the exception rather than the rule. Jacobs, *The Wages of Sin*.

32. The low-dive singer in *The Bride Wore Red* only returns to the poor man after her masquerade as a wealthy socialite is unmasked. McDonald writes that the film "cannot seem to make up its mind whether Anni is a grasping gold-digger or a poor girl who is smart enough to make a grab for what she wants when she gets the opportunity," and that the "ambivalence is never resolved by the narrative." Tamar Jeffers McDonald, *Hollywood Catwalk: Exploring Costume and Transformation in American Film* (New York: I.B. Tauris, 2010), 122. McDonald discusses the relationship of the heroine's costumes in *The Bride Wore Red* to her class passing. See also Berry, *Screen Style*, 34–39.

33. The film was heavily cut by state and municipal boards. Maltby, "The Genesis of the Production Code," 118.

34. Babington and Evans, *Blue Skies and Silver Linings*, 59–64.

35. Jacobs, *The Wages of Sin*, 133–138.

36. Mick Lasalle, *Dangerous Men: Pre-Code Hollywood and the Birth of the Modern Man* (New York: Thomas Dunne Books, 2002), 139.

37. Maltby, "More Sinned Against than Sinning." See also, Jacobs, *The Wages of Sin*, and Ruth Vasey, *The World According to Hollywood, 1918–1939* (Exeter: University of Exeter Press, 1997), especially 131–132.

38. Nick Roddick, *A New Deal in Entertainment: Warner Brothers in the 1930s* (London: British Film Institute, 1983), 65–66.

39. Brauer, "When the Lights Went Out-Hollywood, the Depression, and the Thirties," 29.

40. Smedley, *A Divided World*, 49.

41. Smedley, *A Divided World*, 47, 54.

BIBLIOGRAPHY

Babington, Bruce and Peter William Evans. *Blue Skies and Silver Linings: Aspects of the Hollywood Musical*. Manchester: Manchester University Press, 1985.

Balio, Tino. *Grand Design: Hollywood as a Modern Business Enterprise, 1930–1939*. Berkeley: University of California Press, 1995.

Berry, Sarah. *Screen Style: Fashion and Femininity in 1930s Hollywood*. Minneapolis: University of Minnesota Press, 2000.

Brauer, Ralph A. "When the Lights Went Out-Hollywood, the Depression, and the Thirties," in Michale T. Marsden, Johen G. Nachbar, Sam L. Grogg, Jr. eds. *Movies as Artifacts: Cultural Criticism of Popular Film*. Chicago: Nelson-Hall, 1982, 25–43.

Cavenaugh, Jennifer. "Hooray for What!: A Glimpse into the Golden Age of Sexual Harassment," *Journal of American Drama and Theater* 20.3 (2008): 5–28.

Chafe, William H. *The Paradox of Change: American Women in the 20th Century*. New York: Oxford University Press, 1991.

Clement, Elizabeth Alice. *Love For Sale: Courting, Treating, and Prostitution in New York City, 1900–1945*. Chapel Hill: University of North Carolina Press, 2006.

Crouch, Margaret A. *Thinking About Sexual Harassment: A Guide for the Perplexed*. New York: Oxford University Press, 2000.

Curry, Ramona. *Too Much of a Good Thing: Mae West as Cultural Icon*. Minneapolis: University of Minnesota Press, 1996.

Doherty, Thomas. *Pre-Code Hollywood: Sex, Immorality, and Insurrection in American Cinema 1930–1934*. New York: Columbia University Press, 1999.

——— *Hollywood's Censor: Joseph I. Breen and the Production Code Administration*. New York: Columbia University Press, 2007.

Hanson, Philip. *This Side of Despair: How the Movies and American Life Interrelated during the Great Depression*. Cranbury, NJ: Associated University Press, 2008.

Haralovich, Mary Beth. "The Proletarian Woman's Film of the 1930s; Contending with Censorship and Entertainment," *Screen* 31 (1990): 177–181.

Huettig, Mae E. "The Motion Picture Industry Today," in Tino Balio, ed. *The American Film Industry*. Madison: University of Wisconsin Press, 1976, 228–255.

Jacobs, Lea. *The Wages of Sin: Censorship and the Fallen Woman Film, 1928–1942*. Berkeley: University of California Press, 1997.

Jacobs, Lewis. *The Rise of the American Film: A Critical History*. New York: Teacher College Press 1968 [1939].

Lasalle, Mick. *Dangerous Men: Pre-Code Hollywood and the Birth of the Modern Man*. New York: Thomas Dunne Books, 2002.

Maltby, Richard. "Baby Face or How Joe Breen Made Barbara Stanwyck Atone for Causing the Wall Street Crash," *Screen* 27.2 (1986): 22–45.

——"The Production Code and the Hays Office," in Tino Balio, ed. *Grand Design: Hollywood as a Modern Business Enterprise, 1930–1939*. Berkeley: University of California Press, 1995, 37–72.

—— "Censorship and Self-Regulation," in Geoffrey Nowell-Smith, ed. *The Oxford History of World Cinema*. Oxford: Oxford University Press, 1996, 235–248.

—— "More Sinned Against than Sinning: The Fabrications of 'Pre-Code Cinema'," *Senses of Cinema* 29 (2003) online journal.

—— "The Genesis of the Production Code," in Thomas Schatz, ed. *Hollywood: Social Dimensions: Technology, Regulation and the Audience*. New York: Routledge, 2004, 85–119.

Maule, Frances. *She Strives to Conquer: Business Behavior, Opportunities and Job Requirements for Women*. New York: Funk & Wagnalls, 1934.

McDonald, Tamar Jeffers. *Hollywood Catwalk: Exploring Costume and Transformation in American Film*. New York: I.B.Tauris & Co., 2010.

McLaren, Angus. *Sexual Blackmail: A Modern History*. Cambridge, MA: Harvard University Press, 2002.

Mellencamp, Patricia. *A Fine Romance: Five Ages of Film Feminism*. Philadelphia: Temple University Press, 1995.

Meyerowitz, Joanne J. *Women Adrift: Independent Wage Earners in Chicago, 1880–1930*. Chicago: University of Chicago Press, 1988.

Robertson, Pamela. *Guilty Pleasures: Feminist Camp from Mae West to Madonna*. Durham, NC: Duke University Press, 1996.

Roddick, Nick. *A New Deal in Entertainment: Warner Brothers in the 1930s*. London: British Film Institute, 1983.

Schatz, Thomas. *The Genius of the System: Hollywood Filmmaking in the Studio Era*. New York: Pantheon Books, 1988.

Scheurer, Timothy E. "Goddesses and Golddiggers: Images of Women in Popular Music of the 1930s," *Journal of Popular Culture* 24 (1990): 23–38.

Smedley, Nick. *A Divided World: Hollywood Cinema and Émigré Directors in the Era of Roosevelt and Hitler, 1933–1948*. Bristol, UK: Intellect, 2011.

Vasey, Ruth. *The World According to Hollywood, 1918–1939*. Exeter: University of Exeter Press, 1997.

Vieira, Mark A. *Sin in Soft Focus: Pre-Code Hollywood*. New York: Harry N. Abrams, 1999.

Ware, Susan. *Holding Their Own: American Women in the 1930s*. Boston: Twayne Publishers, 1982.

Wasko, Janet. *Movies and Money: Financing the American Film Industry*. Norwood, New Jersey: Ablex Publishing Corporation, 1982.

CHAPTER 8

The End of the Golden Era and After

Cross-class romance became a less frequent theme of movies after the USA entered World War II in December 1941. A few were made after the war in the late 1940s and early 1950s, and from 1954 they became rare. In recent decades, a number of cross-class romances have been produced but the number has been far fewer than their heyday from 1915 through to the 1920s and 1930s. This chapter will consider the reasons for their decline in numbers and the changes in the films' motifs.

BEFORE AMERICA ENTERED THE WAR

The cross-class romances released in 1940 and 1941 included dramas, comedies and musicals with motifs that had been familiar in the 1930s. The girl in *Music in My Heart* (Columbia, 1940) leaves her wealthy fiancé for an Englishman who is an understudy in a musical and threatened with deportation. *Moon Over Miami* (Twentieth Century Fox, 1941), a musical remake of the same studio's 1938 film *Three Blind Mice*, repeats the story of a girl in search of a millionaire who, when given the choice of a millionaire and a poor man, chooses the poor man. Both the female and male protagonists of *Free and Easy* (MGM, 1941), a remake of *But the Flesh is Weak* (MGM, 1932), aim to marry for money, but although suitable wealthy partners present themselves, they turn them down and marry each other for love. *Maisie Was a Lady* (MGM, 1941) contains the motif of the lower-class girl who sorts out the problems of a wealthy family,

© The Author(s) 2017
S. Sharot, *Love and Marriage Across Social Classes in American Cinema*,
DOI 10.1007/978-3-319-41799-8_8

including the rehabilitation of the drunken playboy son who then has to persuade her that she is a 'lady' before she agrees to marry him.

Fewer prestigious cross-class romance films with major female stars were being made and the formula was being relegated to 'programmers', a low-cost form of an A-level movie, and to B pictures that were intended to appear on the lower half of a double-feature program. *Here Comes Happiness* (Warner, 1941) employed, in the words of a trade journal, "the familiar rich girl-hard working boy formula," and was likely to "amuse audiences while waiting for the main feature to start."[1]

Another programmer was *Unexpected Uncle* (RKO, 1941), advertised as a "shop girl-millionaire romance with enough laughs and dreams-come-true for everybody."[2] The predicament of a gold digger whose conscience weighs upon her when she falls genuinely in love with a millionaire makes an appearance in another low-budget film, *Play Girl* (RKO, 1941). Kay Francis whose stardom had waned plays Grace, a gold digger who realizes that her age is beginning to limit her ability to attract men and she trains a young woman, Ellen, to be her protégé. Grace's plans are spoiled when Ellen falls in love with Tom, a young ranch owner, and runs away when she discovers that he is a millionaire. Some religious leaders complained that the film bordered on an endorsement of prostitution, but the censors let it pass, possibly because of its low status as a programmer.[3]

Two of the major female stars of the 1930s continued to make cross-class romances in these years: Barbara Stanwyck followed the drama *Remember the Night* (Paramount, 1940) with two comedies, *Ball of Fire* (Samuel Goldwyn, 1941) and *The Lady Eve* (Paramount, 1941); and Ginger Rogers followed the dramas *Kitty Foyle* (RKO, 1940) and *Primrose Path* (RKO, 1940) with the comedy *Tom, Dick and Harry* (RKO, 1941). Based on a best-selling novel published in 1939 with the ongoing Depression providing the story's context, *Kitty Foyle* was one of the last examples of the type of cross-class romance that had been a staple during the 1930s and disappeared from the screens after America entered the war. Its central character is a white-collar girl in Philadelphia who dreams of becoming part of that city's fashionable society, its WASP "Main Liners." Her coarse but loving Irish father, Pop, tries to discourage his daughter's fascination with high society and denounces the writers of what he calls "Cinderella stories" who put "crazy ideas in girls' heads" and make them "dissatisfied with honest shoe clerks and bookkeepers." Pop tells her that if the Cinderella does catch her prince the marriage will likely end up in a divorce court. Kitty is not persuaded and becomes involved with Wyn, the rich publisher of the magazine for which she works. Although Kitty is not portrayed as a gold digger and she professes no interest in money, the film shows the appeal of marriage with a wealthy man. When Wyn buys her a glamorous dress and takes her to a ball, Kitty's girl friends talk about Wyn as a "knight in shining armor" and say that Kitty is waiting for him to rescue her.

Pop tells Kitty that men like Wyn "always wind up marrying one of their own kind," and, although Wyn eventually marries Kitty, Pop's forebodings are borne out. A divorce follows Kitty's refusal to follow the plan of Wyn's family to send her to finishing school in order to make her more acceptable in their proper Philadelphia society and Wyn's unwillingness to detach himself from his family's money and position. Kitty leaves him, a child from the marriage is born dead, Wyn marries a woman of his own class, and Kitty opens a branch of a fashion house. Unhappily married, Wyn comes to Kitty and asks her to travel with him as his mistress to South America, but although Kitty is still in love with Wyn she chooses instead to marry a virtuous, unexciting, impoverished doctor. Like many cross-class romance films of the 1930s, *Kitty Foyle* portrays the glamour of the upper-class world together with negative aspects such as snobbishness and superficiality, but in this film the heroine only benefits from that glamour on a temporary basis. Kitty's rejection of the upper-class male in favor of a future of middle-class conventionality and domesticity was a harbinger of post-war values that focused on the middle-class family.[4]

By admitting in a reflexive manner the fantasy elements in the formula, the comedy *Tom, Dick and Harry* (RKO, 1941) assumed that its audience appreciated that the cross-class romance was a fairy tale. The film opens in a darkened movie theater with a full house, and as the camera dollies closer to Janie (Ginger Rogers) and her date Tom (George Murphy) we hear the sound track of the cross-class romance film that they are watching. We hear a male asking a female to come away with him and marry him. The female tells him that they live in two different worlds, that there is a gulf between them because of his money and position. The male replies that their love will build a bridge over that gulf, and the film ends. After they leave the theater, over their ice-cream sundaes, Tom, a car salesman, asks Janie, a telephone operator, if she thinks the film is true to life and if a rich man would really marry a poor girl. Janie replies that of course he would: "He loved her didn't he!" The next day Janie connects a long-distance call for Dick Hamilton (Alan Marshall), the son of the town's wealthiest family, and walking home from work she wishes on a star to marry Dick.

When a man driving an expensive car pulls up alongside the curb, Janie assumes that her wish has been answered; she climbs into the car and agrees to go with the driver for a date that evening. On their date, Janie discovers that the driver is not Dick but Harry (Burgess Meredith), a garage mechanic.

In their conversations, Janie and Harry argue over the possibility of a cross-class marriage. When Janie asks the skeptical Harry why a girl like her cannot marry a millionaire, he explains that there are very few millionaires and millions of girls like Janie who wish to marry one. Janie says that numbers cannot explain everything and that there is no reason why the "accident" of meeting the right fella should not be with a rich fella rather than a poor one. Harry replies that this will not happen because Janie and a rich fella like Dick Hamilton do not move in the same circles. He explains that when the Hamilton family gives a party they do not invite people like Janie but people from their own circle, and if there are not enough of these people from their own town they import them from other towns. Janie proves to Harry that he is wrong. At work, after disconnecting a call between Dick and a girlfriend, Janie succeeds in wrangling a date with him. After a night of drinking and dancing, Dick becomes the third man to propose to her, the others being Tom and Harry. Janie announces to the assembled fiancés that she will marry Dick, but after she hears bells when she kisses Harry farewell, she changes her mind and drives off with Harry on his scooter.

Tom, Dick and Harry satirizes the familiar formula, provides good statistical and sociological reasons why cross-class marriages almost never happen, and makes the fantasy real on screen only to have the heroine reject the rich man for the poor one. Janie also chooses the mechanic over Tom, a workaholic in pursuit of the American Dream. Harry, in contrast, prefers comradely relationships among men to the competition for success; he tells Janie that he does not believe in every man for himself because that would make him lonesome. The scriptwriter, Paul Jarrico, a leftist who would later be blacklisted, wrote that he had critical intentions when he wrote the script: "I believed I was attacking the American success myth and the Cinderella myth in a consciously political way." In a memo to Pandro Berman, the producer, Jarrico wrote that there had been many Cinderellas and Success Stories but "actually there are as few rich men available to millions of romantic girls as there are places at the top of the economic ladder for the millions of ambitious boys."[5] Jarrico admitted later that the film turned out as just another form of the Cinderella myth, of "pure romanticism," and that it "would be an illusion to think that there was anything profound in its observation of society or that it transmitted any real social insight into the mass audience."[6]

Jarrico's script was nominated for an Oscar and, at the time, Jarrico was pleased with it, but he understood that he had not succeeded in undermining the Hollywood cliché of love conquering all. At the end of the film, the girl marries the poor guy, not because of his ideology or view on life but because she hears bells when they kiss.[7] Although it was clear from the start that Jarrico would not achieve his ideological agenda through writing a romantic comedy for a Hollywood studio, the film's reflexivity on the cross-class romance theme indicated that the formula was unlikely to retain its frequency in its naïve forms.

AMERICA AT WAR

Whereas the rapid increase in cross-class romance films from 1915 was not slowed down by America's entrance into World War I in April 1917, America's entrance into World War II in December 1941 appeared to dampen their appeal, although there were already signs of some decline. There were, of course, enormous differences in the levels of American involvement in the two world wars and their effects on American society. America was directly involved for a little more than a year and a half in World War I and its casualties were relatively low compared with the enormous losses of the British and French. America was directly involved in World War II for almost four years; around 14 million men were mobilized and its over 1 million casualties, including nearly 300,000 deaths in battle, were far greater than those the country suffered in World War I. American women had entered 'male' jobs, such as work in munitions and other war-related industries, during World War I,[8] but their participation in the war economy of World War II and the accompanying propaganda campaign to encourage their participation were far more extensive. Between 1941 and 1944, an additional 8 million women joined the workforce and, although a majority entered traditional female work, many entered what had been previously male-dominated sectors such as munitions, shipbuilding, and other heavy production industries. From 20 % of the manufacturing workforce prior to the war, women constituted a third of that force by 1945,[9] and in the war-related industries, women earned almost twice as much as they had before the war in clerical and service work. Married women in particular took advantage of the wartime opportunities to enter occupations previously confined to men and to earn better wages.[10]

In stark contrast with the Depression years, the propaganda campaign of World War II justified the incorporation of women into the paid labor force and encouraged women's entrance into male occupations. Among the foundations of the cross-class romance was a strict separation of gender and the assumption that a woman's mobility depended on marriage to an appropriate man. World War II, temporarily at least, weakened these foundations. Young women found more job opportunities at a time when war service left far fewer men of all classes with whom women could establish stable heterosexual relationships. Working wives separated from their husbands in the armed forces no longer had to choose between marriage and work. From an analysis of wartime fiction published in two magazines, the *Saturday Evening Post*, addressed primarily to the middle class, and *True Story*, addressed primarily to the working class, Maureen Honey found that both magazines published romances in which women entered defense industries and found fulfillment in performing important work for the nation. Whereas employed married women of the 1930s had been portrayed as selfish with negative consequences for their families, the heroines of wartime fictions successfully combined their work with care of their families. In comparison with the heroines of the *Saturday Evening Post*, the heroines of *True Story* were less likely to be found in 'male' occupations and positions of power and were portrayed as less self-confident in their relationships with men. The upward mobility of the *True Story* heroines was focused on males who were appreciative of the heroines' class background and hard work and could raise them through marriage from their clerical or sales jobs into a higher class.[11]

Unlike these magazines, almost all of the few cross-class romance films released from 1942 to 1945 did not place the romance within the context of women's war work, and in most cases the films found little favor with critics or commercial success. *Miss Annie Rooney* (United Artists, 1942) was an unsuccessful comeback film for the former child star Shirley Temple. When Annie's wealthy beau invites her to his birthday party, his mother objects because Annie is from the lower class, and when Annie comes to the party the upper-class girls snub her. The class obstacles that divide the couple are overcome when Annie's father secures their future with an invention and Annie is finally welcomed by the wealthy family. The trade journal, *Film Daily*, criticized the film as "another variation of the Cinderella theme … without any show of inspiration," and as "unadulterated hokum."[12] *And Now Tomorrow* (Paramount, 1944), in which a snobbish daughter of a wealthy family breaks off her engagement to a man of her class in order to marry a poor doctor who has restored her hearing, was criticized in the *New York Times* as "a very stupid film [with] little resemblance to life."[13] The introduction of a cross-class romance into a war context in *The War Against Mrs. Hadley* (MGM, 1942), albeit as just one of a number of intertwined story lines, did nothing to improve the film's critical reception.[14]

Gold diggers were not entirely ignored by the film industry during the war, particularly if they forwent the opportunity of marrying a rich husband in favor of true love with a poor man. In the musical *Happy Go Lucky* (Paramount, 1943), Marjory, a cigarette girl, poses as an heiress in the hope of finding a wealthy husband and in the end chooses her accomplice, a local beachcomber, rather than the yacht-owning millionaire. In *Higher and Higher* (RKO, 1943), another musical, the scullery maid poses as the daughter of a bankrupt millionaire in order to snare a millionaire but her heart belongs to the butler. The musical *Bring on the Girls* (Paramount, 1945) shows a millionaire joining the navy in order to escape gold diggers, but the gold digger who discovers his identity drops him in favor of his guardian and he unites with a nightclub singer, a daughter of a banker, who has also had to fend off greedy suitors.

Once Upon a Honeymoon (RKO, 1942) is an exceptional film insofar as it placed its gold digger, Katie O'Hara (Ginger Rogers), in the struggle against the Nazis. Katie, an ex-burlesque queen from Brooklyn, poses as a socialite from Philadelphia in order to marry an Austrian baron in Vienna in 1938. A foreign correspondent, Pat O'Toole (Cary Grant), reveals to Katie that her husband is working for Hitler. Katie turns spy in order to secure important information from her husband and finally escapes to America with Pat. The mixture of romantic comedy with Nazis, and, in particular, a scene in which Katie and Pat are mistaken as Jews and find themselves momentarily in a concentration camp, was deemed to be of "markedly dubious taste" by a contemporary critic.[15]

A favorably reviewed cross-class romance film, albeit one that pulls back from an emphasis on class differences at the end, was the romantic comedy *No Time for Love* (Paramount, 1943). The title of this film harks back to the objections made about career women in the films of the Depression because the career woman in this case, Katherine Grant (Claudette Colbert), a successful photo-journalist, devotes so much of her time and energy to her job that she has 'no time for love'. On an assignment to photograph 'sandhogs,' who are digging a tunnel under the Hudson, Katherine inadvertently causes the suspension of Jim Ryan (Fred MacMurray), and feeling guilty, she hires him to be her assistant at the magazine where she works. Katherine struggles within herself as she is both attracted and repulsed by Jim's supposedly working-class rough manners and ultra-masculinity. Toward the end of the film, it is disclosed that Jim is an engineer who went to work as a sandhog in order to familiarize himself with construction and that he has invented a machine for tunneling. Thus, when Jim tells Katherine in the last scene to choose between her effeminate fiancé and him, she chooses a man who is both hyper-masculine and a talented inventor. She calls him a "big ape," he replies that that makes her "an ape wife," and he leaves carrying her over his shoulder. One critic wrote that the film was "escapist ... in spades," and another wrote that, although "one might argue that this picture is too frivolous for this day and time," it was to be praised as "a first-class example of the inconsequential put to highly diverting use"[16] (Fig. 8.1)

Fig. 8.1   Still from *No Time for Love* (Paramount, 1943). Career woman Katherine Grant (Claudette Colbert) showing her displeasure with rough, accident-prone, supposedly working-class Jim Ryan (Fred MacMurray). Still courtesy of Derek Boothroyd

POST-WAR

In the romantic dramas made during the war, the impediment to the union of the romantic couple was more likely to be related to the war than to a class difference, which was perceived as inappropriate at a time of national unity. However, the post-war years did not see a comeback of the cross-class romance. There was some increase in the number of cross-class romance films in the immediate post-war years, but the stories in about half of those released in the late 1940s take place in the past, often in Europe, with few set in contemporary America.[17] During the 1950s, the number of cross-class romances released each year was no more than four and they became even more exceptional after 1957 and throughout the 1960s. This was the period of the collapse of the studio system. The antitrust law of 1948 forbade the film corporations from both producing films and owning the cinemas that showed them, and for a number of reasons, including the move to the suburbs and the spread of television, attendance at cinemas began to decline after 1946. Weekly cinema attendance dropped from between 80 and 90 million in the 1940s to below 45 million from 1957. Attendance dropped to the lowest point in the late 1960s and early 1970s when it went below 20 million.[18] With the decline in audiences and without their own cinemas, it was no longer economical for the major film corporations to maintain the factory-like studio system, and from the late 1950s, there was a drop in the number of films they made.

Large numbers of cross-class romance films had been made in the studio system. At the beginning of each year, every studio would decide on the number of films it would make in accord with genres, familiar formulas and its stars. One might argue that fewer cross-class romance films were made simply because Hollywood was making fewer films, but although the number of total films produced began to drop in 1943, until 1953, well over 350 were produced each year. The number of films produced dropped to less than 200 in 1959 and remained below that figure until 1969.[19] During this period, almost no cross-class romances were made. The percentage of cross-class romance films made in the post-war period in relationship to the total number of films produced was far smaller than in the inter-war years. The collapse of the studio system was no doubt one reason for the decline of cross-class romance films, but there are also wider societal and cultural factors to consider.

One reason for the large number of cross-class romance films in the inter-war period was an affinity with the experience of many women who found that the restrictions on their mobility in the work force made marriage with a higher-class male the only opportunity for mobility. The decline in the number of cross-class romance films after the war cannot be explained by an improvement in opportunities for females in the job market. Although many women expressed their desire to remain in their wartime 'male' jobs, they were required to 'step down' to make way for the returning soldiers. A decline in the female labor force in the immediate postwar period was soon reversed, but the postwar re-employment of women occurred primarily in clerical and service occupations. Opportunities for female occupational advancement once again closed up, and the average wage for women declined. Professional schools discriminated against women and very few women were able to enter areas like law, medicine and business. This discrimination was justified by popular writers, including psychiatrists and psychologists, who criticized women who wished to pursue a career with the suggestion that they were lacking femininity and were psychologically damaged. With few professional opportunities, women were given little incentive to earn degrees in higher education. Women constituted 35 % of the college students in 1958, and more than half dropped out of college in order to marry, in some cases in order to support their husbands while the husbands studied for their degrees. Many middle-class women saw college as a means to find and marry men who had good occupational prospects, and those that did graduate were likely to marry within a few years. Some referred to themselves as 'career homemakers', infusing the work of a homemaker with professional virtues that would also contribute to the education of their children.[20]

The dependence of women's mobility on marriage was well understood by Leonora Eames (Barbara Bel Geddes), the department store model in *Caught* (Enterprise, 1949) who enrolls in a 'Charm School' in order to learn the speech and etiquette appropriate to a good marriage. As in many other films, her marrying for money is punished and Leonora finds herself caught as her ruthless, wealthy husband (Robert Ryan) extends his obsession for control from his businesses to his wife. Leonora leaves home, exchanges an enormous, luxury home for a tiny apartment, and finds a low-paid job as a receptionist for two doctors practicing in a poor area. She falls in love with one of the doctors but finds she has been made pregnant by her husband, who threatens to keep the child if she divorces him. She suffers a miscarriage and this sets her free for a future with the doctor (James Mason).

In *A Letter to Three Wives* (Twentieth Century-Fox, 1949), one of the three wives is Lora Mae who escaped from her poor family and work as a department store salesclerk by marrying Porter, her boss who is some years older than her. Like the other two wives, Lora learns from a letter written by Addie Ross, an idealized female whom we never see, that her husband may have left her in favor of Addie. Porter understands that his wife married him for his position and he reveals that he had planned to leave with Addie before realizing, somewhat unconvincingly, how much he loved his wife. Another film from the period that showed the negative consequences of marrying for money was *Ruby Gentry* (Twentieth-Century Fox, 1952). A girl from the wrong side of the tracks who marries a man for his money in a small town in North Carolina does not find happiness after her husband dies from an accident and leaves her his fortune. The man she truly loves—a man from an impoverished upper-class family, who also marries for money—is in the end shot by Ruby's fanatically religious brother. There were few dramas set in contemporary America in which the poor girl ends up happily together with a wealthy male (*One More Tomorrow*, Warner, 1946, *Country Fair*, Monogram, 1950), and comedies and musicals with this theme were only slightly more common (*Something in the Wind*, Universal, 1947, and *Ladies of the Chorus*, Columbia, 1948, were among them).

If the decline in the number of cross-class romance films after the war cannot be explained by greater opportunities for women's occupational mobility, there were changes with respect to women in the workforce that are of relevance as part of an explanation. Prior to America's entrance into the war, two-thirds of female workers were unmarried and most were from the working class, as were the married women who worked. While the number of single women in the labor force declined from 1940–1960, the number of married women, including mothers, in employment increased considerably. By 1960, 30 % of married women were employed and 39 % of all mothers with school-age children were in the labor force. The number of mothers at work rose from 1.5 million to 6.6 million, with the greatest growth occurring among well-educated women from families with moderate incomes.[21] Most of this increase was confined to what was defined as female occupations, but in addition to the effect on many women from their experience of working in 'male' positions during the war, there was an incongruity between the continuous rise of married women in the workforce and the notion of the ideal married woman as a full-time wife and mother.

Joanne Meyerowitz has questioned the portrayal of the 1950s as having a dominant ideology that single-mindedly promoted female domesticity. Her review of nonfiction articles in popular magazines of the period found that "domestic ideals coexisted in ongoing tension with an ethos of individual achievement that celebrated nondomestic activity, individual striving, public service, and public success."[22] Both domestic and nondomestic roles were endorsed, but the nonfiction items about wives that promoted nondomestic accomplishment were more numerous than those that focused on women in their roles as wives and mothers. Arguments for wage work included not just the economic benefits to be gained but also the personal satisfaction to be gained from employment. Negative aspects of domesticity, such as its isolation of women, were included in numerous articles. When she compared the articles of the 1950s with those of the 1930s, Meyerowitz found that, beyond their common themes, there was a difference in emphasis, with a smaller proportion of items in the 1950s focusing on marriage and domestic roles and a higher proportion of items praising the public service of women.

The changes with respect to the position and images of women in the workforce are significant, but hardly sufficient to account for the substantial decline in the number of cross-class romance films. However, these changes were part and parcel of a wider change in American society that marginalized the cross-class romance; a reformulation of the American Dream that focused on the white, middle-class suburban family within a consumerist, domesticated society. The cross-class romance films of the inter-war period that focused on a young, single working woman who escapes from the working class through marriage with a wealthy man were made at a time when a consciousness of class differences was relatively high, and when marriage and birth rates were in decline. Prosperity and consumerism after the war advanced together with the rise in marriage and birth rates, and these changes shifted the focus of popular culture onto the middle-class family.

As we have seen, consumerism advanced considerably in the 1920s and continued to advance during the Depression of the 1930s. However, it was after World War II that mass consumption came to be seen as a major factor defining American society and, by the mid-1950s, unprecedented numbers were participating in consumerism. The national output of goods and services doubled between 1946 and 1956 and doubled again by 1970. Residential construction rose considerably and the proportion of American who owned their home rose from 44 % in 1940 to 62 % in 1960. New car sales quadrupled between 1946 and 1955, and by the end of the 1950s, three-quarters of American households owned at least one car. Consumerism was promoted by television; ownership of televisions grew from fewer than 20,000 families in 1946 to two-thirds of American families in 1953. Many observers at the time concluded that the era of the mass middle class had arrived.[23]

Mass consumption was widely believed to have created a more egalitarian society and as the notion of the 'affluent worker' gained currency, the barriers of class appeared to be breaking down. At first, the post-war suburbia boom resulted in a mix of blue-collar and white-collar families in some suburbs, but as the higher-income sectors moved to upscale suburbs, suburbia became highly structured by class. From about 1955, sociologists began to question many of the assumptions about the embourgeoisement of workers, such as the loss of a distinctive constellation of values and identity among workers, but the belief in a classless prosperity permeated popular culture. The rise in incomes, the production of casual wear for virtually all Americans, the expansion of suburbia, and the increases in ownership of automobiles and home appliances were seen to have created a society in which almost everybody is middle class and in which differences in 'lifestyle' were simply an expression of personal tastes.[24]

The post-war focus on a mass middle class was essentially a focus on the white, middle-class suburban family. Heroines of cross-class romance films in the 1930s justified their refusal to marry their working-class boyfriends with the argument that the boyfriend's income was not sufficient for them to marry and have children, and the heroine either married a wealthy man or finally returned to the poor man as love overcame her initial economic reservations. These arguments were no longer heard after the war, as prosperity enabled many couples to marry and have children without fear of falling into poverty. There was a dramatic rise in the percentage of people getting married and a dramatic drop in the age of marriage; the marriage rate rose by nearly 50 % in 1946, and, during the 1950s, the average age of marriage for men fell to 22 and for women to 20. The very meaning of marriage began to be identified with having children; a 'baby boom' lasted from 1946–1964 with the number of yearly births exceeding 4 million in 1954 and not dropping below that figure until 1965. The image of the comfortable middle-class suburban family with its 'happy housewife' and three or four children dominated magazines and television.[25] The class position of women was still dependent upon the men they married, but with a prevailing image of a prosperous middle class that included almost everybody, the single girl who escaped her working-class background and economic deprivations by marriage with a wealthy men became anachronistic.

CROSS-CLASS ROMANCES OF THE 1950S: THE MALE SIDE

As in all periods, most of the cross-class romance films of the 1950s and subsequent decades focused on the woman, but a few made in the 1950s gave greater attention to the man. Two such films harked back to the industrial settings of many of the first large wave of cross-class romance films from 1915–1919. The nephew of the owner of the steel mill in *Steel Town* (Universal, 1952) works as a laborer to learn the workings of the mill in preparation for an executive position and he falls in love with the daughter of a working-class family with whom he rooms. The nephew wins over his coworkers and the girl after he saves her father's life. The film was photographed in steel mills and scenes detailing the workings of the plant impressed several reviewers. However, one critic complained that the "stunning footage of steel workers in action" was almost blotted out by the "conventional trite romance."[26] Common motifs of films of the 1910s were also evident in the independently produced *Man of Conflict* (Hal R. Makelim, 1953). A capitalist who treats his workers badly has a son who works incognito as an ordinary laborer and falls in love with the daughter of a co-worker. The father and son come to blows over the treatment of the workers, but they are reconciled and the son marries the daughter of the laborer.

In three cross-class romance films of the 1950s, the male is the poorer member of the romantically involved couple. In the comedy *The Mating Game* (Paramount, 1951), it is the working-class status of Ellen (Thelma Ritter), the widowed mother of Val (John Lund), a junior executive, rather than his own class position and potential that is the cause for embarrassment and farcical situations when Val marries Maggie (Gene Tierney). who has been brought up in wealth. As Ellen is aware of Val's concerns about her appearance and class, she does not attend the wedding ceremony, and when she decides to meet her daughter-in-law, Maggie mistakes her for a cook that she is expecting to help her prepare a dinner party. In order to avoid embarrassment, Ellen accepts the role and persuades a reluctant Val to go along with the ruse. Ellen is employed on a full-time basis as the couple's housekeeper and the misunderstandings multiply as Ellen tries to keep her real identity hidden from Maggie and her mother, Fran (Miriam Hopkins), who is upset that her daughter has married beneath her and does all she can to break the couple up. Once the truth comes out, Maggie proves to be the one who scorns class snobbishness and berates Val for being embarrassed about his mother. As Val's boss is drawn to Ellen and a marriage between them can be expected, the class issue is fully solved.

A tragic version of the poor boy–rich girl theme was *A Place in the Sun* (Paramount, 1951), the second film adaptation of Theodore Dreiser's *An American Tragedy* (1925), previously filmed in 1931. Dreiser had objected to the 1931 film as a travesty of his novel and, had he been alive, he would probably have reacted in the same way to the new version. Dreiser's indictment of the class structure and the unrealistic expectations of mobility promoted in America are replaced by a doomed romance between George Eastman (Montgomery Cliff), the ambitious working-class boy, and Angela Vickers (Elizabeth Taylor), the wealthy girl. The boy who, in the novel, is attracted to the girl largely because of her class position, becomes, in the film, a boy whose love appears to have no ulterior motives; the spoiled, manipulative girl of the novel becomes a glamorous, kindhearted girl who is far more sympathetic than Alice Tripp (Shelley Winters), the drab, vulgar working-class girl made pregnant by George. Alice drowns and George is tried and convicted for murder, an act he contemplated but did not commit. Elizabeth visits him before his execution and professes her undying love for him. *Mister Cory* (Universal, 1957) provided another dramatic story of an ambitious, working-class youth who finally fails to unite with the wealthy girl he desires, but in this film the girl's refusal is followed by a happy ending as Cory is consoled by a declaration of love from the socialite's vivacious, non-status conscious younger sister.

CROSS-CLASS ROMANCES OF THE 1950S: PYGMALIONS, CINDERELLA AND GOLD DIGGERS

The motif of the working-class girl who undergoes transformation and moves up into the upper-class under the guidance of a male from that class has been tagged as Pygmalion following the play of that name written by George Bernard Shaw in 1913 and first performed on the stage two years later. The play was adapted to the screen in England in 1938, and an American variation on the theme was presented in *Born Yesterday* (Columbia, 1950), in which Judy Holliday repeated her Broadway success of 1946 as the shrewd 'dumb blonde,' Billie Dawn. Billie is the 'kept woman' of Harry Brook (Broderick Crawford), a junkyard tycoon who comes to Washington D.C. to bribe a congressman to pass legislation that will allow Harry tax exemptions and enable him to expand his business. As a gold digger who plays at being dumb in order to obtain material benefit from men, Billie's lower-class background is evident from her bad taste, ignorance, impropriety and unruliness. Harry hires a newspaper reporter, Paul Verrall (William Holden), as a tutor to make Billie socially acceptable, but Paul's education of Billie goes beyond improving her speech and manners to include the principles of democracy and the evils of corruption. With her new knowledge and values, Billie exposes Harry's crooked business dealings and leaves him for Paul. In place of material capital acquired immorally, Billie acquires cultural capital as well as middle-class restraint taught by Paul. This has been interpreted as the taming of an unruly working-class woman in accord with the middle-class values of domesticity[27] (Fig. 8.2).

The importance of cultural capital in the designation of class is an even more central theme in *Sabrina* (Paramount, 1954), with the difference than the Pygmalion element is incorporated within an overt Cinderella treatment. The film is marked as a fairy tale from its opening when we hear Sabrina's (Audrey Hepburns') voiceover, "Once upon a time ... there lived a small girl on a large estate." Sabrina is the daughter of the chauffeur of the wealthy industrialist Larrabee family, and although she describes the Larrabee estate as a space of unused luxuries ("an outdoor tennis court, an indoor tennis court/an outdoor swimming pool, an indoor swimming pool"), her aspiration is to be part of their world and to be romanced by

Fig. 8.2 Stills from *Born Yesterday* (Columbia, 1950). Billie Dawn (Judy Holliday), the unruly mistress of junkyard tycoon Harry Brook (Broderick Crawford) is educated, Pygmalion style, by newspaper reporter Paul Verrall (William Holden). Images courtesy of Jerry Murbach, http://www.doctormacro.com/

David, one of the two sons of the family. After helping her father wash the family's cars, Sabrina climbs into a tree to watch a party given by the family and to focus her gaze on David (William Holden), her fantasy prince. Sabrina is sent to Paris to take a two-year Cordon Bleu course and while in Paris she is befriended by a wealthy, elderly baron who teaches her European culture and directs her transformation into a beautiful, sophisticated woman exuding confidence, poise and self-possession. On her return to the Larrabee estate, the Larrabees do not at first recognize her and she immediately attracts David with whom she dances at a ball. Sabrina had earlier been warned by her father not to reach for the moon, but now she is seen to "belong up there" as "the most sophisticated woman at the ball." David's attraction to Sabrina upsets his brother Linus (Humphrey Bogart), who unlike his playboy brother is a serious businessman and is depending on David to marry the daughter of a potential partner in a corporation merger. Linus woos Sabrina in order to separate her from David, but the hardheaded businessman's feelings toward her become romantic and, at the end of the film, a softened Linus leaves the business in David's hands to join Sabrina on a ship bound for France[28] (Fig. 8.3).

Audrey Hepburn's star persona has been viewed as well suited to Cinderella roles, which included playing Eliza Doolittle in the musical based on Pygmalion, *My Fair Lady* (Warner, 1964), as her characters' transformation simply reveal what was present from the beginning.

Fig. 8.3 Frames from *Sabrina* (Paramount, 1954). The gamine Sabrina (Paramount, 1954), the chauffeur's daughter, watches from a tree the party given by her father's employers, the wealthy Larrabee family. After her glamorous transformation, Sabrina is wooed by Linus (Humphrey Bogart), the older and more serious brother of the Larrabee family

Beneath her initial appearance in poor clothes, she has 'natural' qualities, including her beauty, that make her the appropriate wearer of the beautiful clothes of the upper class. Rachel Moseley writes that Hepburn provided a model for many women of the period as she was both sexually attractive and classy in acceptable ways. Her combination of boyishness and femininity as well as her 'classy' poise and deportment contrasted with another female star of the period, Marilyn Monroe, who appeared in cross-class romances of a different kind from those of Hepburn.[29] Monroe had played the lead in a cross-class romance, *Ladies of the Chorus,* in 1948 prior to the emergence of her persona, but it was as a gold digger in *Gentlemen Prefer Blondes* (Twentieth Century-Fox, 1953) and *How to Marry a Millionaire* (Twentieth Century-Fox, 1953) that her persona found full expression.

Whereas Hepburn's slim, disciplined body signified her 'natural' classiness in *Sabrina,* Monroe's sumptuous curves and uncontrolled body signified her low status. The song sung by Lorelei (Monroe) and Dorothy (Jane Russell) that begins and ends *Gentlemen Prefer Blondes* informs us that they are "just two little girls from Little Rock [who had] lived on the wrong side of the tracks," but apart from this brief reference, their class background is not made an issue in the film and no connection is made between Monroe's desire to marry a wealthy man and her class origins. Monroe's Lorelei has little in common with the Lorelei of Anita Loo's book, published in 1925. Loo's Lorelei is a female trickster whose pursuit of material goods is unrelenting and who quite consciously plays dumb in order to fool the men she exploits.[30] Although Monroe's Lorelei pursues material goods, especially diamonds, through her relations with men, the consequence of Monroe's persona, one of innocence, vulnerability and artlessness in her sex appeal, is that she does not represent a real threat to men.[31] Monroe's gold digger is also different from the pre-war gold diggers who, however basically good they might be, were highly conscious of their sexual allure and were able to control their sexuality. Many of the pre-war gold diggers were redeemed through love, but the broad comic tone of Monroe's Lorelei did not permit such a serious theme as 'redemption' or the finding of 'true love'.

Although *Gentlemen Prefer Blondes* invites us to laugh at rather than with Monroe's Lorelei, the film appears uncertain about how much of Lorelei's dumb blond is a masquerade. The one scene in the film in which Lorelei appears to admit to performing a masquerade is when she talks to Esmond Sr., the father of Gus, the man she intends to marry. Gus is ineffectual and infantile, and as his father is aware of this he asks Lorelei if she has the nerve to tell him that she is not after Gus' money. Lorelei replies that she is not marrying Gus for his money but for "Your [the father's] money." She explains: "Don't you know that a man being rich is like a girl being pretty? You wouldn't marry a girl just because she's pretty, but my goodness, doesn't it help." This explanation wins over Esmond who says, "Say, they told me you were stupid, but you don't sound stupid to me." Lorelei admits that, "I can be smart when it's important, but most men don't like it." There is little indication in the rest of the film that Lorelei can be smart when she wants to be, but even if her dumbness is a masquerade, her goal to achieve riches is presented as light-hearted rather than as predatory.

Lorelei's focus on diamonds is balanced by Dorothy's desire for true love, but there is little effort on the part of the film to make the non-wealthy object of Dorothy's affections, Malone, as played by the bland Elliot Reid, a man of charm or sex appeal. Perhaps this is of little matter because the only important relationship throughout the film is between the two women. Lorelei and Dorothy achieve their goals in a double wedding at the end of the film, but the last shot comes to focus on Monroe and Russell, with the two men outside of the frame[32] (Fig. 8.4).

In *How to Marry a Millionaire,* Monroe plays Pola, one of three models, the others being Schatze (Lauren Bacall) and Loco (Betty Grable), who lease a posh New York City apartment, which they cannot afford, in order to meet rich men and marry millionaires. Schatze, the most sophis-

Fig. 8.4 Frames from the last shot of *Gentlemen Prefer Blondes* (Twentieth Century-Fox, 1953). The shot begins with the inclusion of the two men that Lorelie (Marilyn Monroe) and Dorothy (Jane Russell) are marrying and ends with their exclusion as the camera has come to focus solely on the female stars

ticated of the three, advises her friends on how to snag a millionaire, but neither of them end up with wealthy husbands. Loco falls in love with a forest ranger whom she believed at first to be the owner of the forest that he supervises, and Pola falls in love with Freddie, who owns the apartment the girls are leasing but is without funds and is a fugitive from Inland Revenue agents. Schatze is pursued by Tom, whom at first she refuses to date because she believes that he has no money; finally, she succumbs and marries him. At the end of the films, the three married couples go out to dinner and Tom discloses that he is a multi-millionaire.

Women pretending to be wealthy in order to capture millionaires, a woman mistakenly believing a poor man to be rich, and a woman mistakenly believing a rich man to be poor are, of course, familiar motifs of the cross-class romance, and *How to Marry a Millionaire* conforms to the formula that all three girls marry for love, indifferent to the economic status of the men. One difference from the films of the 1930s is that none of the characters at any time give an impression of being genuinely poor. We hear that the women have no money but they are able to disguise their poverty by wearing designer clothes and living in a high-end apartment, even if at one point they have to sell the furniture. The film was one of the first in cinemascope and the concern to fill out the screen with extravagance and luxury further removed the film from the working-class ambience of many of the heroines of the 1930s cross-class romance films. Tom, the wealthy man, disguises his wealth by not wearing a necktie, but as casual clothes were being worn across the class spectrum, his poor man subterfuge does not look particularly poor.

The message of *How to Marry a Millionaire* that a woman can expect to be happy if she marries a compatible man, even if he is not wealthy, was familiar, but whereas the heroine's choice of the poor man in the 1930s films was understood to involve a painful economic sacrifice, the 1950s heroines were understood to be sacrificing a sumptuous palace for a comfortable suburban home. At a time when popular culture was promoting 'classless prosperity', a woman's mobility through marriage was no longer seen to be contingent on marrying a millionaire. *How to Marry a Millionaire* was a commercial success, but the expectations of many women that they could look forward to a comfortable lifestyle in the suburbs with a middle-class spouse may have lessened the pleasures of wish-fulfillment provided by cross-class romance films (Fig. 8.5).

Few films of the 1950s took a critical view of middle-class conventionality and consumerism, and it is especially unusual to find such a criti-

Fig. 8.5 Poster for *How to Marry a Millionaire* (Twentieth Century-Fox, 1953). The 1950s-style gold diggers are given an extravagantly, luxurious, cinemascope treatment. Image courtesy of Jerry Murbach, http://www.doctormacro.com/

cal view in a cross-class romance film. Douglas Sirk's *All That Heaven Allows* (Universal, 1955), a film promoted as a 'woman's picture', shows the tribulations of a romance between widowed Cary Scott (Jane Wyman) and her gardener, Ron Kirby (Rock Hudson) who is younger than Cary. Although at the time critics did not appreciate the film as anything more than a weepy melodrama targeted at the female matinee audience, the film has acquired a reputation as a strong critique of rigid conformity and snobbery among the upper-middle class in 1950s America. Cary's efforts to integrate Ron within her country club social circle are unsuccessful and she also faces the opposition of her grown-up children who present her with a television as an alternative to her relationship with Ron. Love wins through over class and age differences, but it should be noted that, although Cary's friends and children see Ron as having an inferior status, Ron is by no means poor or uneducated. He owns a tree farm, he has a college education, his occupation might be described as landscape designer rather than gardener, and he lives a comfortable, refined bohemian lifestyle shared by some good friends. Cary's choice of Ron in the end may have been perceived by her country-club set as a move down in class, but from the perspective of the film Cary was forsaking the empty lifestyle of the country club for the higher, Thoreau-type and far from uncomfortable lifestyle of Ron and his friends.

AFTER THE GOLDEN AGE: THE 'NEW HOLLYWOOD'

From the late 1950s and through the 1960s and 1970s, almost no cross-class romances were made, with *Love Story* (Paramount, 1970) as a highly successful exception. A minor revival in the late 1980s and early 1990s did not prove to be the beginning of a long-term trend. The first 'New Hollywood' period of the late 1960s and 1970s, with its experimentation and controversial themes, was not congenial to cross-class romances. Far fewer romantic dramas or comedies of any type were being made, and although the second 'New Hollywood', post-1975 period with its emphasis on action-packed, effects-filled blockbusters had room for many romantic comedies, few of these were cross-class romances. The only blockbuster to have a cross-class romance at its center was *Titanic* (Twentieth Century Fox, 1997), which focused on the strict class divisions of the past. Among non-blockbuster films, the few cross-class romance films in recent decades have included two enormous commercial successes (*Pretty Woman*, Touchstone Pictures,1990; *Fifty Shades of Grey*, Focus Features, 2015), some moderate successes (*Working Girl*, Twentieth Century Fox, 1988; *Maid in Manhattan*, Revolution Studios, 2002; *The Notebook*, New Line Cinema, 2004), and some less successful films (*White Palace*, Universal, 1990; *Mrs. Winterbourne*, TriStar Pictures, 1996; *Crazy/Beautiful*, Touchstone Pictures, 2001; *Shopgirl*, Touchstone Pictures, 2005; *The Nanny Diaries*, Weinstein, 2007). The remake *Sabrina* (Constellation Entertainment, 1995) was a commercial success and *Stella* (Samuel Goldwyn, 1990), a remake of *Stella Dallas*, was a commercial failure. Thus, cross-class romances have by no means disappeared from the screen and they continue to have an appeal, but as a consequence of changes in the film industry together with wider social changes, especially with respect to the position of women, we can expect cross-class romance films to remain far fewer than during their heyday from 1915 to World War II.

The proportion of women who worked outside the home and the proportion of women who were part of the labor force continued to grow steadily for three decades after 1960 before flattening out in the 1990s and the new millennium. More important than this overall growth were the changes during this period in women's consciousness and their place in society. A signpost of change was the publication in 1963 of Betty Friedan's *The Feminine Mystique* in which she condemned the notion that women found fulfillment in marriage and housewifery as false and wrote that such a notion was an obstacle to women's educational and occupational advancement. Friedan's book has been seen as the beginning of what became known as second-wave feminism, which in the USA lasted through the early 1980s and touched on many facets of women's experience including family, sexuality and work. Women began entering higher education at an accelerated rate from the mid-1960s, and by the mid-1970s the proportion of female students in higher education equaled that of males. For both men and women from lower-income families, the chances of entering higher education, especially prestigious universities, were far lower than those from middle- and upper-income families, but the unprecedented growth of higher education during the 1960s and through the mid-1970s incorporated some students from working-class backgrounds who were the first generation in their families to go to college.

Love Story (Paramount, 1970) reflected a trend that was in an early stage at the time the film was made: college graduates marrying other college graduates from different class origins. *Love Story* emphasizes class differences and includes motifs that have been common in cross-class romances but with the difference that the couple is matched by their educational attainments. The Harvard student from an upper class Boston family and the Radcliffe College girl, daughter of a baker of Italian origins, meet in the Radcliffe library. Despite this setting, the girl, Jenny (Ali MacGraw), immediately senses the differences in their class background. She calls Oliver (Rhan O'Neal) a "preppy" and when he asks her how she knows he went to prep school she replies that he looks stupid and rich, with the implication that his family's connections got him into Harvard. When he responds that he is smart and poor she does not believe him, and states that she is the one who is smart and poor. Oliver is forced to admit that one of the Harvard buildings is named after his family because his great-grandfather gave the building to the University. However, he is concerned that his educational achievements should be based on his intelligence and work and he refuses his father's suggestion to use his influence to obtain a position for Oliver in Harvard law school. Oliver's relationship with his father is distant, tension-ridden and formal (Oliver constantly calls him 'Sir'), and this is in contrast with the warm, close relationship between Jenny and her father.

Pierre Bourdieu has emphasized that each person's childhood class location heavily influences their cultural tastes and sensibilities. In *Love Story*, it is the girl from the working-class background whose tastes are close to those generally associated with the 'high culture' of the upper strata. She is taking a degree in music and emphasizes her love for the classical composers, and although Oliver appreciates her musical interests (which include the Beatles), his principal interest outside of his studies is playing rough games of hockey. The obstacle that threatens their relationship is not their own class sensibilities but their class origins and, as in many cross-class romances, it is the poor protagonist who emphasizes that their class differences are an obstacle. Jenny tells Oliver that she intends to take up a scholarship in music in Paris and that it is inevitable that they will go their separate ways: "You're a preppy millionaire and I'm a social zero." Oliver's response is to propose marriage. When he takes her to meet his parents and they enter the vast ground of his parent's huge mansion, Jenny tells him that she had not thought "it would be like this." He asks, "Like what?" and she replies, "This rich. It's too much for me."

The meeting with Oliver's parents reinforces Jenny's reservations and increases Oliver's anger toward his parents, particularly his father. His father asks Jenny what her parents do and when she tells him that her father bakes cookies and that the name of his business is 'Phil's Bake Shop', Oliver's father responds with a supercilious "How interesting." Oliver's antagonistic relationship with his father is evident and later Jenny suggests to Oliver that he wants to marry her in order to get back at his father. Oliver exclaims, "Don't you believe I love you," and Jenny replies, "Yes, but in a crazy kind of way I believe that you love my negative social status." Oliver's father has a similar view because when Oliver informs him of his intention to marry Jenny, he suggests that Oliver's act is one of rebellion. Oliver replies that he fails to see how marrying a beautiful Radcliffe girl constitutes rebellion. This conversation points to opposing perceptions on class; whereas the father is emphasizing the importance of class origins, Oliver ignores this in favor of class destination through educational achievement. His father asks him to wait until he finishes law school and when Oliver refuses he says that he "will not give him the time of day" and cuts off his financial support.

Jenny decides not to take up the possibility of continuing her music studies in Paris and marries Oliver. As Oliver is refused a scholarship on the basis that he is a millionaire's son, they move to a poor neighborhood and take low-paying jobs to pay for Oliver's tuition fees in law school. Oliver is a success at law school, he obtains a job with an important New York law firm, and they move into a nice apartment. Jenny is found to have a blood disease, and after a short period she dies in her hospital bed in Oliver's arms. The film *Here on Earth* (Fox, 2000) repeated the plot development of the working-class girl in a cross-class romance succumbing to illness. However, with respect to the differences in class origins of students who meet in college, the *Love Story* formula was not adopted in subsequent cross-class romances. Perhaps the impediment of different class backgrounds to the union of a couple who had similar educational achievements was not seen to have much dramatic potential. The tragedy of Jenny's death in *Love Story* was, of course, unrelated to class.

The proportion of women in higher education continued to rise, with women's enrollment in college eclipsing that of men; more women than men in the new millennium were obtaining degrees and enrolling in graduate school. Parity was reached in the law schools with similar changes in medicine and business schools.[33] Beginning in the 1960s, women who went to college no longer saw it as a means to meet a suitable spouse but as a means to embark on a career, and from the early 1970s, the increase in the median age of first marriage was particularly pronounced among college graduates. As women entered professions that had been almost exclusively male, their expectations with respect to employment rose and many sought occupational accomplishment both before and after marriage. Their identity was no longer centered on the family and household, and they now perceived their work in terms of a long-term career, as part of their satisfaction in life, and as an integral part of their social world.[34] Although considerable gender inequality in employment and income remain, the occupational advancement of women has weakened one of the premises of the cross-class romance, namely marriage as the sole means of women's class mobility. However, women's educational and occupational advances have been largely limited to women from middle and upper-middle income families. High status occupations require higher education, and the higher education of students from low-income families, both males and females, is mostly confined to two-year colleges. They constitute only a tiny percentage of students at the most selective colleges and universities. This leaves a large number of young work-ing-class women as potential candidates for mobility through marriage, but with the strengthening of the link between higher education and occupational status the notion of a wealthy male meeting and marry-ing a poor female, or the other way round, has become even more implausible.

Changes in the class characteristics of the cross-class romantic couple reflect changes in the class structure and job market. Although a girl from the working class may still occasionally work in a department store (e.g.,*Shopgirl*) or hotel (e.g.,*Maid in Manhattan*), she is less likely to work for a family-owned business with a boss or boss' son to provide the wealthy partner. If she is a secretary, she may work for a large corporation involved in multi-million dollar deals (e.g.,*Working Girl*), but a large pro-portion of working-class women work in services from waitressing (e.g., *White Palace*) to prostitution (e.g., *Pretty Woman*). The wealthy men in recent cross-class romances are more likely to be hard working executives or professionals than their counterparts, the heirs and dissipated sons, of the 1920s and 1930s; they include an advertising executive (e.g.,*White Palace*), investment broker (e.g.,*Working Girl*), politician (e.g.,*Maid in Manhattan*), and corporate-shuffling businessman (e.g.,*Pretty Woman*). With respect to the class-gender association, the most common pat-tern has continued to be rich boy–poor girl, with very few exceptions (e.g.,*Crazy/Beautiful, The Notebook*), and themes that were common in the cross-class romances of the 1920s and 1930s are still to be found in the more recent versions.

Class 'passing' is restricted in the more recent films to passing as a person from a higher class; upper-class protagonists are not mistaken as lower class as they sometimes were in the older films. The secretary in *Working Girl* passes as her female boss. In *Mrs. Winterbourne*, a remake of *No Man of Her Own* (Paramount, 1950), which made far less of the class issue than its remake, a pregnant girl survives a train crash and is taken in by a wealthy family who believe that she is the newlywed wife of their son who was killed in the crash, whereas, in fact, the wife was killed as well. As in the films of the 1920s and 1930s, class passing is largely accom-plished by wearing the appropriate clothes. The girl in *Mrs. Winterbourne* has the dead rich girl's clothes. When the maid in *Maid in Manhattan* tries on a wealthy woman's dress, the wealthy politician mistakes her as a guest of the first-class hotel. Tess, the *Working Girl*, changes her hairstyle, jewelry and makeup and 'borrows' her boss' clothes in order to pass as her boss. The most spectacular transformation through clothes is made by Vivian, the prostitute heroine of *Pretty Woman*, who changes her working prostitute clothes, signaling tasteless low class, for an array of stylish outfits including a red ball gown with accessories (white silk gloves, glistening necklace, stylish clutch bag) worn for the opera sequence. This outfit represents the pinnacle of her transformation from prostitute to 'lady'.

Pretty Woman demonstrates yet another theme common to cross-class romances in their heyday: the redemption of the upper-class male by the working-girl female. The type of redemption has changed with the times. The wealthy men in the 1930s were redeemed by the virtuous heroines from sins such as living a self-indulgent, wasteful, work-shy lifestyle. Vivian in *Pretty Woman* transforms the super-wealthy Edward from an unethical, corporate raider to a more 'traditional' moral type of capitalist who invests in the production of goods that satisfy human needs. Vivian, a prostitute, is virtuous and 'chaste'; the film encourages us to forget that she has probably had sexual intercourse with numerous men because we only see her ply her trade or have sex with the man she redeems.[35]

The enormous success of *Pretty Woman* showed that the formula could still work, but one reason it worked was that it provided a self-conscious and somewhat ironic reflection on the formula. The film opens with a chorus-like male yelling out, "Welcome to Hollywood. Everybody has a dream. What's your dream?" and ends with the same man announcing, "Some dreams come true, some don't ... This is Hollywood. Always time to dream, so keep on dreamin'." As an example of what has been called the 'new romance,' *Pretty Woman* emphasizes its artifice by invoking and incorporating other familiar romantic fictions. Edward takes Vivian to the opera *La Traviata*, itself a romance between a courtesan and a young bourgeoise, and the film includes scenes similar to those in *Pygmalion* and its musical version, *My Fair Lady*. Vivian tells Edward that she wants the "fairy tale," and when she asks her friend Kit if she can tell her of one person for whom her kind of relationship with Edward has worked out, Kit can only come up with "Cindafuckin'ella." Vivian's wish for the fairy tale is fulfilled at the end when Edmund arrives like a prince in a white limousine and ascends the fire escape with a bouquet of red roses to embrace Vivian. In reply to his question of what happens after the prince climbs up the tower and rescues the damsel, Vivian answers, "She rescues him right back."[36] *Pretty Woman* concludes like most cross-class romances with the union of the couple, but this is accompanied by its admission that this is only possible in the dream world provided by Hollywood.

NOTES

1. *Independent Exhibitors Film Bulletin*, April 5, 1951, 27.
2. *Motion Picture Daily*, September 17, 1941, 10.
3. *Film Bulletin*, January 11, 1941, 4; TCM article on *Play Girl*.
4. Katherine Rogers-Carpenter, "Re-envisioning 1930s Working Women: The Case of *Kitty Foyle*," *Women's Studies*, 37.6 (2008): 707–730; Michele Schreiber, *American Postfeminist Cinema: Women, Romance and Contemporary Culture* (Edinburgh: Edinburgh University Press, 2014), 28–36.
5. Larry Ceplair, *The Marxist and the Movies: A Biography of Paul Jarrico* (Lexington, KY: University of Kentucky Press, 2007), 49.
6. Larry Ceplair and Steven Englund, *The Inquisition in Hollywood: Politics in the Film Community, 1930–1960* (Berkeley: University of California Press, 1983), 302.
7. Ceplair, *The Marxist and the Movies*, 49.
8. Kimberly Jensen, *Mobilizing Minerva: American Women in the First World War* (University of Illinois Press, 2008), 13–14.
9. Martha May, *Women's Roles in Twentieth-Century America* (Westport, CT: Greenwood Press, 2009), 15.
10. Elaine Tyler May, "Pushing the Limits, 1940–1961," in Nancy F. Cott, ed., *No Small Courage: A History of Women in the United States* (New York: Oxford University Press, 2000), 479.
11. Maureen Honey, "The Working-Class Woman and Recruitment Propaganda during World War II: Class Differences in the Portrayal of War Work," *Signs* 8.4 (1983): 672–687.
12. *Film Daily*, May 27, 1942, 8.
13. *New York Times*, November 23, 1944.
14. *New York Times*, November 26, 1942.
15. Review by Brosley Crowther, *New York Times*, November 13, 1942.
16. *Variety*, December 31, 1943; *New York Times*, December 2, 1943.
17. Eighteenth-century England was the setting of *Kitty* (1946), the nineteenth century was the setting for *Dragonwyk* (Twentieth Century Fox, 1946), *The Imperial Lady* (Paramount, 1947), and *The Heiress* (Paramount, 1949), and the early twentieth century was the setting for *Of Human Bondage* (Warner, 1946) in London, *Three Little Girls in Blue* (Twentieth Century Fox, 1946), another musical remake of *Three Blind Mice*, this time set in Atlantic City, and *The Late George Apley* (Twentieth Century Fox, 1947) in Boston.
18. Cobbett Steinberg, *Film Facts* (New York: Facts on File, 1980), 46.
19. Steinberg, *Film Facts*, 42–43.

20. May, *Women's Roles in Twentieth-Century America*, 19; May, "Pushing the Limits" 496–500; Elaine Taylor May, *Homeward Bound: American Families in the Cold War Era* (New York: Basic Books, 2008 [1988]); Andrea S. Walsh, *Women's Film and Female Experience 1940–1950* (New York: Praeger, 1984), 75–78.

21. William Henry Chafe, *The Paradox of Change: American Women in the 20th Century* (New York: Oxford University Press, 1991), 188, 192, 194; Susan M. Hartman, "Women's Employment and the Domestic Ideal in the Early Cold War Years," in Joanne Jay Meyerowitz, ed., *Not June Cleaver: Women and Gender in Postwar America, 1945–1960* (Philadelphia: Temple University Press, 1994), 86.

22. Joanne Meyerowitz, "Beyond the Feminine Mystique: A Reassessment of Postwar Mass Culture, 1946–1958," *The Journal of American History* 79.4 (1993): 1457.

23. Lizabeth Cohen, *A Consumers' Republic: The Politics of Mass Consumption in Postwar America* (New York: Vintage Books, 2003).

24. Roland Marchand, "Visions of Classlessness, Quests for Dominion: American Popular Culture, 1945–1960," in Robert H. Bremner and Gary W. Reichard, eds., *Reshaping America: Society and Institutions, 1945–1960* (Columbus: Ohio State University Press, 1982), 163–190.

25. Jessica Weiss, *To Have and to Hold: Marriage, the Baby Boom, and Social Change* (University of Chicago Press, 2000), 17–20; Jane Mersky Leder, *Thanks for the Memories: Love, Sex, and World War II* (Westport, CT: Greenwood, 2006), 157–158.

26. *New York Times*, May 10, 1952.

27. Kathleen Rowe, *The Unruly Woman: Gender and the Genres of Laughter* (Austin: University of Texas Press, 1995), 172–177.

28. Moseley writes that although Sabrina becomes "classy" this does not mean that she attains the social status of the Larrabees. Mrs. Larrabee acknowledges Sabrina's transformation but also puts her down when she tells her that she should come and cook something special for the family. Moseley notes that there is little suggestion at the end of the film that Sabrina and Linus will marry, and that Sabrina's future social status remains uncertain. Rachel Moseley, *Growing Up with Audrey Hepburn* (Manchester: Manchester University Press, 2002), 155–156. See also Smith who interprets *Sabrina* as supporting a merger of American capitalism and European culture. Dina M. Smith, "Global Cinderella: 'Sabrina'(1954), Hollywood, and Postwar Internationalism," *Cinema Journal* 41.4 (2002): 27–51.

29. Moseley, *Growing Up with Audrey Hepburn*, 134–135.

30. Lori Landay, *Madcaps, Screwballs, Con Women: The Female Trickster in American Culture* (Philadelphia: University of Pennsylvania Press, 1998), 156.

31. On Monroe's persona see Richard Dyer, *Heavenly Bodies: Film Stars and Society* (New York: St. Martin's Press, 1986), 19–66.
32. Rowe, *The Unruly Woman*, 172–182.
33. Thomas A. DiPrete and Claudia Buchmann, *The Rise of Women: The Growing Gender Gap in Education and What it Means for American Schools* (New York: Russell Sage Foundation, 2013).
34. Claudia Goldin, "The Quiet Revolution That Transformed Women's Employment, Education, and Family," *American Economic Review* 96.2 (2006): 1–21.
35. Discussions of recent cross-class romance films are found in J. Emmett Winn, *The American Dream and Contemporary Hollywood Cinema* (New York: Continuum, 2007); Thomas E. Wartenburg, *Unlikely Couples: Movie Romance as Social Criticism* (Boulder, CO: Westview Press, 1999); Hilary Radner, "Pretty Is as Pretty Does: Free Enterprise and the Marriage Plot," in Jim Collins, Hilary Radner and Ava Preacher Collins, *Film Theory Goes to the Movies* (New York: Routledge, 1993), 56–76: Diana I. Rios and Zae Alicia Reyes, "Jennifer Lopez and a Hollywood Latina Romance Film: Mythic Motifs in *Maid in Manhattan*," in Mary-Lou Galician and Debra L. Merskin, eds., *Critical Thinking about Sex, Love and Romance in the Mass Media: Media Literacy Applications* (Mahway, NJ: Lawrence Erlbaum Associates, 2007), 107–118; Wuming Zhao, "Gendered Dreams and the Hollywood Cross-Class Romance," in Kevin Cahill, Lene Johannessen, eds., *Considering Class: Essays on the Discourse of the American Dream* (Berlin: LIT Verlag, 2008), 117–129; Wuming Zhao, "The Cinderella Narrative in Eighties' Hollywood," *Doshisha American Studies* 39 (2003): 93–108.
36. James MacDowell, *Happy Endings in Hollywood Cinema: Cliché, Convention and the Final Couple* (Edinburgh: Edinburgh University Press, 2014), 104–111.

BIBLIOGRAPHY

Ceplair, Larry. *The Marxist and the Movies: A Biography of Paul Jarrico*. Lexington, KY: University of Kentucky Press, 2007.
Ceplair, Larry and Steven Englund. *The Inquisition in Hollywood: Politics in the Film Community, 1930–1960*. Berkeley: University of California Press, 1983.
Chafe, William H. *The Paradox of Change: American Women in the 20th Century*. New York: Oxford University Press, 1991.
Cohen, Lizabeth. *A Consumers' Republic: The Politics of Mass Consumption in Postwar America*. New York: Vintage Books, 2003.
DiPrete, Thomas A. and Claudia Buchmann. *The Rise of Women: The Growing Gender Gap in Education and What it Means for American Schools*. New York: Russell Sage Foundation, 2013.

Dyer, Richard. *Heavenly Bodies: Film Stars and Society*. London: British Film Institute and Macmillan, 1986.

Goldin, Claudia. "The Quiet Revolution That Transformed Women's Employment, Education, and Family," *American Economic Review* 96.2 (2006): 1–21.

Hartman, Susan M. "Women's Employment and the Domestic Ideal in the Early Cold War Years," in Joanne Jay Meyerowitz, ed. *Not June Cleaver: Women and Gender in Postwar America, 1945–1960*. Philadelphia: Temple University Press, 1994, 84–100.

Honey, Maureen. "The Working-Class Woman and Recruitment Propaganda during World War II: Class Differences in the Portrayal of War Work," *Signs* 8.4 (1983): 672–687.

Jensen, Kimberly. *Mobilizing Minerva: American Women in the First World War*. Champaign, IL: University of Illinois Press, 2008.

Landay, Lori. *Madcaps, Screwballs, Con Women: The Female Trickster in American Culture*. Philadelphia: University of Pennsylvania Press, 1998.

Leder, Jane Mersky. *Thanks for the Memories: Love, Sex, and World War II*. Westport, CT: Greenwood, 2006.

Marchand, Roland. "Visions of Classlessness, Quests for Dominion: American Popular Culture, 1945–1960," in Robert H. Bremner and Gary W. Reichard, eds. *Reshaping America: Society and Institutions, 1945–1960*. Columbus: Ohio State University Press, 1982, 163–190.

May, Elaine Tyler. "Pushing the Limits, 1940–1961," in Nancy F. Cott, ed. *No Small Courage: A History of Women in the United States*. New York: Oxford University Press, 2000, 473–528.

———. *Homeward Bound: American Families in the Cold War Era*. New York: Basic Books, 2008 [1988].

MacDowell, James. *Happy Endings in Hollywood Cinema: Cliché, Convention and the Final Couple*. Edinburgh: Edinburgh University Press, 2014.

Meyerowitz, Joanne J. "Beyond the Feminine Mystique: A Reassessment of Postwar Mass Culture, 1946–1958," *The Journal of American History* 79.4 (1993): 1455–1482.

Moseley, Rachel. *Growing Up with Audrey Hepburn*. Manchester: Manchester University Press, 2002.

Radner, Hilary. "Pretty Is as Pretty Does: Free Enterprise and the Marriage Plot," in Jim Collins, Hilary Radner and Ava Preacher Collins, eds. *Film Theory Goes to the Movies*. New York: Routledge, 1993, 56–76.

Rios, Diana I. and Zae Alicia Reyes. "Jennifer Lopez and a Hollywood Latina Romance Film: Mythic Motifs in *Maid in Manhattan*," in Mary-Lou Galician and Debra L. Merskin, eds. *Critical Thinking about Sex, Love and Romance in the Mass Media: Media Literacy Applications*. Mahway, NJ: Lawrence Erlbaum Associates, 2007, 107–118.

Rogers-Carpenter, Katherine. "Re-envisioning 1930s Working Women: The Case of *Kitty Foyle*," *Women's Studies*, 37.6 (2008): 707–730.

Rowe, Kathleen. *The Unruly Woman: Gender and the Genres of Laughter.* Austin: University of Texas Press, 1995.

Schreiber, Michele. *American Postfeminist Cinema: Women, Romance and Contemporary Culture.* Edinburgh: Edinburgh University Press, 2014.

Smith, Dina M. "Global Cinderella: 'Sabrina'(1954), Hollywood, and Postwar Internationalism," *Cinema Journal* 41.4 (2002): 27–51.

Steinberg, Cobbett. *Film Facts.* New York: Facts on File, 1980.

Walsh, Andrea S. *Women's Film and Female Experience 1940–1950.* New York: Praeger, 1984.

Wartenburg, Thomas E. *Unlikely Couples: Movie Romance as Social Criticism.* Boulder, CO: Westview Press, 1999.

Weiss, Jessica. *To Have and to Hold: Marriage, the Baby Boom, and Social Change.* Chicago, IL: University of Chicago Press, 2000.

Winn, J. Emmett. *The American Dream and Contemporary Hollywood Cinema.* New York: Continuum, 2007.

Zhao, Wuming. "The Cinderella Narrative in Eighties' Hollywood," *Doshisha American Studies* 39 (2003): 93–108.

———. "Gendered Dreams and the Hollywood Cross-Class Romance," in Kevin Cahill, Lene Johannessen, eds. *Considering Class: Essays on the Discourse of the American Dream.* Berlin: LIT Verlag, 2008, 117–129.

CHAPTER 9

Conclusion: Formula, Genre, and Social Experience

THE FORMULA IN DRAMAS AND COMEDIES

The reflexivity of *Pretty Woman* on the formula to which it conforms is more likely to be found in romantic comedies than in romantic dramas that are unlikely to want to undermine the seriousness and belief of the romance by irony or pastiche. However, not just cross-class romantic dramas but romantic dramas in general have become a rarity in comparison with romantic comedies. For most of the twentieth century, romantic dramas were more numerous than romantic comedies, but after a fallow period in the 1960s and 1970s, the number of romantic comedies increased significantly in the 1980s, and in the 1990s and thereafter they have exceeded the number of romantic dramas. As we have seen, there were almost no cross-class romance comedies until the late 1910s of the twentieth century, and the cross-class romance dramas continued to predominate until 1926. Comedies predominated in the late 1920s followed by a predominance of dramas in the early 1930s and a return to a predominance of comedies in the late 1930s. In the 1940s and 1950s, there was about an equal number of dramas on the one hand and comedies and musicals on the other. With respect to the very few cross-class romance films made in recent decades, there has been an approximately equal ratio of dramas and comedies. Whereas the decline in the number of cross-class romance dramas is in accord with the decline of romantic dramas in general, cross-class romantic comedies constitute a tiny minority of the large number of romantic comedies that have been made in recent decades.

© The Author(s) 2017
S. Sharot, *Love and Marriage Across Social Classes in American Cinema*,
DOI 10.1007/978-3-319-41799-8_9

The explanation of James J. Dowd and Nicole R. Pallotta for the general decline of romantic drama is relevant not only for the decline of cross-class romantic dramas but also for the decline of cross-class romantic comedies. They point to the "disappearance" of the social impediments and risks that, in the dramas of the past, served to separate the lovers or make their romance difficult. They write that the significant obstacles that appear in romantic dramas take two forms. Firstly, the most common obstacle is that one or both of the lovers is married. As recent decades have seen a growing tolerance toward separation and divorce and many cohabiting couples remain unmarried, marriage has become less credible as a factor that would keep couples apart. The second type of obstacle is the social background or identity of the two lovers, such as their race, ethnicity, clan, social class or age. Dowd and Pallotta argue that this type of obstacle has also become less convincing as a dramatic device because, since the 1960s, such impediments have been "swept aside" by egalitarian movements, particularly the feminist movement. As the obstacles become less significant in contemporary society, the few romantic dramas that were made in the late twentieth century, such as *Titanic* (1997) and *The English Patient* (1996), were often set in the past. This leaves the comedy as "the only viable form that the conventional, romantic films can take."[1]

Dowd and Pallotta may have exaggerated the decline of romantic drama, and since the publication of their article in 2000, one can find many examples, such as *Eternal Sunshine of the Spotless Mind*, 2004 and *Her*, 2013. There is no doubt, however, that romantic comedies continue to predominate over romantic dramas.

In comparison with its frequency in romantic dramas in general, the obstacle of marriage in cross-class romance films is rare; the wealthy man is married in *Forbidden*, 1932, and in *Backstreet*, made three times in 1933, 1941 and 1961. Most cross-class romance films, both dramas and comedies, have ended with the couple about to marry and their life after marriage (the 'happy ever after') is rarely shown. The minority of cross-class romance films that continue after marriage have varied in their themes. A few have tensions arising from the couple's class differences: the working-class husband resists the wasteful, wealthy lifestyle of his wife (e.g., *Kept Husbands*, 1931, *Platinum Blonde*, 1931); the wife from the poor background resists the class-derived pressures put on her by her husband's family (e.g., *Splendor*, 1935, *Kitty Foyle*, 1940); and the wealthy husband has to overcome the class prejudices of his wife's middle-class family (e.g., *The Idle Rich*, 1929, and its remake *Rich Man, Poor Girl*, 1938).

Once married, the girl with a working-class background may set about reforming her wealthy husband in some way, from being work shy (e.g., *Brief Moment*, 1933), from being a workaholic (e.g., *She Married Her Boss*, 1935), or from alcoholism (e.g., *The Girl from 10th Avenue*, 1935). The wealthy husband may turn out, however, to be cruel and violent (e.g., *She Wanted a Millionaire*, 1932, *Caught*, 1949). Adultery is a rare theme to arise for a cross-class married couple, but in *Passion Flower* (1930) the husband, the former chauffeur of his wife's family, leaves his wife for her wealthy cousin, and in *Case Timberlane* (1947), the wife from the wrong side of the tracks starts an affair with her husband's friend. Most of these examples are dramas. Cross-class romantic comedies, like most romantic comedies in general, do not address what happens after the marriage of the romantic couple.

In arguing that social movements have reduced the relevance of the class impediment in romantic films, Down and Pallotta are not denying the continuation of class differences and inequality, which in fact has grown in recent decades. Their argument is that egalitarian values have meant that class has fewer negative repercussions for lovers in the postmodern world. This argument would appear to apply more to comedies such as *Pretty Woman* (1990) and *Maid in Manhattan* (2002) than to dramas such as *White Palace* (1990) in which the advertising executive tries to keep his love for a diner waitress a secret from his upper-middle-class Jewish circle of family and friends, and when she forces him to take her to a family dinner it is a disaster. As noted, within the general category of romance films, romantic comedies are now more numerous than romantic dramas. In most of the romantic comedies of the last decades, the two romantic leads are presented as coequals, most often from the same middle or upper-middle class and having an equal share as active shapers of the story's trajectory. The couple have to overcome relatively mild obstacles, such as the existing engagement or relationship of one of them to someone who is shown to be an unsuitable partner.[2]

Genre, Spectators and the 'Real World'

We may assume that the overt portrayal of the artifice of the cross-class romance formula in *Pretty Woman* is not informing audiences of something that they do not know already. Even without self-conscious pastiche or, as it were, a wink to the audience, spectators of both romantic dramas and comedies have learnt what to expect: the impediments will be overcome or set aside, and at the end the couple will unite in a happy ending. There are, of course, exceptions, particularly in romantic dramas, but audiences may also have learnt to recognize signs that will lead them on certain occasions to expect an unhappy ending. Even before the first wave of cross-class romance films, from about 1915, spectators were familiar with the formula from written fiction and the theatre, and even though some romances ended tragically, in the vast majority of cases, the expectations of readers and spectators regarding the lovers' happy union were in the end fulfilled. Spectators of romantic films have no doubt taken a similar stance to that found among readers of popular romantic novels; readers readily admit that the world of romantic fictions bears little resemblance to the world that they inhabit, but they will be dissatisfied if a particular fiction deviates from the formula, such as ending with the separation of the romantic couple.[3] Investigators of peoples' conceptions of love have found that many express skepticism and sometimes distance from the 'myth' of romance associated with Hollywood, but the same people who reject Hollywood romantic films as remote from reality tend to call upon the mythic view of romance when describing their own romantic relationships.[4] Like the film *Pretty Woman*, many people vacillate between dismissing as unrealistic and assenting to the notions of popular romance.

The contextual reality of the heyday of cross-class romance films was one in which large numbers of young, unmarried women were entering the work force, class divisions and conflict were sharp, and there was little questioning of the gender stratification and inequality in the occupational structure. The solution proposed for young working girls by cross-class romance films was one that acknowledged the reality from which many of them would have liked to escape, especially during the Depression. In contrast with a number of popular genres of the inter-war years, such as historical romances, horror films and westerns, most cross-class romance films were anchored in the audiences' time and space. Many were comedies, but unlike the anarchic early 1930s films of the Marx brothers and some of the screwball comedies of the mid- and late 1930s, characters in cross-class romances were not distanced from audience realities by outrageous behavior. Although the occasional cross-class romance film had a European setting, most were set in contemporary America and some acknowledged the prevalence of harsh conditions. Some of the cross-class romances of the 1930s included direct references to the Depression, and there were frequent indications of hard conditions such as unemployment, the problems of finding work and the joy of being served a decent meal.

Many cross-class romance films connected to reality by including explicit and vivid portrayals of widespread social behavior. A number of the films of the late 1910s of the twentieth century showed the sexual harassment of young female workers by bosses, male co-workers and customers, and films of the early 1930s showed the pressures on female workers to provide sexual favors in exchange for employment. The conflicts or dilemmas faced by the heroines in these films were familiar to many of the films' female spectators. Marriage was seen by many young working women as an escape from an oppressive working environment, and although few expected that marriage would propel them into the upper class, cross-class romance films addressed, albeit in an utopian fashion, their reasonable hopes of class mobility through marriage.

The ways in which female spectators could identify with the heroines of cross-class romances was reinforced by the ways they identified with hugely popular stars, such as Joan Crawford and Barbara Stanwyck, who played them. The congruence between the class background of the stars, as identified and reported in the fan magazines, and that of the characters they played can be related to the spectators' or fans' recognition of similarities and differences between themselves and the stars. Fans valued both the perceived similarities, which enabled them to recognize qualities they believed they already had, and the differences, which allowed them to imagine a fantasy self and better life.[5] This identity was facilitated by the fans' knowledge that the stars, like the characters they played, had often moved from a working-class background, shared by many of the fans, into a high-class milieu of wealth and glamour.[6] Just as fans identified with stars they recognized as both different and similar to themselves, female spectators could identity with the working-girl heroines the stars portrayed as both different and similar to themselves. The heroines were different insofar as they married an upper-class man or millionaire, but they were similar insofar as many women experienced or expected some degree of mobility through marriage.

Cross-class romance films spoke to the dilemmas of many in the audience who had made some movement from one class to another, often from a blue-collar background to white- or pink-collar occupations, or had aspirations of some upward mobility. The heroines and, in a minority of cross-class romances, the heroes from working-class backgrounds learnt to dress, talk and behave in appropriate ways as they moved into a higher class, but they would often also express their pride in the more 'authentic' culture of their class of origin. In a number of cross-class romances, the working-class heroine shows her ability to 'pass' as an upper-class lady, and even though the plots enabled her to revert to her working-class persona, in most cases she still retained the love of the upper-class male. These films expressed the dilemmas of the upwardly mobile and those with aspirations of mobility: should one conceal one's class origins in order to rise socially, and to what extent does social mobility involve a 'performance' of dressing, talking, and acting like a person from a higher class? In a few films, the upper-class participant, sometimes the female but more often the male, 'passes' as working class, and this demonstrates his or her worthiness as a partner for the authentic working-class protagonist. Either way, class passing was made possible by a consumer culture that encouraged the notion of fluid class boundaries and of movement up the social scale by the purchase of appropriate clothes, cosmetics, toothpaste, mouthwash, and so on—items that were advertised in fan magazines and sponsored by stars.

Dilemmas of mobility and authenticity are expressed in cross-class romances in the tensions between material considerations and 'true' love. From its beginnings in the modern novel of the eighteenth century, the cross-class romance formula dealt with the contradiction between interests of wealth and social status on the one hand and the value of romantic, disinterested love on the other. The common solution, in which the poor protagonist is rewarded for her or his disinterested love by a successful union with the wealthy protagonist, might be termed a wish fulfillment. This particular wish fulfillment may have been especially pleasurable to particular audiences (i.e., urban, female, with aspirations to mobility) because it was grounded in a reality of class and gender inequality, which, given the limited opportunities for women in the labor market, made the social mobility of women dependent on marriage. Unlike most cases of women's mobility through marriage in society, the films represent mobility through cross-class romance as long range, and whereas the boundaries between the highest and lowest classes in society are formidable, they prove surmountable in cross-class romance films. Audiences may have identified or felt some involvement with the heroines and heroes as they finally surmounted the class barriers to achieve union with their love object, and they were unlikely to feel dejected by a comparison with their own situation because they had learnt to experience the formula as an entertainment without continually comparing it with their own experience. The cross-class romance films provided their intended audiences with a dilemma that was familiar in their real world and an ideal solution that overcame the ambiguity, uncertainty, and limitations of that world. Cross-class romance films continued to unequivocally support disinterested love over material interests, but that the resolution in favor of disinterested love had to be repeatedly re-enacted exposed the continual confrontation of values by material interests and suggested that, in the real world at least, the contradiction could never be finally resolved.

NOTES

1. James J. Dowd and Nicole R. Pallotta, "The Demystification of Love in the Postmodern Age," *Sociological Perspectives* 43.4 (2000): 549–580, quote on p. 563.

2. Examples of romantic comedies provided by Dowd and Pallotta in which the two lovers are presented as coequals are *Sleepless in Seattle* (1993), *One Fine Day* (1996), *Chasing Amy* (1997), and *You've Got Mail* (1998). Dowd and Pallotta, "The Demystification of Love in the Postmodern Age," 566–567. Schreiber writes that one of the characteristics of the "postfeminist romance cycle" is the luxurious life-style of the female protagonists who are firmly situated in an upper-middle-class milieu. Michele Schreiber, *American Postfeminist Cinema: Women, Romance and Contemporary Culture* (Edinburgh: Edinburgh University Press, 2014), 15, 145, 160–162, 175. Deleyto writes that the greater emphasis on equality between men and women has meant that "the perfectly codified conventions" of romantic comedy have lost much of their meaning and that there has been a tendency in recent years, best exemplified by *My Best Friend's Wedding* (1997), for friendship to be viewed as an acceptable alternative to love within the genre. Even if the female protagonist loses her boyfriend, life goes on and she still has her best friend. Celistino Deleyto, "Between Friends: Love and Friendship in Contemporary Hollywood Romantic Comedy," *Screen* 44.2 (2003): 181–187.

3. Janice Radway, *Reading the Romance: Women, Patriarchy and Popular Literature* (Chapel Hill: University of North Carolina Press, 1991).

4. Swidler's interviewees lurched between the 'mythic' view of love propagated by Hollywood and what they considered a 'realistic' view of love. Anne Swidler, *Talk of Love: How Culture Matters* (Chicago: University of Chicago Press, 2003), 114–118; See also, Eva Illouz, *Consuming the Romantic Utopia: Love and the Cultural Contradictions of Capitalism* (Berkeley: University of California Press, 1997), 153–181; James MacDowell, *Happy Endings in Hollywood Cinema: Cliché, Convention and the Final Couple* (Edinburgh: Edinburgh University Press, 2014), 137–140.

5. Jackie Stacey, *Star Gazing: Hollywood Cinema and Female Spectatorship* (London: Routledge, 1994), 126–134, 145–159.

6. Stephen Sharot, "Social Class in Female Star Personas and the Cross-Class Romantic Formula in Depression-era America," *Screen* 56.2 (2015): 172–194.

BIBLIOGRAPHY

Deleyto, Celistino. "Between Friends: Love and Friendship in Contemporary Hollywood Romantic Comedy," *Screen* 44.2 (2003): 181–187.

Dowd, James J. and Nicole R. Pallotta. "The Demystification of Love in the Postmodern Age," *Sociological Perspectives* 43.4 (2000): 549–580.

Illouz, Eva. *Consuming the Romantic Utopia: Love and the Cultural Contradictions of Capitalism*. Berkeley: University of California Press, 1997.

MacDowell, James. *Happy Endings in Hollywood Cinema: Cliché, Convention and the Final Couple*. Edinburgh: Edinburgh University Press, 2014.

Radway, Janice. *Reading the Romance: Women, Patriarchy and Popular Literature*. Chapel Hill: University of North Carolina Press, 1991.

Schreiber, Michele. *American Postfeminist Cinema: Women, Romance and Contemporary Culture*. Edinburgh: Edinburgh University Press, 2014.

Sharot, Stephen. "Social Class in Female Star Personas and the Cross-Class Romantic Formula in Depression-era America," *Screen* 56.2 (2015): 172–194.

Stacey, Jackie. *Star Gazing: Hollywood Cinema and Female Spectatorship*. London: Routledge, 1994.

Swidler, Anne. *Talk of Love: How Culture Matters*. Chicago: University of Chicago Press, 2003.

INDEX

© The Author(s) 2017   267
S. Sharot, *Love and Marriage Across Social Classes in American Cinema*,
DOI 10.1007/978-3-319-41799-8